Advance Praise for
Shift: The Beginning of War, The Ending of War

I hold deep admiration for the great pioneering work of Dr. Judith Hand for a world without war which is possible when people believe passionately and work for it. We can create for our children safe, secure, and healthy communities free from violence. *Shift: The Beginning of War, The Ending of War* explains "Why?" and "How?"

> Mairead Maguire
> Nobel Peace Laureate

Judith Hand marshals knowledge and insight from biological, cultural, and political sciences to argue persuasively that now is the time in human development to extinguish the fires of war. Not only does Dr. Hand demonstrate that such a mammoth shift of human spirit and politics is possible, in fact crucial to human survival, but she invites each and every one of us who cares about the future of the human family to take part in this historical psychological, social, and institutional shift toward resolving differences through law with justice instead of bullets and bombs.

> Douglas P. Fry, Ph.D.
> Director of Peace, Mediation and Conflict Research
> Åbo Akademi, University in Vasa, Finland
> Author of *Beyond War: The Human Potential for Peace*

On a level with Rachel Carson's *Silent Spring*, *Shift* raises the questions and sets the agenda for future studies. The depth and breadth of knowledge in *Shift* makes it essential reading for anyone interested in war and the possibilities of peace. From a biological and anthropological perspective, this remarkable book challenges myths surrounding the more traditional understanding of why we, as a species, make war and our propensity for violence. *Shift* offers grounds for hope that we may be close to permanently ending our love affair with war.

> Sean English, Ph.D.
> Former Director of Saor-Ollscoil (The Free University of Ireland 2000-2007)
> Convener, Peace Theories Commission of the International Peace Research Association (IPRA)
> Academic Director, National College of Business Administration (NCBA)
> Author of *The Collapse of the War System* (2007)

In *Shift: The Beginning of War, The Ending of War*, Judith Hand has written a book for the ages, and our time on earth might be shorter than we'd like if we don't heed her warnings and follow her outlines to a world free of war…forever! Many of us have been waiting years to read a book like this. Only a biologist understands the dangers of ignoring the implacable elements of evolved human nature. She demonstrates that the current century blesses us with a rare but narrowing opportunity to end war. Do it now or it may be too late. I heed her rallying cry and hope you join us.

> Clarence "Sonny" Williams
> Sr. Executive, Commercial Insurance Industry

The scientific method has changed our moral landscape. Before we knew how to find out why we behave the way we do, we lived in a state of ignorance. Evolution, a blind and amoral process, shaped us to want and need certain things in order to reproduce." With these words, Judith Hand goes to core of the any debate on the origins of conflict and war. Judith Hand brings the all important woman's perspective - a perspective central to understanding the origins of war - and more importantly, the means to avoid war.

> Malcolm Potts, Ph.D.
> Professor, Population and Family Planning, UC Berkeley
> Author, *Sex and War*

Judith Hand's *Shift: The Beginning of War, The Ending of War* offers meaningful insights on a topic of great importance for all of humanity: why we go to war and what can be done to avoid war. She brings to bear a biologist's training and perspective and years of research and thought. The notion that we might actually be able to end war may seem—may in fact be—utopian, but Dr. Hand lays out a strong case that this achievement is possible. This argument deserves widespread attention. *Shift* will be an important book and deserves publication by a major publishing house.

> Robert S. McElvaine
> Professor of History
> Millsaps College
> Author, *Eve's Seed: Biology, the Sexes and the Course of History*

Judith Hand has laid out in this book a plan for the next great abolition movement, a movement both possible and necessary for the survival of human civilization. With the success of this movement to abolish war, we may discover that what we have heretofore called civilization, however, quickly begins to look primitive and destructive in comparison with what we are able to develop.

> David Swanson
> Activist, author of *War Is A Lie* and *War No More: The Case for Abolition*

SHIFT

The Beginning of War
The Ending of War

Judith Hand, Ph.D.

Questpath Publishing
San Diego, California

Questpath Publishing, P.O. Box 270074, San Diego, CA 92198-2074

Copyright © 2014 by Judith Hand

More information about this title is available at afww.org/shift.

Text and cover design and layout by Robbie Adkins, Adkins Consulting, Temecula, California

Cover illustration by Robbie Adkins, Adkins Consulting, Temecula, California

From *The Argument Culture* by Deborah Tannen, Copyright © 1997 by Deborah Tannen. Used by permission of Random House, Inc.

From *Anatomy Of Love: The Natural History of Monogamy, Adultery, and Divorce* by Helen E. Fisher. Copyright © 1992 by Helen E. Fisher. Used by permission of W. W. Norton & Company, Inc.

From web page of Peggy Reeves Sanday. Used by permission of Peggy Reeves Sanday.

Reprinted with the permission of The Free Press, a Division of Simon & Schuster, Adult Publishing Group, from *The End Of History And The Last Man* by Francis Fukuyama. Copyright © 1992 by Francis Fukuyama.

Excerpts from *On Aggression* by Konrad Lorenz, copyright ©1963 by Dr. G. Bortha-Schoeler Verlag, Wein, English translation by Majorie Kerr Wilson, Copyright © 1966 by Konrad Lorenz, reprinted by permission of Harcourt, Inc.

Hand, Judith, 1940-

   Shift: The beginning of war, the ending of war / Judith Hand.
   Includes bibliographical references, tables, and index.
   ISBN 978-0-97000-31-8-8 (softcover) 1. Origins of war. 2. War and society. 3. War (Philosophy) 4. Women and war. 5. Peace (Philosphy) 6. Sex differences (Psycholoyg)

First Edition, 2014 Printed in the United States of America

This book is dedicated
with grateful love
to my greatest hero,
my husband and best friend,
Harold Hand,
and to my niece
Annamaria Alfonso.

Judith Hand, Ph.D., is a scientist, novelist, and visionary peace apologist. Dr. Hand earned her Ph.D. in biology from UCLA. Her specializations as an evolutionary biologist are in animal and human behavior, communication, conflict resolution, and gender differences. She subsequently spent a year as a Smithsonian Post-doctoral Fellow at the National Zoo in Washington, D.C. and then returned to UCLA as a research associate and lecturer. Her undergraduate major was in cultural anthropology. As a student of animal communication, she has written on the subject of social conflict resolution. She has also worked as a technician in neurophysiology laboratories at UCLA and the Max Planck Institute, in Munich, Germany.

Her massive website, A Future Without War.org, and her book, *Women, Power, and the Biology of Peace*, explore war from a biological and anthropological perspective that explains why we make war and presents evidence explaining why we can end war. Essays, a blog, book and film reviews, and more on the website explore how to achieve that goal. She brings this hopeful message to audiences through the use of video and lectures.

All of her novels and screenplays feature strong female heroines matched with a strong male partner. To research the historical novel *Voice of the Goddess,* Dr. Hand worked at the archeological museum on Crete and visited temple sites at Knossos, Phaestos, and Gournia. She interviewed the principal investigator of the Minoan excavation on Santorini (Thera) and visited museum and goddess sites in Turkey.

An avid movie and classical music fan and birdwatcher, she currently lives in Rancho Bernardo, California.

For more information about the book, the author, or how to contact her, see her web site, www.AFutureWithoutWar.org. More biographical information can be found at: http://en.wikipedia.org/wiki/Judith_Hand, and http://www.shesource.org/experts/profile/judith-hand

Also by Judith Hand:
  Book - *Women, Power, and the Biology of Peace* (2003)
  Book - *A Future Without War: The Strategy of a Warfare Transition* (2006)
  DVD – "No More War: The Human Potential for Peace" (http://tinyurl.com/caft8uh)
  Blog – afww.wordpress.com

Paradigms are underlying assumptions that guide and motivate our lives and which we accept without thought as being true—whether or not they are.

In the case of war, the current maladaptive, underlying paradigm we must shift is:

Domination of others using force and violence is inevitable and hence to be endured/accommodated/worked around.

The paradigm which would undergird and sustain enduring peace in homes and communities is:

Using force and violence against others is anathema, intolerable under any conditions.

Judith Hand
"Shaping the Future"[1]

TABLE OF CONTENTS

ACKNOWLEDGMENTS

Parts of *Shift* are excerpts from my previous book, *Women, Power, and the Biology of Peace*. That book owes its existence to my friend and colleague Peggy Lang who has, through many years, unswervingly encouraged and supported me. Her brilliant editing has made *Shift* clearer, more compelling, and more interesting to read.

I was generously given time by individuals who criticized sections or full drafts of *Women, Power, and the Biology of Peace*: Stephanie Budin, Drusilla Campbell, Mark Clements, Donna Erickson, Barry Friedman, Robert Goodman, Sara Blaffer Hrdy, Pete Johnson, Deanna LeCoco, Sheila Mahoney, Raymond Pierotti, Jay Sheppard, and Paul Shen-Brown.

They don't all agree with everything I have to say, and I am solely responsible for the ideas presented, but the comments of all greatly improved my effort, and that is true for others whose valuable talents and insights contributed to *Shift*: Kathleen Barry, A.B. Curtiss, Douglas Fry, Joseph R. Jehl, Judith Levine, Mary Liston Leopold, Winslow Myers, Irene Pepperberg, Peter Verbeek, and Maynard Wade. To Clarence Williams I owe a special debt for his painstaking and insightful comments and suggestions.

The name I used to embrace the concept of a global people's movement to end war is F.A.C.E. It is an acronym of "For All Children Everywhere," and I am grateful for its creation to Annamaria Alfonso, A. B. Curtiss, Donna Erickson, Robert Goodman, Nicole Jones, Peggy Lang, and Andre Sheldon.

Over many years my work on the website A Future Without War.org was made easier by the advice, skills, and thoroughly professional approach of Ame Stanko, my website creator and manager and a good friend.

I am especially grateful to my colleague Sarah Blaffer Hrdy, not only for her seminal works on women in her books *Mother Nature: a History of Mothers, Infants, and Natural Selection* and *Mothers and Others: On the Origins of Mutual Understanding*, which greatly influenced my thinking, but also for her encouragement and moral support. Sarah quickly agreed, when I mentioned reading John

Horgan's new book *The End of War*, that it was time for me to write this update. Grateful thanks also go to Douglas P. Fry whose books *The Human Potential for Peace: an Anthropological Challenge to Assumptions about War and Violence* and *Beyond War: the Human Potential for Peace* similarly influenced my thinking and gave me a foundation to build on. As my editor he also shepherded my paper, "To Abolish War," through publication in the *Journal of Aggression, Conflict, and Peace Research.*

I extend a special "thank you" to authors of secondary sources listed in the bibliography. I chose these references with the intention that, if possible, *Shift's* readers should be able to access these works from any good central library. Where possible, I provide links to resources available on the Internet.

I also take this opportunity to recognize my debt to the thousands of scientists and other specialists listed in the extensive bibliographies of these secondary sources. These are the lovers of knowledge and the quest for truth who dedicated years of toil, sometimes in extraordinarily difficult circumstances, in the search for knowledge. The Jane Goodalls, Edward O. Wilsons, Jared Diamonds, and thousands of names we don't recognize, all of whom have done their part to bring light where there was darkness.

I acknowledge and thank, posthumously, Joan B. Kroc for her foresight and generosity in funding the Joan B. Kroc Institute for Peace and Justice in San Diego. The Kroc Institute's Women PeaceMakers Program has brought peacemaking men and women from all over the world to San Diego, and I could not have done my work without this extraordinary resource. Funding for the Institute's Women PeaceMakers Program for its first nine years was generously provided by the Fred J. Hansen Foundation.

Finally, I am deeply grateful to my professor at UCLA, Thomas R. Howell, who accepted me as a doctoral student when others "were not taking female candidates," and to Eugene S. Morton who sponsored my post-doctoral fellowship at the Smithsonian Institution in Washington, D.C. where I made the Laughing Gull observations recounted in *Shift*.

PREFACE
A Vision of a Peaceful Future and How to Get There

In *Shift* I explore the basics required to permanently eliminate war, a paradigm shift as great as the Agricultural and Industrial Revolutions. Elsewhere I suggested two possible names for such a monumental change: the Egalitarian Revolution and The Nonviolence Revolution.

Some people argue that a bit of war now and then is a beneficial evil, a necessary engine that drives all sorts of creativity. I make no attempt to argue pros and cons of that opinion. My view is that modern war is an unmitigated tragedy, sheer folly, a demon from our evolutionary past.

Because I'm a female offering a harsh assessment of male aggression, I want to address an issue of possible bias on my part that might occur to some readers. I've been told by friends and colleagues that the defining features of my life—the disciplines I've studied, the professions I've practiced, the experiences I've had as a woman raised in a male-dominated culture—all these make me uniquely qualified to write on this subject. While the biologically based tendencies described in *Shift* are often associated with one sex or the other, they exist in all of us. And the book's theme, which I stress, is that *what war-weary humanity needs for best results is male/female partnership in decision-making and leadership within our public lives.*

Humans are not doomed by our nature to be wracked repeatedly by vicious and destructive armed conflicts. In *Shift* I explore this false premise and my point is positive:

(a) A practical and achievable path to a future without war does exist.

(b) There is a powerful biological underpinning for this path.

We are living in extraordinary times. The tide of history for the last ten millennia is turning with respect to relationships between men and women. It's time for that shift to include our relationship with war.

J. L. Hand

PART I - WHY WE MAKE WAR

War is at best barbarism ... Its glory is all moonshine. It is only those who have neither fired a shot nor heard the shrieks and groans of the wounded who cry aloud for blood, more vengeance, more desolation. War is Hell.

William Tecumseh Sherman
Graduation Address
Michigan Military Academy, 1879

CHAPTER 1 – WHY I WROTE THIS BOOK

Did the pathway that led us to advanced social behavior and conquest make it inevitable that we will destroy most of what we've conquered? That is the question of questions. I'm optimistic. I think that we can pass from conquerors to stewards. We have the intellectual and moral capacity to do it, but I've also felt very strongly that we needed a much better understanding of who we are and where we came from. We need answers to those questions in order to get our bearings toward a successful long-term future, that means a future for ourselves, our species and for the rest of life.

Edward O. Wilson
2012 - Carl Zimmer Interview[2]

What if someone could convince you that we actually have the power to permanently end war? What if someone could convince you that once we resolve to make that happen, we could free ourselves from war in two generations or less? If either of those concepts intrigues or excites you, I write this book for you.

Foot-dragging, Obsolete Mindsets, and Global Decision-making

I also write this book because we live in a time when experts from many fields offer an ominous number of extraordinarily dire warnings, some relating to modern warfare. We ignore dire warnings from experts at our peril. And regrettably, we do so quite often.

Ivor van Heerden, a hurricane expert at Louisiana State University, warned for years, along with his colleagues, that dikes in New Orleans, Louisiana, could not weather a slow-moving, category 3 hurricane.[3] Their warnings were ignored. In 2005, hurricane Katrina hit along with torrential rains, and Heerden's worst nightmare came true. A Noah's flood engulfed much of New Orleans, bringing with it over 1,800 deaths.

Events can also speak to us, if we choose to listen. The nuclear disaster in 2011 at Fukushima, Japan, offers a dire warning about insufficient protection of nuclear plants. In the U.S. coastal state of Massachusetts, safety advocates living in the vicinity of the Pilgrim Island Nuclear Power Station, concerned for their personal welfare, looked into safety features in their own nuclear backyard.[4] They have not been happy with their findings. They want to have filtered vents installed in the concrete containment buildings surrounding the nuclear reactors. They accuse officials and politicians of dragging their feet, generating much talk and no action. Do these officials expect appropriate installations to spontaneously take place on their own? No. They're just procrastinating. Or perhaps they hope to avoid having to pay the financial costs of responding. Like we humans often do, they keep fingers crossed and hope for the best.

Globally, the stakes for us when it comes to our continuing embrace of war are much higher. As I hope to show, it's time to look at our mindsets and resources, and if we do, we can devise a plan that will keep us from blasting ourselves into the kind of apocalypse cropping up in so many books, movies, and documentaries. In our hearts, we know some of those dire scenarios could happen—but, well, maybe things will just sort themselves out….Or maybe not.

The literature on human violence and war is woefully outdated. At a recent book signing, a bright man engaged me in conversation about war. He kept citing his main authority on the subject, Robert Ardrey. Ardrey was a science writer in the late 1960s in the field of paleoanthropology. He famously wrote *The Territorial Imperative* and *The Hunting Hypothesis*.[5] These embraced the idea that humans have an aggressive nature and our ancestors were making war even in our deep, paleo-past, when we were still confined to Africa or in the early stages of our journeys into Europe and points east. The implication is that war is a genetically built-in, evolved trait.

Since Ardrey's time, anthropologists, paleontologists, geneticists, behaviorists, neuropsychologists and economists have vastly increased our knowledge of human nature and history. Yet knowledgeable people who wouldn't dream of relying on fifty-year-old telephones are content with fifty-year-old research on basic human nature—on which they base major decisions. A serious updating on the nature of human aggression and war written for laymen, women, and all policy makers is most definitely needed.

Two remarkably positive books, one by neuropsychologist Steven Pinker and the other by science journalist John Horgan, contribute nicely to that updating. Before I purchased Harvard neuropsychologist Steven Pinker's 2011 book *The Better Angels of Our Nature: Why Violence Has Declined*, I had already read several reviews of it.[6] Assuming reviewers were correctly describing Pinker's work in *Better Angels*, I felt sure I would agree with much of what he would present. I worried, however, that I might find him suggesting that we, as a species, are growing less violent. He might present evidence, as others have done, that we are killing fewer people in wars *per capita* and that the frequency of wars is declining, with which I would agree.[7] As a biologist, however, I would disagree that we are becoming less violent by nature. That is to say, I suspected that his case might be strong in the area of history, but weak in the area of biology. I was pleased to discover that Pinker did get the biology right: he does not attribute the change to any alteration in our genes. As for his overview of history, particularly of our ancient past, I disagree, as I'll explain later.

Having purchased the 2012 book by the science writer John Horgan, *The End of War*, I settled into bed with Vivaldi playing in the background and dove in.[8] By the time I finished reading, I felt that in his positive book—which concludes that we can end war if we choose to—Horgan downplays the role of biology in a way that undermines efforts to permanently end the behavior.

It took me only one restless night's sleep to wake up compelled to write a follow-up to my own previous work and to the contributions of these two authors. My perspective differs from theirs; it's the perspective of an evolutionary biologist.

In recent decades discussions about human nature have broadened to include consideration of our capacities for cooperation, empathy, and sharing—to consideration of our peacemaking and peacekeeping behavior. Scholars reveal how these skills have evolved along with changes in social structure from nomadic foragers to settled farmers to modern civilization, from simple third party mediation in tribal communities to the sophistication of the United Nations.[9]

Cutting edge thinking on aggression suggests that war is preventable, but we can't make sane decisions about it, let alone permanently end war if we blunder forward, encouraged by a vision like Pinker's in which history is incorrectly portrayed as an ever increasing downward trend in violence. Or buoyed by unsupported New Age belief in an inevitable human evolution to some higher, less violent plane of human psyche as suggested by thinkers like the physician, public speaker, and writer Deepak Chopra.[10] If we are to deal with war's complexity with sufficient sophistication to abolish it, our thinking needs updating so we correctly connect the dots between causes and cure. That begins with understanding the role of biology. Contrary to the sense of ease that Horgan gives us, for example, that we have the means to end war and now all we need is the will to do it, ending war will not be easy. In *Shift* I first explore the biology of war and then what it will take to permanently cast it into history's trashcan.

Cultural Norms Can Change

To begin, we can be encouraged by the fact that cultures can and do change. For thousands of years, slavery was assumed to be normal and natural. Now it is at least officially outlawed. Most of the world no longer accepts that it is just to cut off a man's hand for stealing a loaf of bread to feed his family. Drawing and quartering are no longer considered acceptable punishments. We don't burn people at the stake.

In *Shift* we explore the possibility of freeing ourselves from war and do so using nonviolent means. If you are doubtful, allow me to encourage you to keep your mind open. Two examples within the last century of the kind of shift I'm talking about were the efforts of suffragists in the United States who opposed any use of violence to secure the vote for women (e.g., Alice Paul), and Mohandas Gandhi who, in India, led a nonviolent struggle for independence from Great Britain.[11]

One of the most succinct explanations of Gandhi's efforts can be found in a pamphlet, *Hope or Terror, the other 9/11*, by retired Berkeley philosophy professor Michael Nagler.[12] Nagler also cites figures from the book *Peace is the Way* showing that the number of such movements has grown since 1948 both quantitatively and qualitatively.[13] He notes that in one year alone, 1989-1990, there were thirteen uprisings against despotic rule and all but one were essentially nonviolent. "The exception, Rumania," he points out, "was by far the most violent revolution of the post-Communist transitions—and characteristically accomplished the least. All but one of the remaining twelve, the disastrous Tiananmen uprising in China—led their participants to freedom."

Nagler also notes that these uprisings (in, among other places, Latvia, Bulgaria, Kazakhstan, Hungary, Indonesia, and Chile) affected some 1.7 billion people, or 1/3 of the planet. He sums up: "If we step back and look at the whole past century, getting India also into the net, an astounding 3.3 billion people, or more than half the human population on the earth, now enjoys freedoms that were formerly denied to them (and in most cases could never have been secured by force) thanks to the use of nonviolent strategy and tactics." Learning what this strategy is and the tactics it uses has stimulated activists across the globe. The original protestors in Egypt's Tahrir Square in 2011 engaged in nonviolent protest, crying out "Nonviolent! Nonviolent!"

Human history clearly is not fixed. Cultures are not fixed. We humans have experienced even greater changes in the past. Witness the Agricultural and Industrial Revolutions. In light of all of the above, we will explore in *Shift* why we are poised right now to experience another great revolution. As recent changes brought about using nonviolent protest prove, we have the ability to consciously act to produce a result of our choosing. If you will, we can establish a global "new normal" in which war is never a tolerated option.

In the second half of *Shift* we explore, in depth, the means for creating a future without war—something generations before us have repeatedly been unable to do. But to be equipped to achieve that goal, we need to see how our biology relates to the cultures we create. Exploring that relationship is the focus of *Shift's* first half.

And we start with a review of how heredity relates to behavior in general, looking not at humans but at examples from other animals.

Heredity and Environment – My Background, and a Real-World Example

Experience has taught me that to understand how genes relate to behavior, it is almost a necessity that a person has watched some animal species in its natural environment or in a situation that approximates its natural social context. When you watch wild animals engrossed in the serious business of survival and reproduction—and you know that behind everything they do is a long, evolutionary history that selected some genes and eliminated others—you get a real-world sense of what extraordinary actions those genes can generate. You also begin to appreciate the remarkable range of behavioral flexibility a highly evolved nervous system can generate.

People lacking that kind of intimate observation of another species in a reasonably "natural" context and who also lack a background in genetics can find it hard to see how genes relate to behavior. Seeing this relationship accurately is critical to the biological arguments in *Shift*. It's why, in this book about war, I spend significant time on basic genetics and the biology of behavior.

As an undergraduate at Wheaton College in Illinois, my first love was cultural anthropology. Only in my senior year did I switch to a biology major. I began serious work as a student of animal behavior by taking a masters degree at UCLA in general physiology. This introduced me to fundamentals of neurophysiology, including how the brain works, and what was then known about genes and behavior. Subsequently, one of my tasks in the laboratory of Professor Detlev Ploog at a Max Planck Institute in Munich, Germany, was to observe a small group of squirrel monkeys. The lab's research focused on using brain stimulation to map brain areas responsible for producing behavior, including vocalizations, and we wanted some idea of how the monkeys used the vocalizations. My subjects were held unrestrained and unbothered in a small enclosure with a glass front. I watched them daily for hours. One female became pregnant and gave birth to an adorable baby. I published two papers on my subjects' mating behavior and sexual play.[14]

It was in Munich that I fell in love with the study of whole animal behavior. I returned to the United States determined to study chimpanzees. Circumstances diverted me instead into doing my dissertation on vocalizations and other behavior of Western Gulls. One of my papers from this work had to do with conflict resolution by mated pairs. The question was whether the male—which is always the larger of the two birds—dominated his mate when they had conflicts over nest duties or food. To my knowledge, my papers on the egalitarian nature of conflict resolving behavior of mated gulls were the first to document an egalitarian relationship in wild animals.[15]

I found this exception to the usual case in animals—where larger individuals dominate smaller ones in virtually all relationships between two individuals—particularly fascinating. I set out to further explore possible forms of egalitarian conflict resolution by applying for a Smithsonian Post-doctoral Fellowship at the National Zoo in Washington, D.C. The zoo's spacious flight cage (approximately 37 meters in diameter) holds several bird species. Among them at that time were 24 gulls of two species, Silver and Laughing Gulls. The two species were breeding successfully. In fact, they had interbred and produced hybrids.

The zoo wanted to identify the hybrids in order to remove them from the cage. I wanted to study the relationship between breeding mated pairs. To do that, I needed a population where I could identify and determine the sex of every individual. My needs and the zoo's nicely overlapped. We trapped the gulls, the zoo veterinarian sexed them, and I gave them colored leg bands to identify them individually. While they were anesthetized so a tiny incision could be made to see if they had a testis or ovary, I noted and measured traits that identify hybrids. The birds were released again into the flight cage. After I completed my research, the keepers removed the hybrids.

Now comes the example of behavior that so impressed me, and which I wrote about.[16] There were nine Laughing Gulls, only two of which were breeding age females. This is a highly unnatural sex ratio; in nature the ratio of breeding-age males to breeding-age females would be roughly one to one. From a perch on a high rock overlooking the expanse of the flight cage, I watched the birds enter breeding season. Males and females of both species went through their usual species-typical courting behavior. This involves a variety of vocalizations, including a call associated with a dainty upward tossing of the head by the female. Her Head Tossing display encourages a potential mate to feed her a bit of food, like a small piece of fish or a juicy mealworm. Days passed and males and females sorted themselves into pairs.

Eventually males began to mount their partners for mating. This was accompanied by coordinated moves in which the female, on the bottom, allowed the male on her back to oppose his cloaca to hers to transfer sperm while the male uttered a distinctive "copulation call." After a bond has formed, mated pairs fetch scraps of plant material which they bring back to a site where they construct a nest. They also share the duty of driving other gulls away from the plot of ground around this nest that they consider their "territory."

Even before courting or mating began, I noted that two Laughing Gull males were "keeping company." When these birds "keep company" they approach each other, circle about and exchange a couple of special displays, and then withdraw to rest together slightly apart from other birds. One day, to my absolute astonishment, these two males began to engage in "courtship feeding." Their courtship feeding differed from that of heterosexual pairs in that the two males passed the meal worm back and forth many times before it was torn apart or one swallowed it. Together they constructed a perfectly fine nest and shared the defense of their ground. Soon, to my further, jaw-dropping amazement, both males engaged in mounting, one male mounting the other. These mountings, which included copulation calls, were never completed. The male on top never lowered his tail to attempt cloacal contact, or he fell off.

Several other aspects of their behavior suggested that they were not fully "satisfied" with this relationship. For example, they would intrude into neighboring Laughing Gull territories and give slow copulation calls as they stood near the territory residents. Or while on the neighboring territory and in the presence of the resident female or pair, one male might mount the other.

In all species of gulls in which pair bonds were studied to that point…and there were a number of such studies on several species…the bonds were uniformly heterosexual and monogamous. But in this *altered environment* of an extremely skewed male/female sex ratio, these males demonstrated remarkable behavioral flexibility. Three and possibly five behaviors were "new." That is, they were not the species-typical result of a long history of evolution by natural selection:

- A male took food from a potential mate (was fed by another individual). In nature, no adult male ever feeds another adult male, and no adult male accepts food from another individual.
- A male allowed another bird to mount its back.
- A male entered an adjacent territory and made copulation calls but was not actually copulating. In nature, copulation calls are only heard from copulating males.
- If it's possible that gulls can distinguish sex from external appearance (that they can tell males from females, and observations indicate that they do), allowing another male to remain on one's territory would be novel.
- If it's possible that gulls can distinguish sex from external appearance, "keeping company" with another male would be novel.

The most lasting impression made on me was the critical realization that in complex behavior like courting, territory defense, and mating, genes of species with large brains do not directly produce behavior in some one-to-one, evolved link from genes to action. *That if you change the environment or social context in which individuals of a species have been shaped by natural selection for thousands of generations, complex nervous systems can produce an impressive variety of novel responses.* In this case, of the three other male Laughing Gulls lacking a Laughing Gull female with which to mate, two simply did not pair and one paired with an immature Laughing Gull female.

The end of the story is equally amazing. I placed two fertilized eggs, one each taken from two other nests into the nest of the bonded males. They performed typical nest reliefs to incubate the eggs, both of which hatched successfully, and then the males shared in feeding the chicks.

The bottom line here with respect to heredity and behavior: if you change an environment sufficiently, the genes that produce a species-typical behavior in one context can underlie very different behavior in that altered environment. What's interesting about this example of behavioral plasticity, as we shall soon see, is that it has relevance when we take up the subject of exactly when, and why, we started making war.

Why Our Need to Understand Ourselves and End War is Great

Perhaps you are among many who look into the years ahead with concern or even dread, aware of monumental, self-inflicted problems that seem to be spinning us out of control, even threatening our existence: abject poverty that triggers revolution and wars, the cruelty of the slave and sex trades, the waste of lives to drug addictions, violence in our homes and communities, the unsustainable consumption of life-sustaining resources. Then there are the potential horrors of newfangled weapons of mass destruction, a global pandemic, or global economic collapse triggered by global climate change and factors such as drastic imbalances in the distribution of wealth.

Our problems are super-sized, many are planet-wide in scope. Our disagreements are numerous and severe. On Christmas Eve 1968, Apollo 8 astronauts beamed a message to earth, including the famous photo, *Earthrise*. This image of our tiny blue-and-white globe against the vast darkness of space is a powerful image that speaks to something critical about our human journey: we evolved in a tiny corner of one continent, in Africa, we spread throughout a planet originally empty of humans, and now, in the words of ecological economist Herman Daly, our globe is full.[17] This is our only home into the foreseeable future, and we have been fruitful and multiplied so that our kind now occupies every niche capable of sustaining a human community.

Our environment is radically changed. Like those male gulls, we are challenged with something very new. On our lovely blue-and-white, full world, many people—thoughtful futurists or just plain folks—sense that ways of living that worked for us during our long journey out of Africa…well, those behaviors aren't working so well anymore. Our political, cultural, and ecological world is shifting with such speed that we can scarcely catch our breath, and the shifting can't be stopped.[18] The scary truth is that we may not have time to adequately respond should any of these onslaughts escalate into catastrophic proportions.

And our prime dilemma? We have nowhere to flee. There are no unoccupied lands with fresh resources and no other human competitors. Pioneering a new frontier has always been part of our survival strategy. It encouraged our ultimate occupation of the globe. As long as parts of our world remained empty of humans, we could move to where unexploited resources of food, water, and shelter of the kind we needed were available. And where we could escape from other humans with whom we had conflicts if we wanted to avoid killing and war. In fact, one hypothesis that emerges in *Shift* is that when it came to resolving major resource conflicts, the *key to early* Homo sapiens' *success was not war, but dispersal. In situations when competition was so intense that a survival option might have been to take up weapons to kill each other, the preferred choice of successful groups, which contributed to the success of individuals in those groups, was that some or all members of the group would pack up and move on.* If you will, the primary adaptation to severe resource competition was most likely dispersal.[19]

Now, on our full world, this option is for all practical purposes no longer workable. The elimination of the possibility of leaving human competitors behind has enormous consequences for not only our quality of life but our survival. From Malthus's 1798 predictions of the demands of population growth exceeding our available resources to the 1968 modern-day Malthus, Paul Ehrlich, who gave us his book *The Population Bomb*, we have had some modest reprieves.[20] For example, the "Green Revolution" gave us added crop productivity. A spreading "demographic transition," part of which involves women reducing the number of children they have, also slows our global increase in population size. But the planet's basic resources—most notably now, water—are not limitless, and the potential for conflict escalates.[21] Our populations continue to grow and consume. "Business as usual" may fail to mitigate, let alone prevent, cataclysmic changes, thereby halting the march of civilization—even conceivably, ending Earth's experiment with highly intelligent and highly technological life.

Joseph Rotblat was one of eleven scientists who, led by Bertrand Russell and Albert Einstein, issued a statement which became known as the Russell-Einstein Manifesto.[22] Concerned about nuclear proliferation and weapons of mass destruction, possibly global annihilation of our species, they posed the question, "Shall we put an end to the human race, or shall mankind renounce war?" In 2006, Rotblat again addressed the importance of ending war:

> To safeguard the future of humankind we have to eliminate not only the instruments for waging war, but war itself. As long as war is a recognized social institution, as long as conflicts are resolved by resort to military confrontation, the danger is that a war which begins over a local conflict – for example, over Kashmir – will escalate into a global war in which weapons of mass destruction are employed. The probability of this happening at any given time may be very small, but the consequences – should it happen – are so enormous that we must do everything in our power to eliminate the risk. In this nuclear age we can no longer tolerate war, any war. With the future of the human species at stake, this becomes a matter of concern to each of us.[23]

Faced with enormous challenges, which include the threat of a global annihilation event, continuing to devote the Earth's and our limited resources to war is now hugely maladaptive if not suicidal.[24] War can now be genuinely considered a form of social insanity. It is now obsolete, a reality explored recently by the author and peace activist David Swanson in his book *War No More: the Case for Abolition*.[25] Our need to understand ourselves so that we can permanently end it is a survival imperative.

Despite many challenges, there is hope. We are a supremely adaptive species—without peers in adaptability—and our survival instinct has been aroused. In some quarters, it is in over-drive. In a recent NPR Radio blog entitled *Is War Inevitable? A View from the Stars*, astrophysicist Adam Frank commented on contrasting views on war by biologist E.O. Wilson and science writer John Horgan in articles in *Discover* magazine, Wilson suggesting war *is* inevitable and Horgan suggesting it is not. From a planetary perspective, Frank suggests that changes we are making to Earth's planetary systems may be creating a behavioral bottleneck through which we must pass, that this new environment we've created may require a "cultural evolution that provides metaphors organizing humanity into new collective behaviors that don't include war." That "an astrobiological perspective, which is also a planetary perspective, might suggest that either war goes, or we do."[26] Globally, many organizations, groups, and individuals are broadcasting similar alarms and searching for change that will save us from ourselves.

Preview of Subjects to Be Covered

The first half of *Shift*, "Why We Make War," explores the origins of war from biological, anthropological, and paleontological perspectives, and considers differences of men and women as these relate to war. The second half, "How We Can End War," explores areas of concern that must be addressed to end war, strategy and tactics of nonviolent social transformation which are the means to be used to end war, and a call to action that describes a plan for ending war based on a mechanism developed by the International Committee to Ban Landmines (ICBL).

This chapter has explained my personal motivation for writing *Shift* and reasons why our global community is hungering for and needs to experience a major paradigm shift in our approach to resolving our differences.

Chapter 2 begins with a definition of war as used in *Shift* and distinguishes it from other forms of violence not covered in *Shift*, such as murder, revenge killings, raiding, dueling, or ritualized juridical "battles." The causes of war can be studied from three different perspectives: psychological, proximate, and ultimate causation. Chapter 2 briefly reviews psychological causation, including a definition of "warmonger," and issues of group emotions and war, and masculinity and war.

Chapter 3 explores proximate causation, the question being, what are the immediate triggers for wars? Twelve of many theories historically offered are listed. Stressed is that there are many such causes and that addressing them will be integral to a plan for ending war that is presented in subsequent chapters. Peace, often thought to be war's opposite, is defined, and an explanation is offered for why a campaign to end war is not the same as waging peace.

Ultimate causation refers to the biological roots of war. Chapter 4, on ultimate causation, is the longest causation discussion. This reflects *Shift's* biological orientation, which stresses significant biological differences between men and women in how they relate to using physical violence. I review the link between genes and observed behavior, then consider how traits of men and women can be compared using the bell curve. Looking at neurobiology and observed behavioral differences between human males and females, a "female preference for social stability" hypothesis is presented to explain why war is overwhelmingly a male preoccupation and activity. This critical, systematically unrecognized gender difference plays an important role in later chapters as we work toward requirements for and a doable outline for mounting a campaign to make war for future generations little more than a bad memory. Positive aspects of human aggression are briefly mentioned. Finally, stressed again is that to be successful in achieving the goal to end war, we need to understand our biology as well as our cultures.

Chapters 5, 6, and 7 plunge into questions such as: Have humans always made war? If we did not, when did we begin and why? Chapter 5 examines relevant behavior and anatomy of close relatives (chimpanzees and bonobos), and physical characteristics of a very ancient ancestor, *Ardipithecus ramidus*.

In Chapter 6 we consider the origins of human cooperative behavior, asking whether some survival or reproductive advantage provided by killing our fellow humans (war) explains why we developed our impressive abilities to cooperate—a "man-the-warrior" hypothesis is compared to a "humans-as-cooperators" hypothesis. The hypothesis introduced above, that for early humans faced with serious social conflicts dispersal, not war, was the behavior of choice, is given support. Chapter 7 explores several possible hypotheses for why and when we started making war.

Chapters 8 and 9 tackle a seeming contradiction: how women seem to avoid physical violence, and yet under some conditions they engage in it or encourage men to engage in it. Solving this puzzle entails looking at how women use power, and the ways in which they have historically engaged in wars. The puzzle of women and war is solved when we understand that women do not oppose war *per se*: they are adapted to prefer social stability. This "preference for social stability" hypothesis is explained further, and hypotheses for testing it are suggested, and examples of how this shapes women's responses to social conflicts or potential conflicts are offered.

Having established that war is not a genetically evolved adaptation but a relatively recent cultural invention and the roles of the two sexes with respect to war, we begin the second half of *Shift*. Chapter 10 offers an approach to ending war that groups war's many proximate causes and addresses them through nine foundational cornerstones: Embrace the Goal, Empower Women, Enlist Young Men, Foster Connectedness, Ensure Essential Resources, Promote Nonviolent Conflict Resolution, Provide Security and Order, Shift our Economies, and Spread Liberal Democracy. I argue that unless we simultaneously attend to all of these areas of human need and endeavor, any campaign to establish enduring peace is unlikely to succeed. A few of the many organizations already working on these cornerstones around the globe and who could become partners in a campaign to end war are listed.

Grounds for Hope, Chapter 11, offers reasons why our time in history is actually poised to end war. It boldly asserts that it is entirely possible for us to meet this enormous challenge if we are willing to apply sufficient human and financial resources because of six major historical changes, going back roughly 700 years to the Renaissance and Reformation. Then examples of rapid human social transformation make the case that we could accomplish this huge shift in two generations or less from the time we resolve to do it.

All previous chapters lead to Chapter 12, a call to action to embrace a mechanism, called F.A.C.E.. This mechanism provides a means to unite a critical mass of global citizens to directly take on and dismantle the war machine (however long it takes). The chapter addresses: 1) a need to bury the "just war" concept, 2) the major barriers to ending war; 3) the nature of approaches needed to end war (Constructive and Obstructive Programs); 4) a call to action that outlines F.A.C.E., modeled on the "massively distributed collaboration" used successfully by the International Committee to Ban Land Mines (ICBL; 5) suggestions for a radical change in tactics social transformers can use, viz. putting women on the front lines whenever possible, and finally; 6) four critical keys to prevent backsliding once we've reached the goal of no ongoing wars.

The final chapter reviews how natural selection worked to end us up where we are now, pointing out that we did not consciously choose war: the dictates of biology and the need to survive and reproduce have delivered us to this state. Now, however, we have sufficient knowledge that we can, if we choose, alter our societies in ways that will abolish this killing beast. Stressed is that the key to success will be partnership between men and women as leaders, activists, and citizens so that male and female built-in biological proclivities work for us, not against us.

In Appendices II and III, I compare the nine cornerstones outlined in *Shift* with elements that reduce violence, including war, described in Steven Pinkers's book *The Better Angels of our Nature* and characteristics of peace systems described in Douglas Fry's article "Life Without War."

PART I – WHY WE MAKE WAR

"The trouble with people is not that they don't know,
but that they know so much that ain't so..."

Josh Billings (Henry Wheeler Shaw)

CHAPTER 2 – PSYCHOLOGICAL CAUSES OF WAR

To know psychology….is no guarantee that we shall manage our minds rightly.

William Glover
Know Your Own Mind - 1915

War Defined

Many violent acts get lumped into the category "war" which, in fact, should not be included. Because the range of violence we inflict on others of our kind covers a remarkably diverse array of actions, we need a clear definition of what we're talking about in *Shift*. Douglas Fry, in *Beyond War*, offers a succinct discussion of why and how "war" should be distinguished from "homicide," "revenge killings," and "feuds."[27] It should also be distinguished from "raiding." Here are summaries of the distinctions I draw, which are similar to Fry's.

Homicide or murder, a one-on-one killing, doubtless goes back in our lineage to the time before we were humans, and it is not war.

Revenge killing describes cases where one person, or a few, gang up on and kill another specific individual or individuals because of some perceived wrong the victim/s did to them. This is also sometimes called "redress for specific grievances." This can include "execution," where the wrong being redressed is a homicide. These actions are not war.

Feud describes cases in which members of one group (but often not the entire group or with its permission) punish specific members of their group or some other group and the latter retaliate. When this is extended into a vicious cycle it becomes feuding, but it is also not what I consider to be war: the focus of the killing is on a specific individual or individuals deemed to be at fault for some perceived wrong, and the retaliation for that killing is again directed at those who did the killing or their relatives. Victims are not targeted indiscriminately as is the case with war (defined below).

Raiding is distinguished from war because the raiders' intent is not to kill members of another group but to take something from that group and then leave.[28] Most importantly, raiding does not involve the entire community giving official sanction to the raiders to indiscriminately kill members of the other group. Raids can easily escalate into revenge raids, but again, the two sides do not arm and prepare themselves to kill enemies.

Some other behaviors, for example dueling and juridical encounters are also not war. *Juridical encounters* use ritualized display to end conflicts. Outsiders and some ethnographers often mistakenly described these as war because more than two people are involved and so are weapons. Someone has been aggrieved. Often sexual problems are involved, as when a husband whose wife had eloped with another man would call a meeting to ask for help from his relatives and clan members. The members of the "enemy" group, to which the other man belongs, would also be informed. A date and time would be set for the "battle."

Typically after much brandishing of and then an exchange of thrown spears, which do not actually hit anyone, the battle is considered decided and members of both groups camp together for the night. These juridical encounters are a form of ritualized conflict resolution, the function of which is to resolve conflicts without loss of life. They involve weapons, they display relative power, but they do not usually result in anyone getting seriously hurt. They are personal, involving specific individuals and their kin; they are a form of group redress for a grievance. They also are not war. They save face and they save lives. They resemble, to a biologist, the ritualized behavior seen by males of many species.[29] [Biologists reading descriptions of these weapon-brandishing bouts often facetiously call them "penis waving."]

I define war as Fry does in *Beyond War*:[30] "A group activity carried on by members of one community against members of another community, in which it is the primary purpose to inflict serious injury or death on multiple nonspecified members of that other community, or in which the primary purpose makes it highly likely that serious injury or death will be inflicted on multiple nonspecified members of that community in the accomplishment of the primary purpose." War, the subject of this book, by its nature is not personal. It is taking up weapons and indiscriminately killing members of some other group.

Other Forms of Violence

How are we to deal with other forms of violence: e.g., rape, torture, modern slavery, domestic violence, the violence associated with organized crime? Each will have to be dealt with on its own terms, attacking its own roots in our biology and life experience. But two things are surely true. First, part of the process of ending war is teaching children from early childhood the philosophy and practice of nonviolent conflict resolution. Consequently, as adults they will be skilled in these arts. Their behavior will inevitably be less violent. Surely this will affect the occurrence of other forms of violence. And second, if we stop wasting financial and human resources on war, they can be used to combat these other social sicknesses that so demean the human spirit.

The Causes of War Can Be Studied on Several Levels

War's causes are, of course, many. This is central to why ending it permanently is an enormous challenge. We can study the reasons we take up weapons to kill from three difference perspectives: Psychological Causes, Proximate Causes, and Ultimate Causes. I begin with consideration of psychological causes. Because I am not a psychologist, the psychology of why some individuals start a war or why human communities agree to make war is not an area of my direct expertise. What I present is, therefore, a simple introduction to issues about how and why wars are launched or supported.

Warmongers

*Monarchs ought to put to death the authors and instigators of war,
as their sworn enemies and as dangers to their states.*

> Elizabeth I, Queen of England, To the French
> Ambassador Chamberlin, *The Sayings of Queen
> Elizabeth*, 1923, C. 13.

If a country or group is attacked and they take up weapons to defend themselves, there is no great mystery as to why they are waging war. The critical question to ask is, what motivates individuals to strike that first physical blow that crosses the line between shouting words or simply brandishing a spear, sword, or nuclear device to actually using the weapon to kill?

Individuals who beat the drums for war, who urge the members of their group to take up weapons and begin the killing, are warmongers.[31] What motivates them? What stirs them to rouse members of their community to kill members of another group? Each person making such a decision—whether a king, tyrant, chief oligarch, president, or part of an inner circle bent on war—is an individual with his or her own genetic inheritance and life history.

So to study the causes of wars on the psychological level requires that we dig deep into the personal history of warmongers. We will find many superficial differences. But in the end, one commonality frequently emerges: the desire, for whatever personal reason, to dominate another group, to control another group, and quite often in the process, to take some vital resource or resources from that other group. Controlling key or highly desired resources brings power to the warmonger (financial gain, enhanced social status or both). As described in later sections, humans have an evolved aversion to killing other humans indiscriminately, that is to say, killing other individuals who have not specifically wronged them. A warmonger is defined in *Shift* as an individual driven by desire for power that overrides this general human disinclination to kill other people: he (or she) is willing to stir up people to begin a war. These are wars of conquest or aggression, not fighting in defense.

Warmongers are willing to kill, or persuade others to start the killing or do the killing for them, to achieve their goal.[32]

Consider the most recent example of a war of aggression begun by the United States, the 2003 invasion of the Middle-Eastern, Muslim country of Iraq, a country that had not attacked the United States. Arguably the principle resource in question was oil. The USA is a democracy, so the decision to make war could not be made without the consent of many individuals, including substantial numbers of the U.S. Congress and financial supporters of the decision-makers. In this instance, the major players urging the country to war were the United States President, George W. Bush, the United States Vice President, Richard B. Cheney, the United States National Security Advisor, Condoleezza Rice, and the United States Secretary of Defense, Donald H. Rumsfeld.

To understand why each agreed that they must rouse the nation to preemptive war (that is, a war begun without any violence having been done to those launching the war), we would need to get them on the psychologist's couch. It can be amusing to speculate on their motivation. What mix of inborn personality traits and life experiences within their families and among their peers has shaped them? But only a psychologist who had studied them in detail would know what factors influenced their choice. It would NOT be the same for all of them. Besides power and wealth (markers of status), there are a number of other possible personal motivators: revenge, fear, pride, to establish one's "manhood," to curry favor from someone else. I've left some out. In each case it's possible, even probable, that more than one of these motivators was involved.

Without question, the greatest warmonger behind the Second World War was Adolph Hitler. Again, to understand why this man started a war would require a study of his life and his innate temperament. But in the end, the desire to control others, to have power—out of fear, ambition, addiction to power, and/or enslavement to some ideology—would likely characterize his psychological condition.

It's important to repeat that willingness to kill indiscriminately, for whatever reason, is a defining characteristic of a warmonger. In Chapter 12, I estimate how rare I think this willingness is. Those who have not been wronged but are nevertheless willing to kill and do it on a small, individual scale are sociopathic or psychopathic murderers. *Those who have not been wronged but are willing to initiate indiscriminate killing and do it on a community or state level are warmongers.*

Do these cheer leaders for war view themselves as evil? Rarely would any of the legions of warmongers in human history have described himself (or herself) as starting a war for the sheer pleasure of it, for the sole desire to exercise control over the lives of their fellow humans, or for the love of revenge or power/status. Virtually always they would justify their actions as being in the cause of some great good (e.g., protecting their people by acquiring a buffering territory of nearby land; securing for their people some vital resource without which they would be doomed; upholding the honor of their people; protecting their homeland from the threat of imminent annihilation; creating a better, stronger, more glorious human race). In the case of the second Iraq war, those calling for war presented "evidence" that Iraq was planning an imminent attack on the United States using weapons of mass destruction, evidence that proved not only flimsy but in some cases fabrications. Manufacturing made-up threats is a common practice of individuals or groups seeking to start a war.

In *Blood Rites*, essayist Barbara Ehrenreich reviews conditions in the transitional time period in our ancient past when our forebears started making war. Exactly when this occurred or the conditions under which it occurred are a topic of much debate. But she arrives at the same conclusion about the prime mover of struggle for status (for humans, I equate a struggle for status with a struggle for power):

> *So we may be in better conformity with the facts to say that war arises....at least in part, as a new source of prestige for men who might otherwise have been employed as hunters and as defenders against wild animals. Which is to say that war served not only to enrich the victorious community as a whole, but to enhance the status of a specific group within it: the men who fought or led the fighting.*[33]

Arguably the quest for status/power/control remains the principle cause of war. How does a particular individual arrive at that point in life? Everything from being born sociopaths who most often don't even understand why they kill, to the ambitious male who rises so high in a power hierarchy that he becomes power-drunk to the point of losing his moral compass.

Studies have shown that sociopaths are born lacking a sense of empathy or are able to readily cut themselves off from empathy.[34] It's said they lack an "empathy chip." They don't relate to other peoples' emotions and their own are often stunted. They certainly don't all become serial killers but they can kill without remorse; John Horgan notes that they can make very good soldiers.[35] Many learn to hide their lack of empathy by imitating the actions we associate with empathy. They can be likeable, even charming. They can become very successful, and generally ruthless, heads of corporations. Some succeed in politics. A high level sociopathic politician is a great danger to his or her entire community.

In the case of the vast majority of people who do have the usual "empathy chip," the environment into which they are born and their life experience, if brutal, can nevertheless cause, in an individual with a susceptible temperament, emergence of a willingness to kill. Some will be willing to launch their people into war, especially if they can convince themselves that they have a just cause. And arguably, when it comes to heads of state, the cause may, in fact, sometime *be* just…although whether that is true can be the subject of much debate. Committed pacifists can give good argument that even the Second World War could have been avoided.

In non-warring societies, the likelihood that a warmonger will emerge is extremely slim, no matter what a given child's genetic endowment or inclinations toward dominance and violence may be. We humans create warmongers via culture and life experience just as much as we create career criminals and murderers.

Group Emotions of War

In *Blood Rites*, Barbara Ehrenreich masterfully describes the emotional similarities between religion and war.[36] Entire communities and nations can get caught up in war fervor. Referring to the enthusiasm for war in 1914 among the British citizenry and such notables as Rainer Maria Rilke, Anatole France, Isadora Duncan, the suffragist Isabella Pankhurst, even briefly Sigmund Freud, Ehrenreich writes, "The emotions that overwhelmed Europe in 1914 had little to do with rage or hatred or greed. Rather they were among the 'noblest' feelings humans are fortunate enough to experience: feelings of generosity, community, and submergence in a great and worthy cause."

Fascinatingly, this sense of sharing in a profoundly important "great something" larger than self is eerily similar to reinforcing emotions aroused by religion. How this emotional transformation is achieved is an important subject of study in its own right.[37] What is clear is that as a group-living species, we are susceptible to both religion and war. Moreover, the ability to glorify war so an entire community is moved to support it is something warmongers rely on.

Another innate trait warmongers count on is our tendency to bond when threatened by an outside force. Ehrenreich continues by exploring how our pre-human ancestors responded to the threat of attack by the big predators—lions, wolves, bears, tigers.[38] She describes how in species living socially, the perception of danger may trigger powerful feelings of group solidarity, at least in most individuals, as when male Colobus monkeys prepare for group resistance to a predator by running to and hugging one other. She describes nonhuman primates driving away dangerous intruders by "mobbing" them: group members close ranks and use threatening noises and gestures. Baboons mob and chase intruders. Ehrenreich invokes the image of unarmed human campers confronting a bear by banding together, shouting, and pounding on pots and pans.

A warmonger uses this innate aspect of human group psychology to bond against a common threat by dehumanizing the enemy against which he wishes to rouse the people. Military trainers find it absolutely essential to use every means possible to dehumanize the enemy they are preparing soldiers to kill.[39] Derogatory names are used of course (gooks, japs, krauts, rag-heads, infidels), but often they also use true or even false stories of the enemy's evil ways: they are cannibals or they fornicate with animals or they worship an evil god. In his book *On Aggression*, Konrad Lorenz, one of the fathers of the modern field of ethology (animal behavior), describes the danger in allowing humans to kill at a distance, such as using bombs dropped from a plane. It separates them from the face-to-face context that triggers our built-in empathy and unwillingness to kill another human. The contemporary use of drones also increases this separation and is a stealthy means that can be used by the war business machine to attempt to keep us killing each other.[40] Keeping the killing distant by any means is a way to counteract the humanizing, personalizing effect of global communication and travel that teaches us that we are all one.

Another innate trait that warmongers count on is our tendency to be suspicious of the strange or unusual. In our deep past, this trait would have survival value for the obvious reason that the strange or unusual might be dangerous. When this is translated into a sense of group identity that separates "our group" from "not our group," we call it xenophobia. Warmongers can use it effectively to create fear of those not belonging to the warmonger's group, sufficient fear to be willing to kill the "others" in the name of safety. To end war we will have to enlarge the human sense of "group self" to embrace a oneness with all of humanity.[41]

Using an understanding of group psychology in order to move people to war has a long history, two of its most famous students of the past being Sun Tzu and Niccolo Machiavelli. Nationally syndicated columnist Norman Soloman, in *War Made Easy: How Presidents and Pundits Keep Spinning Us to Death,* presents a modern critique. He uses primarily case studies of the United States and its wars to show how individuals determined to make war can convince citizens to accept a war's necessity. These techniques include such things as convincing citizens that their country is a fair and noble one, that their leaders will do everything they can to avoid war, that the country's leaders would never tell people outright lies, that opposing the war means siding with the enemy, and that their military elements fight wars as humanely as possible.[42]

Masculinity and War

A number of writers have developed the proposition that making war, indisputably a male behavior, fills a psychological need for men to define what it means to be a man. Personal identity becomes wrapped up in a warrior model of behavior.[43] For example, historian Robert McElvaine, in *Eve's Seed: Biology, the Sexes, and the Course of History*, proposes that war serves the function of giving men a "male" identity distinct from women, and that when men no longer could define masculinity as the heroic behavior of hunting, they shifted the definition of masculinity to war.[44] They also transferred any trait that didn't reinforce this warrior image of masculinity to being female; the ultimate insult for a man was to be accused of being a woman. Clifton Kroeber and Bernard Fontana make this same connection between creating a cultural male identity and war.[45]

Ehrenrich in a section entitled "Masculinity and War" provides many examples of how war is often not fought for resources, concluding, "Thus war-making is not simply another occupation that men have monopolized. It is an activity that has often served to define manhood itself."[46]

While this aspect of male psychology may hinder the will to end war, may even lead us to feel that it's not possible to end war, as we shall see later, there are cultures that have devised ways to provide satisfying masculine roles other than warrior. We can learn from these people how to put similar means to work for those of us living in "warrior cultures" as we tackle the war monster and subdue it.

CHAPTER 3 – PROXIMATE CAUSES OF WAR

You can't say civilization don't advance ... in every war they kill you in a new way.

Will Rogers
New York Times, Dec. 23, 1929

What's All the Fighting About?

If people are attacked, it is abundantly obvious why they fight back. Self defense, particularly if there is no option to flee or move elsewhere, is a legitimate response, necessary for survival. In *Shift* however, we're looking to understand why any individual or group *initiates* a war.

We've looked using the perspective of psychology and will soon look at ultimate causes. In this chapter we consider proximate causes. We're asking, what are the immediate triggers of a war? What are the war's instigators fighting over? What set the whole mess off? What is the *casus belli* that caused someone to strike the first blow?

Experts and lay people have labored mightily to figure this out. The result is a plethora of answers. None, by the way, indicate that we make war so that we can live in peace, although some people do buy into this fallacy when their leaders suggest it as the reason to break out the weapons.

Here is a list of some reasons offered:

- We humans fight because many males simply enjoy a good war; they find it addictive (it's in our biology – i.e. it is actually linked to ultimate causation)
- We fight because we possess a gene (or genes) that directs us to make war (again, a biological theory)

- We fight because in some cultures, engaging in war and making a kill signifies the transition from being a boy into a man, or from being a man into being a warrior – for a change in status (a cultural theory)
- We fight when a leader (or leaders) seeks symbols that can give him (or her) power (status) (e.g., scalps or heads of defeated enemies) (a cultural theory)
- We fight over worldview or religious differences, to dominate others by forcing them to accept ours or to free ourselves from domination by others (a cultural theory)
- We fight over ethnic or lifestyle differences, to dominate others by forcing them to accept ours or to free ourselves from domination by others (a cultural theory)
- We fight to exact revenge on others who first attacked us (a psychological theory)
- Capitalism and economic inequality trigger wars (Karl Marx – an economic theory)
- Poverty leads to war (Jeffrey Sachs – an economic theory)
- We fight when a leader (or leaders) seeks control of a critical or highly valued resource that can give him (or her) power (e.g., land, water rights, salt, gold, women, slaves, diamonds, oil, precious metals – this list can be very long) (an economic theory)
- We fight "because we can," meaning societies with high military preparedness tend to make war more frequently compared to states with low military readiness (an economic and political theory)[47]
- We fight when a leader (or leaders) under pressure from their subjects need to find a distraction to unite the people behind the leader (a political theory)
- Competition over scarce resources triggers war when population size or droughts or any other factor causes basic environmental resources to become scarce (Steven LeBlanc, Azar Gat - an ecological theory with many proponents)
- We fight out of a fear of a possible scarcity of resources, not actual scarcity (Ember and Ember - a psychological theory related to economics).

Armies of experts have mounted substantial efforts to analyze proximate triggers, some actually hoping to find a single, pivotal cause that could be attacked to end human slaughter.[48] Clearly, any search for one single cause was and, I believe, will remain, a futile exercise. One might just as eagerly seek the single reason why people love each other.

Of all of the above possibilities, John Horgan describes one I find most interesting and provocative. He recalls a discussion with two anthropologists, Carol and Melvin Ember.[49] The Embers for many years oversaw the Human Relations Area Files, a massive source of information gathered over two centuries by ethnographers on over 300 societies. The Embers looked to see if there was a strong correlation between actual resource scarcity and the outbreak of war. They found none.

What they did find was a strong correlation with unpredictable natural disaster—floods, droughts, earthquakes, insect infestations—that had disrupted food supplies in the past. It wasn't disasters themselves that triggered war, the Embers emphatically explained. Rather it was the memory of past disasters and the fear of future ones. The fear of scarcity. Horgan quotes the Embers as writing, "Societies with only the threat of disaster with a memory of unpredictable disasters, but no actual disaster during a twenty-five-year period, fought very frequently."

Maybe it is not actual lack of oil that is triggering armed (proxy) struggles taking place in the Middle-East for example, but a fear of lack of oil (or of a resource that can supply affordable energy). Maybe something people need to avoid going to war is assurance that they will not lack something they consider essential.

What is certainly true is that many of the listed proximate causes are involved at one time or another at some level in the calculations of those initiating a war. That's why the plan presented to dismantle the war machine in Chapter 12 is built around nine "cornerstones," challenges that must be tackled simultaneously. The cornerstones address the proximate causes listed above and several additional problem areas as well. Failing to address any of them will make ending war unlikely, and it will guarantee backsliding. That is, were we to achieve a global peace, we would not be able to sustain it over time if any of the essential cornerstones of peace was allowed to crumble. We'll return to proximate causes in some detail when we take up the plan.

Peace

Although the subject of *Shift* is war, a word needs to be said about what is generally thought to be its opposite: peace. Specifically, it needs to be noted that a struggle to end war is not the same thing as waging peace.

"Peace" has many definitions. In *The Collapse of the War System*, J. J. English reviews different definitions of peace and provides a thorough review of the history and philosophy behind the study of peace and the study of war.[50] The ethologist Peter Verbeek provides another good introduction to its meanings and how the study of peace can be approached.[51] Verbeek defines peace as "….the behavior through which individuals, families, groups, communities, and/or nations experience low levels of violence and engage in mutually harmonious interactions."[52]

The Nobel Peace Laureate Oscar Arias Sanchez describes peace as "…. a never-ending process, the work of many decisions by many people in many countries. It is an attitude, a way of life, a way of solving problems and resolving conflicts."[53]

In a major review of behaviors generally distributed in an array of animal species (e.g., peacemaking, reconciliation, tolerance, peacekeeping), Verbeek injects balance into the study of social interactions by showing that peace and making peace is a natural phenomenon, every bit as important as aggression.[54] For example, male chimpanzees compete strongly for dominance. They can engage in vicious fights. If, however, a group is to maintain cohesion—which is important to all members—reconciliation has to take place. The biologist Frans de Waal was the first to describe the chimpanzee reconciliation process, which involves the subordinate male grooming the dominant male. It is noteworthy that often it is a female who initiates the grooming session between the males: she acts as peacemaker.[55]

Globally the numbers of peace institutes and classes on peace education are growing. This trend seems to reflect the growing global sense of unease and even alarm mentioned in the introduction, that our old ways of behaving have become dangerously maladaptive, and that we urgently need to find new, less destructive ways to relate to each other.

English, in his introductory "To the Reader," writes about the ideology of violence, the ideology of war, and a culture of peace:

The collapse of the ideology of war will of course not automatically bring about the collapse of the ideology of violence, but it surely follows that a culture of peace cannot be built on a culture of violence. The ideology of war is one of the central foundations of the ideology of violence and just as the horse comes before the cart, the collapse of the ideology of war will be a major step in the collapse of the ideology of violence.[56]

I agree completely. A culture of peace cannot be built on a foundation that includes war…actual war or tolerating the concept of initiating war for any reason as something legitimate. In short, a campaign to end war is not the same as peace education or promoting nonviolent conflict resolution. However ending war is to be accomplished, it is a necessary *prerequisite* for establishing a culture of peace.

There is, of course, much overlap in the work of ending war and the work of teaching peace. For example, both stress promoting nonviolent conflict resolution, fostering a sense of a shared humanity of all people, and pursuing basic human rights that we associate with liberal democracies. Both efforts—doing the work of ending war and doing the work of promoting peace—can and, I will argue, must be pursued simultaneously. But teaching peace will not end war; the war machine in the past has repeatedly trumped all efforts using education, or example, or rational debate to create cultures of peace. What the *Shift* ending-war campaign aims to do is create, for the first time in millennia, a suitable environment for nurturing peace by mounting a concerted and focused effort to dismantle the war machine and thereby put an end to war.

CHAPTER 4 – ULTIMATE CAUSES OF WAR

The genes hold culture on a leash. The leash is very long, but inevitably values will be constrained in accordance with their effects on the human gene pool. The brain is a product of evolution. Human behavior—like the deepest capacities for emotional response which drive and guide it—is the circuitous technique by which human genetic material has been and will be kept intact.

Edward O. Wilson
On Human Nature (1978), 167

Biological Roots – Ultimate Causation

From a rudimentary, simple perspective it is obvious that at some level genes must influence whether we make war or not. We're not rabbits, or deer, or butterflies. If we were these species, we would not have it in us to make war. We simply would not have the genetic makeup required.

In this chapter we explore the relationship of genes (heredity) to observed behavior. If someone asks, What about their heredity causes animals to behave the way they do? They are asking about biological roots. They are asking what survival or reproductive advantage in the evolutionary, deep past of the species favored the behavior we observe. When we focus on the selective advantage provided in the evolutionary past by genes that created the sense organs and nervous systems that produce the behavior we now observe, we're searching for the *ultimate* causes of behavior, for evolutionary origins.

Actions we see—like a bird building a nest or mating or migrating, a chimpanzee using a twig to fish termites from a termite mound, a mother nursing her baby, or humans making war—these are the product of genes and environment acting together but in differing amounts. By "environment," I refer to all of life experience, everything that impinged on an animal—physical, chemical and social—even from the time before fertilization of the egg that eventually became the adult.

For humans, culture (one facet of environment) has tremendous influence on our actions because we are so very good at learning. In fact, each culture we create is a kind of new environment within which each individual must behave so as to survive and reproduce.

Note again that all observed behaviors are not adaptations (they aren't all the result of being selected in the past via "natural selection"). Natural selection acts by favoring some genes over others because those genes produced a behavior (or structure or physiological process) that promoted the survival and reproduction of the particular animal possessing those genes. Many behaviors that are not "adaptations" can be the result of learning (but keep in mind that the brain that did the learning was itself genetically built to be able to learn). And some, like the compensating behaviors of the male Laughing Gulls, are the result of putting a nervous system that evolved in one environment into a radically altered, new environment. Natural selection of the new behavior those males performed was not involved.

Determining how much of a human behavior is the result of genetics and how much is the result of learning has been and continues to be a major problem because the relationship, in most instances, is so complex. This isn't just a problem for non-biologists, it's a problem even for biologists who specialize in the study of animal behavior.

How does this relate to understanding war? All behavior rests on an animal's fundamental genetic base, including the capacity for learning.[57] So if someone proposing to explain war does not realize the extent to which ALL behavior has both biological and environmental (experiential) underpinnings, their explanations about war will fall short. For that reason, what follows is a basic, but essential, review of how genes relate to (produce) behavior, and why considered as groups (not individuals), human males and females have some significantly different built-in genetic proclivities with respect to using physical violence and avoiding war.

Martian Men and Venusian Women

Virtually everyone concedes that throughout history war has been an overwhelmingly male activity. Men have also overwhelmingly been in charge of our governing bodies. So is there any reason to think women might be biologically geared to react differently than men when it comes to war? Isn't it possible that if women had governing power in our societies, perhaps they would also succumb to the seductive sway of power and act exactly like men, including the launching of wars?

John Gray wrote a popular and often cited relationship book, *Men are from Mars. Women are from Venus.*[58] The book suggests how men and women can understand their differences in order to communicate better and get along. Some differences between men and women are superficial (changing fashion can quickly alter them—e.g. American men don't use hair dye) or the differences are cultural (not based heavily on genetics) and thus changeable, although often not easily so (e.g., women don't fight on front lines in American wars). But this much-copied book does express an important kernel of biological truth. Some differences between men and women have deep genetic origins and are, for all practical considerations, unchangeable.

To Save Ourselves from Ourselves We Must Know Ourselves

To fix a problem or cure a disease, knowing symptoms or even contributing factors isn't enough. To end war requires that we understand what it is about us that leads us to the killing. In *The Social Conquest of Earth* (2012), the masterful scientist Edward O. Wilson proposed to answer three existential questions: "Where did we come from?" "What are we?" and "Where are we going?"[59] Answers to all three of these queries are also central to *Shift's* analysis of war and how to end it permanently.

From a biological perspective, one of the things we are NOT is a monolithic species composed solely of males. Our species' behavior and the cultures we create are products of two very different groups: males and females. One half of our species has brains significantly suffused with testosterone and one half has brains significantly suffused with estrogen. Men and women also differ significantly with respect to blood levels of oxytocin, a neurohormone that has many profound effects on our social behavior, from pair-bonding to levels of empathy and trust. Women have consistently higher levels of oxytocin, which the neuroeconomist Paul Zak, who has studied its effects, has dubbed the "moral molecule."[60]

These hormonal differences underlie the fact that groups of men and women confronted with the same situation often respond differently. Natural selection favors behavior that increases reproductive success, and behavior that, over thousands of years of evolution, produced reproductive success for men often differs in significant ways from behavior that fostered the reproductive success of women. As a consequence, behavior choices of groups of men can be very different from the behavior choices of groups of women. This is markedly evident when it comes to using physical aggression: groups of women, for example, are consistently less likely to attempt to solve conflicts using violence and war than are groups of men.

A reader may be amazed to discover that in the majority of discussions of why we make war, women are scarcely mentioned, if mentioned at all. Three notable exceptions are books on war by Joshua Goldstein and the co-authors Malcolm Potts and Thomas Hayden and a section about "feminization" in Stephen Pinker's book (see Appexdix II).[61] I've called the tendency of scholars to generally overlook women a problem of "hidden females."[62] Women tend to be systematically lumped into the words *humans, humanity, human, mankind* or *humankind*.

This blinkering characterizes and hinders many areas of study and thought. For example, in his analysis of the evolution of political systems, *The End of History and the Last Man*, political scientist Francis Fukuyama suggested that history is moving, albeit in fits and starts, toward universal liberal democracy. But he makes no mention of women or how their exclusion from governing in illiberal democracies might have influenced history. In his book *War is a Force that Gives us Meaning*, Chris Hedges similarly makes no mention of women; we are left to assume that the force of war has the same meaning for women as it does for men. His index does not even have an entry for women.

Even E. O. Wilson's *The Social Conquest of Earth* lacks an index entry for women and the words *woman*, *women*, and *female/s* are mentioned scarcely a dozen times, and then only in passing and usually in the context of tribes exchanging women. His explanations of our origins could have been significantly enhanced by considering separately the contributions of men and women in the same detail with which he describes participation of casts of social ant species. Likewise, John's Horgan's *The End of War* provides no discussion of how the differing biology of men and women might relate to ending war.

This biological blind spot in our understanding makes it impossible to answer the question so fundamental to comprehending the root cause of war: "What are we?" We begin to answer that question by considering some fundamental principles of biology and evolution that relate to differences between the sexes.

The Biological Logic – Why Men and Women Respond Differently to Conflict

Evolutionary biologists have for years explored what they call male and female reproductive strategies. It is universally the case across the animal kingdom that males can produce a great many sperm compared to females' more limited production of eggs. These fundamental biological differences create different priorities and pressures on the two sexes. The result produces differences in their behavior that are dramatic, and are often described as a "battle of the sexes."

The anthropologist Sarah Blaffer Hrdy wrote a broad survey on human reproductive behavior, *Mother Nature: A History of Mothers, Infants, and Natural Selection*.[63] She focused on priorities of and pressures on women. One thing to note from the outset is that in

Mother Nature, Hrdy dismantles the idea that women are made of sugar and spice and everything nice while men are less delightful, made from snips and snails and puppy dog tails. She makes clear that women are aggressive beings, that they create dominance hierarchies and defend them. And most remarkably, women under a variety of social and physical pressures will abandon or even kill their offspring, something almost never seen with other primate females.[64]

Furthermore, cross-cultural studies reveal that men in many cultures care for children, and men who bond early with their children can be very nurturing. Barry Hewlett, for example, studied father-infant bonding in Aka pygmies and finds that fathers there bond with their children by regular hugging, kissing, and soothing care."[65] So we begin our exploration into gender differences and how these may relate to war by dismissing any idea that women are innately nicer or more nurturing than men…or for that matter, more moral. If in our search to understand our capacity for peace or war we find differences in how men and women use physical aggression and relate to war—and we will find differences—it won't be because women are sugar and spice and men aren't.

Mother Nature presents in detail a list of references as well as evidence that forms the backbone of the following biological logic. Deborah Blum's introduction to her book *Sex on the Brain* provides another brief discussion of most of the following biological points.[66]

Keep in mind two biological facts: first, we are mammals because like all female mammals, our females produce milk to feed their offspring. And second, we're primates, related to chimpanzees, bonobos, gorillas, orangutans and more distantly to baboons and other monkeys. Keeping these biological facts in mind, the biological logic is this:

1. For all living things, the **basic biological bottom line is to reproduce and have offspring that in turn have offspring**. Genes of individuals that fail to reproduce are eliminated from the great evolutionary game of life. This means that behavioral inclinations coded in those genes are not passed to subsequent generations. There are some subtleties here—for example, highly social animals (bees, humans) can often

contribute some genes to the future by aiding close relatives who possess the same genes rather than reproducing themselves—but such subtleties don't alter the basic biological reality.

2. For female mammals, and certainly **for female primates, reproducing successfully is a very expensive proposition**. Female primates carry an offspring to term, protecting and nourishing it within their body, often for many months. They must risk the hazards of childbirth. Then they provide milk to nourish it for weeks if not months or even years more. They must protect it, care for it, and support it sometimes for many additional years before it is old enough to reproduce. Women must bear, protect, and care for a child for a minimum of twelve to thirteen years before that child is capable of reproduction, and in bearing, giving birth to, and rearing offspring, women risk and invest far more than men do. For every parent raising children, whether in the United States, Brazil, Thailand, or Ghana, the costs involved (in time, energy, risk, and resources) resonate deeply. And then, in most cultures, once a child is raised, females especially remain involved in ensuring that the offspring of their offspring—their grandchildren—survive. For females, this is, beyond doubt or argument, an extraordinarily expensive process.

3. Therefore, **the ideal condition for female primates is social stability for long periods**. Serious social turmoil, anything that threatens the life of these expensive offspring before they can reproduce is hugely counterproductive. What this has meant in women's evolutionary history is that any serious turmoil—which certainly includes a war that might result in the woman's death or the death of her children—has been highly counterproductive. War for our female ancestors as well as for modern women is an extraordinarily dangerous threat to reproduction.

4. For male mammals, including male primates, the biological game is usually quite different, because **they do not invest as heavily in the survival of their children as females do**. In some primates, fathers contribute nothing beyond their

sperm, which are in plentiful supply. While human males often become involved in support and protection of their young, this isn't the case in all cultures (see, for example, the Mosuo described by Hua[67] where technically there isn't even an institution of marriage). In few cultures does a father's investment approach that of a mother, though there are some notable primate exceptions, tamarins for example. But compared to females, male mammals including male primates are generally more involved in spreading their seed widely than investing heavily in any given offspring. Should males lose offspring as a consequence of conflict or war, they can more easily sire replacement offspring than females can bear, give birth to, and raise replacements.

5. Therefore, for many male primates, including men, **social stability is not as high a priority as it is for females**. In most modern cultures, for example, much of men's social lives centers around rearranging the social order in their dominance hierarchies to achieve greater social status.[68] Joshua Goldstein's *War and Gender* provides a comprehensive review of the importance of forming dominance hierarchies by male primates, and that includes humans.[69] Hrdy, in her book *The Woman that Never Evolved,* defines dominance as "the ability of one individual to influence or coerce the behavior of others, usually by threatening to inflict damage but also by promising to give (or withhold) rewards."[70] Sometimes this involves using physical violence. In humans, dominance does equate with status, and with the ability to control others. By extension, war is an expression of the inclination to control/dominate others carried out on a grand scale.

So one possible biological explanation for this sex difference, with men more tolerant of social turmoil than women, relates to the male urge to rise in rank. The rationale would be that if a male's struggle to rise in rank within the group succeeds, it pays off because he is able to mate with more females, thus spreading his seed.[71] Goldstein, reviewing data on the relationship between reproductive success and the obsession with dominance relationships in male primates indicates that this hypothesis does not seem to be the explanation.[72] Another hypothesis explaining this male struggle for higher status, or to avoid sinking to lower status, is that it results in greater access to resources such as food or safe resting or sleeping sites. A recent study suggests that wounds of high-ranking male baboons heal faster than wounds of males of low rank.[73] Goldstein, reviewing studies on primate hierarchies, says that as a general rule, "human males may be more hierarchical—oriented towards competition and status—whereas females are more empathetic, although with a 'great deal of plasticity' in gender roles."[74]

It's possible, even probable, that higher status conveys different advantages to different species, and different advantages in different situations.[75] Whatever the reason, men today in the vast majority of cultures still compete regularly to overturn the social order, to rise in rank if possible or to avoid losing status, and they are much more inclined than women to use physical aggression to do so. Male groups, unless restrained by police, strong social prohibitions, or both, fight to dominate other male groups. In short, and to repeat, the overall result of these different biological pressures and priorities is that social stability is not as high a priority for men as it is for women.

Other inherited traits also underlie our ability, and willingness, to wage war. One of these is an inclination for male bonding associated with aggressive action. Certainly for ancestors in our deep past it would have facilitated certain kinds of hunting, especially of large animals. Goldstein provides a lengthy review of male bonding in humans as this relates to war.[76] He points out that small-group bonding is very important to combat effectiveness. Combat veterans will say that they fought, and if necessary killed in combat, in order to protect their comrades, not out of patriotism or hatred of the enemy. Military hierarchies attempt to extend this aggressive male bonding to the larger-unit scale with concepts like *esprit de corps*, the idea of upholding group honor. Close-order drill is also used to create a sense of group cohesion.

Note that women display these same inclinations for status and bonding, only that in women they are not as consistently or strongly expressed; they are more characteristic of or take a stronger form in men in general.

We see this tendency for aggressive male group action expressed in men's love of aggressive team sports, in young males that get together to do pranks, and when angry men form a mob—after a stolen election or simply after a soccer match. These angry mobs are very unlikely to be composed mostly of women.

Two other biological traits also facilitate the building of armies. One is an admirable trait: altruism in the form of willingness to defend or rescue other individuals of the group, even possibly at the risk of one's own life. There are many examples of humans of both sexes performing this sort of self-sacrifice not only for family members but for members of their group, or for the group itself, which may not be composed of close relatives at all.

Goldstein describes the other trait, the willingness to work in hierarchies, a characteristic of which is willingness to follow orders of members of higher rank.[77] Horgan also points out the importance of this trait to the functioning of armies.[78]

In J. J. English's introduction "To the Reader" of his book *The Collapse of the War System*,[79] he writes, "In fact, all the information, knowledge and wisdom that is required for us as individuals and for our societies to live in peace are well known and freely available." Yet this useful exploration of the history of the philosophy of war and peace makes no significant mention of how our biology makes us susceptible to war. Nor does it explore how reproductive pressures and priorities of men and women might differ in ways that relate to war. Horgan concedes that biology has some place in figuring out how to end war, but he also fails to explore the profound significance of gender differences. A central purpose of *Shift* is to fill this yawning gap in our "information, knowledge, and wisdom" of what is required if we are to end war permanently so that we may, in fact, live in a future far more peaceful.

War Is Not Innate

Before reviewing more specifically how genes relate to behavior, we can unequivocally say one thing about war itself. War is not innate in the sense that it is inescapable. The most incontrovertible proof we have that it is not is the existence of societies anthropologists have found to be without war. For example, in *The Human Potential for Peace* and *Beyond War*, Douglas Fry lists over 70 of these societies and describes many of them.[80] His article on lethal aggression in mobile forager bands with his colleague Patrik Söderberg in a 2013 article in *Science* also mentions a number of warless societies.[81] The website *www.peacefulsocieties.org* provides introductory descriptions of over 20 societies deemed to be extremely peaceful.[82] The red dots on a map at my website indicate the centers of distribution of over 80 such peaceful cultures.[83] These exist in a wide variety of habitats.

None of these societies is a utopia. None are without human conflicts. Anthropologist Raymond Kelly reviews the motivations for arguments in non-warring societies that can erupt into fights or even homicide and he finds a wide range of reasons for conflicts.[84] No single pattern applies to all of these cultures. Kelly does indicate that male-female (typically spousal) conflicts are the most prevalent, and that fighting between men is only a little more frequent than fighting between women.[85] What is key is not that these societies are without conflict or even rare violence, but that many societies are without war, as war is defined in *Shift*.

You may know the names of some of these people: Amish, Hutterites, Hopi, Laplanders (or Sami), Nubians. Most of their names are totally unfamiliar to us since they aren't taught in our schools. It's almost as if the dominant, warring cultures would like to keep their existence a secret lest we get revolutionary ideas. Simply put, if war is an inescapable aspect of human nature, such societies would not and could not exist.

The trailblazing anthropologist Margaret Mead knew about non-warring people and came to this same conclusion. In her essay *War is Only an Invention – Not a Biological Necessity,* she calls war a cultural *invention*.[86] Ehrenreich suggests the term *meme*, a word coined by the biologist Richard Dawkins to describe self-replicating cultural units (ideas, concepts) analogous to genes that seek to copy themselves as widely as possible.[87] Others having looked at biology agree: war is not innate. It is an extremely bad habit/social disease/invention/meme.

In summary, what are the innate, inheritable traits that do make us susceptible to making war?

- Dominance and Obedience - An inclination to form dominance hierarchies, and to defer to superior authority.
- Passionate bonding - Male tendencies for aggressive bonding, critical for some forms of group defense and hunting and able to be manipulated into the service of war.
- Personal sacrifice - Willingness to sacrifice oneself for the survival of the group.
- Xenophobia - A tendency to be wary or suspicious of unknown individuals or groups, which can be used by warmongers to stir up fear of the "dangerous other."

It is the combined presence of the above traits, the first three in men especially, that allows warmongers to build armies and launch wars. This is clearly very different from saying that the savagery that is war is inevitable.

Links Between Genes and Behavior – The What-Feels-Right Principle

We should never underestimate the power of feelings. Earlier I indicated that observing wild animals in a natural environment can help us understand how genes relate to behavior, and that the relationship is a distant one. In a classroom setting when teaching Animal Behavior, I often illustrated the "feeling" link between genes and behavior using the example of the mind-blowing complexity of African Weaver Bird nests.

At UCLA where I was teaching, biology professor Nicholas Collias had a captive colony of this small African species. A young male weaver without previous experience in nest building, in the absence of even an example of how a nest should look, can right off select the right plant material and construct a perfectly typical, tightly woven hanging pendulum with an entrance nicely arranged to make it difficult for snakes to enter. This behavior clearly is not learned by example. So how do they do it? I call it the "what-feels-right" principle. What we observe is that the young male begins to build by experimenting. He picks up plant materials, for example, seemingly at random in the beginning. But those pieces that don't "feel right" (apparently to him too stiff, or too flabby) he drops. Or he may insert a piece only to pull it out and reinsert it in a slightly different way. He works and works guided by what "feels right" to his touch and eyes. We, too, are run to an impressive extent by the "what-feels-right" principle.

What does that mean? There is no gene for "doing war" or for "fostering social stability." Rather, genes affect behavior at a distance by directing the construction of brains and endocrine organs and sense organs. It takes many genes working in concert to direct the growth and assembly of these body structures, including delicate brain architecture.[88]

Once a brain is constructed during embryonic development, it becomes the body's decision-maker. Sense organs detect environmental stimuli—our ears, eyes, touch receptors, and so on. The quality or "amount" of a stimulus is coded as electrochemical signals passed along nerve cells to the brain, our astounding analyzing, decision-making, and action-executing organ—an organ said to possess more cells than there are stars in our galaxy—and each and every one of us has one of these wondrous brains sitting atop our shoulders!

There, inside our skulls, the brain decodes and manipulates the signals. The location where these impulses end up determines how the input is interpreted. Impulses coming from the eyes are interpreted as visual signals. If signals arrive at areas linked by neural paths to the nose, the brain interprets the input as smell. All this information from our sense organs is subsequently processed in a variety of complex ways.

This processing often produces an emotional response. The brain's structure, the result of numberless generations of natural selection, determines whether we experience the incoming stimuli as pleasing or noxious, delightful or revolting. On a bitterly cold day, the heat of a campfire is pleasing, and the offer of a bowl of ice cream is something we can pass up. We feel as we do, not because of single genes for those reactions, but because many genes acting in concert constructed for us sensory organs to pick up information from our environment and a brain that makes assessments, many of them emotional.

Another result of processing can be a decision, a conscious or unconscious one, about how to respond. We huddle closer to the toasty fire. We decline the chilly ice cream.

It is the architecture and chemistry of a human brain that determines which physical or social conditions a given brain finds satisfying, pleasurable, exciting, stimulating, cool, worth doing, worth repeating, worth working for. Such stimuli or conditions are said to be "reinforcing," and they drive our behavior. We respond to positive reinforcers (food, safe hiding place, a good-looking man or woman) and to negative reinforcers (pain, scolding, social isolation).[89] And we are motivated to do what "feels right."

How reinforcement works is becoming a fascinating area of research on a biochemical level. Neuroeconomist Paul Zak, for example, studies the reinforcing effects of hormones, especially oxytocin. He reports on years of work in his enlightening and entertaining book *The Moral Molecule*, looking at such behaviors as risk-taking, use of aggression, trust, and empathy.[90] His research documents a clear link between the release of oxytocin in the brain and its reinforcing effects on human interpersonal relations, and he asserts that "the Golden Rule is a lesson the body already knows, and when we get it right we feel the rewards immediately."[91] He also documents the antagonistic effects of testosterone on oxytocin. The interplay between these two chemicals in the brain and their effects on our bodies underlies much of human behavior, including as mentioned earlier some broad general differences between men and women. Although Zak does not address the issue of war directly, his neurochemical approach to empathy and morality definitely has important implications for students of war.[92]

Vast swaths of our behavior are for the most part guided, subconsciously, by "what-feels-right." Ultimately the results of all this processing fosters survival and reproduction.

If evolution produced a male tendency (inclination) for this and a female tendency (inclination) for that, we would find that the brains of males and females respond differently to the same stimulus context—in this case, a choice to go to war or not—with males more inclined in one direction, females more inclined in another,[93] depending on how he or she feels, consciously, or more often subconsciously.

Inclinations, the Bell Curve, and Male/Female Differences

What is quite evident is that differences between men and women in the traits in question are not either/or. It's not that one sex has it while the other doesn't. Both tendencies—the thrill of bonding together to go make war on a perceived enemy and the capacity to take pleasure in social stability—are present in both men and women. After all, men who do live in communities with children they have fathered would benefit by that community remaining secure and stable. And women can be roused to fight in defense of their offspring or the community where they are raising their offspring.

All humans have a "masculine side" and a "feminine side." How individual traits, which different cultures decide to call masculine and feminine, are mixed together is part of what makes each individual unique. The question is whether men and women differ sufficiently *on average* in expressing these traits so that letting one or the other sex express its tendencies unchecked for millennia leads to disastrous results.

So can we visualize quantitative or qualitative differences in traits between males and females? Consider what we'd find if we were to measure the eye color of men and women, from extremely light blue to darkest blue, and plot the number of individuals having a given eye color on a graph. We would find that the measurements for men and the curve for women would overlap virtually perfectly. We would find no significant difference between men and women in eye color.

But if we were to measure the amount of fat and glandular tissue lying between the nipple and underlying breast muscle in adults, adjusting the measures to account for different levels of obesity, and plot those distributions, the male and female curves generated would hardly overlap at all. Only a few men have a breast measurement that overlaps even those women who develop small breasts.

A good way to vizualize differences between men and women in any trait—height, weight, upper body strength, ability to do math, facility with language, facility with solving spatial problems—is the bell curve. It is a graph which presents, for a given ability or trait, the distribution of the measurements of many individuals. Online is a short review by K. H. Grobman, with an illustrative graph, that summarizes results of comparing studies of gender differences.[94] When plotted, the distributions typically show measurements of a few individuals on either extreme (very high measurements and very low measurements). The majority of people fall somewhere in the middle. The result is that the curve produced looks like a bell.

When no difference exists between two groups, such as men and women, and you place the curve of one group on top of the other, the curves overlap perfectly. If the frequency of occurrence of traits of individuals from the two groups is not the same—if for example, one group has individuals that have much higher scores than any individuals in the other group—the curves will not match; when you try to place one group's curve on top of the other, there will be an offset.

When we plot occurrence frequencies of different traits for men and women the curves almost always overlap, sometimes a lot, sometimes very little. And that's the heart of the question here. Just how much do inherited male and female tendencies for engaging in war or striving for social stability match up? If there is a difference, how great is it? And how can we measure such inclinations?

Trying to evaluate the degree of difference becomes particularly complicated because learning profoundly influences the ways humans express these two opposed tendencies. Trying to determine just how much of any human behavior is determined by genetics (nature) and how much is due to learning (nurture) continues to bedevil us. This is nowhere more evident than when investigators try to sort out the extent to which men and women do or do not differ with respect to personality traits and behavior as opposed to physical traits like height or upper body strength.[95]

What has been shown to be a reliable gender difference relates not to rates of aggression, but to the willingness to use *physical* aggression. For example, Eagly and Steffen did a meta-analysis of many studies on using direct and indirect aggression.[96] The analysis shows that men are more physically and verbally aggressive than women. The difference is largest (although still relatively small) when the aggression used was physical rather than indirect. In other words, the curves do overlap; there are greater differences in using both indirect and physical aggression within the sexes than there is between them. *But the curves do not overlap completely.*

The relationship between learning and expression of the desire to go to war, or instead to make peace, is even more complex to study. It is simply impossible to make direct measures of innate, biologically inherited differences in these inclinations. Too many factors influence how any individual decides in a given social context. Nonetheless, we can consider what data we do have that indicate the existence of sex differences in several aspects of biology and behavior, which I do in sections to follow.

A reminder is appropriate here. Individual men and women are wonderfully unique. Each is a distinct, astoundingly complex combination of what members of various cultures choose to call male and female traits. How gender differences relate to culture and how personality traits are molded and modified by learning are subjects covered in such texts as *Cultural Anthropology* by Carol and Melvin Ember or the similarly titled one by William Haviland.[97] One fundamental and clear fact is that through the influence of learning, culture is a powerful determinant of what behavior for adults of the two sexes is considered normal and acceptable.

But culture is not all-powerful. One of the central goals of the Women's Liberation Movement has been the struggle to let each person be whatever he or she wants to be—to free individuals from stereotyped expectations imposed by the cultural norms of a particular society that often don't suit the temperament or talents of a given man or woman. Although many, including my younger self, felt the point being made by the movement was that there were no fundamental gender differences beyond sexual behavior (primarily because so much focus was on freeing women from stereotypes), the fundamental goal of the movement was grander. It was to give scope to the wealth of human individuality: liberation was to be for both sexes, that women so inclined could be CEO's and men could be house dads.

This book, however, does not focus on unique individuals. It is concerned with statistically significant male/female differences over long periods of (evolutionary and historical) time and within large groups of individuals as these relate to war and to how the differences shape our cultural lives.

Given that men and women have differences, how might differences be reflected in our brains?

Differences in Brain Structure

A veritable mountain of research in the past three quarters of a century has put to rest any idea that men and women are born into this world as blank slates upon which culture draws up the person we know as an adult. This *tabula rasa* idea described the notion that nurture was all and nature nothing. We've learned that humans are not infinitely moldable into whatever shape a society (or parents) might like to dictate. Nature does count. And the latest research is clear: male and female babies, on average, emerge from the womb different and become more so as parents, friends, and culture mold their behavior.

One of the most exciting things that can happen to a scientist is to have an epiphany. One such experience I had concerned sex differences and brains. When I began graduate school, I was absolutely certain that while the bodies of men and women were different, their minds were essentially the same, distinguished only by individual differences and learning. I could cite you study after study showing how parents treat male and female children differently, causing them to develop in ways that fit culturally defined roles.[98] I could cite criticisms of studies from the past about brain size that had been used to argue that women were intellectually inferior to men, criticisms that showed clearly how investigator bias—the belief that women were inferior—had influenced the investigator's analysis and conclusions.

I could cite studies showing that even before children are born, we treat boy and girl babies differently and have different expectations for them. I vividly recall shopping for a gift for the birth of a nephew. I found a perfect, cuddly outfit. But it was pink, and they didn't have a blue one. I simply could not bring myself to buy pink for a boy. Instead, I settled on a yellow blanket.

And I chalked the experience up to one more example of how our expectations and treatment of the sexes differ, even when we might want to treat them the same. I was utterly convinced that at birth the "minds" of men and women are not different by sex, it's just different treatment that explains the gender differences we see in the interests of adults.

Then when I was doing Master's work at UCLA, I attended a seminar by Jerre Levy, a young neurobiologist. The subject was brain architecture. Levy claimed to be finding clear differences in the structure of a particular brain area. The clear differences were between the brains of males and females. I remember as if it were yesterday storming enraged out of the seminar. I was furious with Levy, thinking her a traitor to her sex because she was reinforcing the notion that mentally women were different from men—that is, somehow inferior.

But time proved Levy right. I followed the literature on brain architecture through the years until one day my epiphany struck. The weight of the data had become overwhelming and incontrovertible. Here and there, in this slight way and that, male and female brains were different! And not merely in regions involved in sexual behavior. My world turned upside down. I was going to have to deal with that unsettling fact.

My assumption was wrong, however, that difference would be taken to indicate female inferiority. The brains are simply different. They are not inferior or superior.

The clear implication, however, is that if the brains are built differently, men and women may do some things slightly, or even significantly, differently. They may think about some things slightly, or even significantly, differently. They may feel about some things slightly, or even significantly, differently.

Here are four sample differences in structure from studies of preserved adult brains. Other differences and references to original research can be found in Helen Fisher's *The First Sex*, Anne Moir and David Jessel's *Brain Sex*, the section on fetal brain development in Linda Mealey's *Sex Differences*, a particularly thorough discussion in Deborah Blum's *Sex on the Brain*, and the books by Louann Brizendine, *The Female Brain* and *The Male Brain*.[99]

- One region of the pre-frontal cortex is larger in women. Fisher believes this may reflect something she calls "web-thinking" in women, versus "step-thinking" in men.[100]
- Women have greater neuron density in the posterior temporal cortex, an area involved in differentiating sounds involved with language processing. This seems to correspond with studies showing that women do, on average, tend to have better linguistic abilities.[101]
- The anterior commissure is 12% bigger in women.[102]
- An area of the corpus collosum is somewhat larger in women.[103]

The last two findings were made early in these new investigations into sex differences in the brain. They are particularly interesting because these two thick bands of tissue, the anterior commissure and corpus collosum, connect the brain's right hemisphere with the left. They are the principal media through which the right and left halves of the brain talk to each other.

Some investigators have speculated that the thicker connections in women do seem to relate to a constellation of traits where women seem to be better than men, namely for multitasking and "intuition." These two talents may depend upon the ability of the two hemispheres to communicate particularly efficiently, which may be something female brains are specialized to do. Men seem to have more "lateralized" brain function; for a number of tasks, they rely somewhat more on one hemisphere than the other.

Differences in Brain Function

Researchers have also discovered a number of behaviors, abilities, or tendencies in which one sex, on average, scored higher than the other. All are tasks carried out by our brains. (Remember that the curves for the sexes overlap—there is often more difference between individual boys and girls, individual men and women, than there is between the two sexes). Fisher discusses many of these features, suggesting why evolution *may* have favored that skill in one sex or the other:[104]

- Men tolerate acute pain better.
- Women tolerate long-term discomfort better.
- Women are better able to decipher facial expressions.
- Women are more capable at multi-tasking.
- Women are more inclined to long-term planning.
- Men are more inclined to focus tightly on a problem.
- Men exhibit more emotional control.
- Women have better intuitional judgment.
- Men are more likely to take risks.

The cutting edge on the study of brain function has gone high-tech. Volunteers are asked to perform tasks—let's say something verbal—and they are studied with either a PET scanner or an MRI scanner. These are live-brain tests. Deborah Blum describes, for example, the work of Sally and Bennett Shaywitz, who looked at gender differences and language processing.[105] They asked subjects to do a rhyming task while under an MRI scanner. In most men, as they matched words with appropriate rhymes (cake, bake), a small center called the inferior frontal gyrus (behind the eyebrow) lit up only on the left side. For women, the tendency was for this region to light up in both hemispheres.

Note that we can't know whether all, some, or none of the structural differences I described above are the result of genes directing the brains' construction, or rather that the brains are anatomically different in adults because of a lifetime of learning. Learning affects brain structure, and the anatomical studies referred to were done on the brains of deceased adults.

Similarly, most live-brain function studies have been done on adults who, as Blum emphasizes in *Sex On The Brain*, had been subjected to a lifetime of learning. Ideally what we need are similar PET and MRI studies involving infants, where learning cannot be the explanation for differences. Given current technology, where the subject must lie still for a long period in a strange contraption, restless infants don't make ideal subjects, but some progress is still being made.

Studies on Infants and Cross-cultural Studies of Children

We are barely at the beginning of the age of exploring this extraordinary inner world of the mind, and we will surely find many more male/female differences. MRI and PET studies with infants will be critical. Also important are cross-cultural studies looking at gender differences in behavior in infants and young children. If we detect differences in infants, very young children, and across cultures, we secure strong evidence that the differences are the result of nature rather than nurture.

A Field Guide to Boys and Girls by Susan Gilbert, a fine book for parents, describes just how early in time some major sex differences in behavior begin to appear,[106] as does Blum in *Sex on the Brain*. Note again that the differences between sexes are usually not large. One of the biggest differences, for example, is that boys, cross-culturally, engage in more rough and tumble play than girls do. They are more likely to pummel, wrestle, and pretend-fight. But only a small percent of the boys—15-20% in one study cited by Gilbert—score higher than did any girls. Most boys' and girls' scores overlap.

These studies do show, however, that materials for building an adult are not exactly the same in populations of very young males and females. Some examples taken from Gilbert:

The INAH-3, a tiny pin-prick-size cluster of cells is the same size in male and female babies but begins to enlarge in boys when they are about ten. The implication is that the genetically timed increase in testosterone secretion associated with puberty causes the changes in boys. The cluster has one half to three times more nerve cells in adult men than women, and it is thought to be involved in regulating sexual desire.

The two brain hemispheres develop at different rates in girls and boys. The left, the one most involved in language processing, develops more quickly in girls. The right, the side critical to many spatial tasks, develops more quickly in boys.

Within hours of delivery, girls, on average, seem more social than boys in that they maintain eye contact longer with people and are more responsive to other people and to sounds.

- Boys cry more, become more easily upset, and stay upset longer, on average, than girls.
- Girls' fine motor skills develop, on average, faster than boys'.

On average:

- Girls talk earlier than boys.
- Girls develop emotional or impulse control sooner than boys.
- Boys are more physically aggressive than girls.
- Girls are more verbally aggressive in the form of gossip or fighting words.
- Boys are more openly and physically involved in establishing dominance, while girls prefer to "get along" with a network, a friend, or a few friends, and to establish dominance by indirect, more subtle means.

Here, taken slightly modified from Debra Tannen's *The Argument Culture,* is a description of a play session that, while it involved older students, typifies what one sees even with young children.[107]

Two boys and a girl who were friends were playing a game of blocks. Each had built a structure, a unique design. Suddenly, one boy threw a block at the other boy's structure to knock it over. The second boy retaliated by throwing a block at the first boy's structure. The first boy then threw a block at the girl's. She put her arms around her building to shield it from flying blocks. The two boys happily destroyed each other's buildings but couldn't get hers because they didn't want to hit her with the blocks. A third boy came over and asked her why she didn't throw blocks back, and she said she didn't like to play that way and didn't find it fun.

As Tannen says, it's not that boys are insensitive and mean. It's a kind of game for them. It was fun. Note that the girl's reaction was not to flee, but to defend her building. I discuss later the powerful inclination women have for defense (see Women as Warriors).

Blum describes the work of Martin Hoffman who studied the emotional responses of day-old infants to various sounds: animal calls, the weird droning voice of a computer, and babies crying.[108] The strongest response of these day-old infants was to the sounds of human crying. And it was the *female* infants who reacted most strongly to the sounds of human distress. Certainly in these cases, learning cannot be involved.

Gilbert cites studies that show that parents of the children in these studies do a variety of things that encourage girls to speak and discourage boys from doing so, and that parents have many more face-to-face "conversations" with infant daughters than sons. Peers are also critical. One study looked at the popularity of children in fourth to sixth grade. Boys who fought back were popular. Girls who fought back weren't.[109]

It is culture—in the form of parents, siblings, friends, and the social environment at large—that takes these overlapping yet different beginning materials and shapes them. We then end up with little boys who grow into men having the male characteristics expected by their culture and little girls who grow into women having the expected female characteristics.

Testing the Female Preference for Social Stability Hypothesis

It was in *Women, Power, and the Biology of Peace* that I first proposed the hypothesis that women have a strongly evolved inclination for social stability.[110] That during our long paleo-past, natural selection associated with differing reproductive pressures and priorities of men and women gave women a suite of evolved traits/proclivities that work—over time and expressed by women in their communities—to maintain a socially stable (safe) environment in which to raise children.

I had wrestled for years, along with a lot of other people, to figure out why women are, for example, universally responsible for fewer homicides.[111] The psychologist Anne Campbell examined the use of aggression across many societies. Women, much more than men, prefer to avoid physical aggression and killing, and Campbell pointed out that evolutionarily, this serves to protect the women, their families, close associates, and especially their children from harm, a serious reproductive hazard.[112] So why do women tend to prefer keeping the peace but when sufficiently riled, will attack their husband with a frying pan or urge men to make war? How could I explain that when I attended scientific meetings composed 95% of men, the general atmosphere was competitive, and on occasion verbally combative, compared to meetings with romance writers composed of 95% women, where the atmosphere was generally cooperative and helpful? Why is that?

The key to the puzzle came one day in the shower, where I do a lot of creative thinking. I serendipitously attacked the issue from a fresh angle. I asked two biological questions that, oddly, I'd never asked myself before. Not counting the obvious driving urge to find a good man, I asked, "Biologically speaking, what do women want, and why do they want it?" What fundamentally motivates them?

To my surprise, I immediately thought of an answer: aside from that driving urge to find a good mate, women want safe and stable family and community and they want sufficient resources, both of which are essential to raise their (biologically expensive) children. Mind on fire, I hurried out, dried off, and wrote down the questions and the answer. I even made some quick initial mental tests as to how those biological needs—those female reproductive imperatives—would translate into behavior when it comes to using physical aggression…and maybe even other social behavior as well.

The general answer: women are geared by natural selection to do *whatever is necessary* to foster social stability. Anything that would threaten the life of her children or a mother's own life, especially war, would be an unacceptable risk to successful reproduction. Thus women would have to continually accommodate the need for social stability (the security of her community and family) with the need for sufficient resources.

Feeling certain I was on the right track, I started applying these two imperatives in a variety of contexts. To my pleased amazement, women's behavior, even seemingly strange contradictions, made sense. For example, if a disagreement develops over how to divide up a resource that two women both claim as theirs, a physical fight between the two of them—much more than a verbal screaming match—would more likely rile up and involve close kin and allies in physical fighting. The possible result would be that one or both of the women, or perhaps one or more of their children, might be wounded in the ensuing melee. Wounds can often be outright fatal or lacking modern medical care become seriously infected, resulting in death. It would be far more adaptive over the long (evolutionary) haul for the two women to find a way to compromise, perhaps with the aid of an outside third party. Indeed, the outside third party might have a stake in keeping the women from physical fighting because of her (or his) own interest in maintaining the peace. If starvation or the threat of starvation were at hand, however, women might well fight over the resource. Women would not avoid fighting in all contexts.

An immediate question arises. Wouldn't the rule against physical fighting apply equally to men? Yes, provided there is no incentive for men to engage in physical fights. But *Homo sapiens* is a primate, descended from a primate lineage in which males compete aggressively, including fighting physically, for dominance. That our men still inherit that predisposition is evident; it is something all cultures work to suppress or at least control. That our females prefer to compromise rather than fight physically is a trait that perhaps goes equally far back into our lineage since early recourse to fighting physically likely did NOT generally serve the reproductive or survival interests of human females who were living in cooperatively breeding groups (see "Cooperative Breeding" defined in Chapter Six) while male/male fighting sometimes, maybe often, did.

This same sort of analysis can be applied to conflicts in other contexts. For example, it can explain the phenomenon of soccer moms who vote for preemptive war. "Go to war," they will say to the men if they can be convinced that their community, where they are raising their children, is in imminent danger (e.g., of starvation or attack). It can explain choices of conservative thinking women who oppose politically progressive causes that would give them more individual power, such as the right to vote or a right to reproductive choice, because they prefer to avoid potentially serious disruptive or dangerous changes in the familiar social order even more than they seek personal power.[113]

This preference-for-social-stability hypothesis can be tested. The eight hypotheses (H) listed below state that the traits in question are (or are likely to be) more characteristic of women, keeping in mind individual differences and the moderating influence of culture. Although on the surface seemingly unrelated by any common function, they all have the potential to produce or foster social stability. The hypothesis predicts that when traits are found that universally show statistically significant differences between men and women, analysis should reveal that some that are more characteristic of women undergird social stability, either immediately or over time.

The first three (H1-H3) are already well documented cross-culturally. They were the facts that stimulated this social stability hypothesis. The remaining five have some support but need further study.

Although learning can reinforce their use, these traits are not learned behavior. Think of the situation being similar to language: the aptitude/inclination for the behavior is innate but learning reinforces and brings it out in full form in a particular culture. What is critical is that these inclinations/proclivities would produce the observed behavior because doing them is positively reinforcing to the person acting under their influence (doing so produces feelings of satisfaction), or not doing them is negatively reinforcing (failing to do so produces feelings of disquiet or dissatisfaction)."

- H1 - Forms of conflict resolution: More frequent or quicker use of win-win conflict choices of behavior (negotiation, mediation) or compromise that diffuses conflict.
- H2 - Dominance hierarchies: More stable than those of men and formed without using physical aggression.
- H3 - Physical violence: Less use of physical violence in interpersonal or community conflicts.
- H4 - Reconciliation: Willingness to more quickly forgive/reconcile over small crimes but harshly or seriously punish violent crime or crimes against women; greater concern to

bring about reconciliation between individual fighters or groups.

- H5 - Sympathetic concern: After a fight, more likely to console losers (e.g., with words or friendly embrace), reducing the recipients' stress level and facilitating continued group cohesion.[114]
- H6 - Budgeting choices: for example, more money spent on things to reduce violent neighborhood crime rather than spending on something that would enhance prestige, like acquiring a sports team for the community or a new city hall building.
- H7 - Foresight: Less emphasis on winning a conflict now in contrast to more emphasis on making sure the solution chosen now will also mean less conflict later (foresight regarding potential conflicts) (this kind of foresight coupled with women's concerns about having sufficient resources may explain the bias women have for supporting "green" or conservation issues).[115]
- H8 - Justice: less focused on the punitive and more focused on understanding an offender's problems, which places less emphasis on the letter of the law and more on individual justice based on circumstances (empathy for defendants)

Consider an amusing example that reflects women's preference for conflict resolutions that can foster return to social stability as quickly as possible. During the discussion session at a conference on why humans make war, a colleague told this story of an incident she experienced when working at the United Nations. She was observing negotiations between two parties. Both sides wanted to reach some resolution, but it was clear they were not making progress. Noting that no women were at the negotiating table, she suggested to the men that they include some women. The immediate response from the men on both sides was, "Oh no. We can't do that. The women would compromise."

Investigating these hypotheses won't be easy. It requires study of very complex behaviors of the two sexes cross-culturally, and setting up appropriate controls. For example, someone might ask concerning reconciliation (H4), "Don't some male elders exhibit this trait as well? Even more than a young women might?" But it would be inappropriate to compare young women with older males; the preferences or inclinations of young women should be compared with those of young men, and older males with same age females having similar life experiences. If detecting whether such differences exist and whether they are statistically and behaviorally significance were easy, they would already be well known and understood.

Foresight is another important trait to head off conflicts. Consider that quite commonly men and women have different responses to a night of wild and unplanned-for sex—men mostly focused on the moment, while women tend to anticipate the drastic changes that might occur in nine months. Over countless generations women have, via natural selection, honed the female skill of planning ahead for many contingencies. Men who are good or great leaders are just as skilled at anticipating problems. One might say that they are in touch with their "feminine side." But in *The First Sex*, anthropologist Helen Fisher cites studies showing that women CEOs are, in general, more inclined than male CEOs to look forward on a *habitual* basis. Says Fisher, this enables these female CEOs to anticipate where problems may arise. They use this forward-looking habit to get ahead of the potential conflict curve. Looking forward to defuse potential problems is part of the win-win, keep-the-peace tendencies of our female heritage, a reason why we need to harness female inclinations for the public sphere.[116]

To create a satisfying and more peaceful future, it will be the task of all leaders, of both sexes, to think proactively and creatively to uncover the seeds of social unrest and implement programs to prevent them from sprouting. Environmentalists doubtless hope to put in place forward-thinking leaders who will care for our planet's future. Without them, we may so seriously alter the environment for short-term gain in ways hostile to our well-being that we cause our history to end brutally despite our best social and political efforts to achieve peace.

The origins of the differences I've stressed here are not cultural. They are deeply rooted in our evolutionary past and are the outcome of different reproductive priorities of the two sexes. Given free rein and uncurbed by social or ecological forces, these opposed tendencies—with males more preoccupied with dominance/status/control which results in the turmoil of changing the social order, and females inclined to seek social stability over the long haul—will play themselves out in our group behavior. Not to take them into consideration when discussing the question of war and how to make a lasting peace is an error of profound consequence.

Positive Aspects of Aggression

So what would the world be like if women, with their preference for social stability, ran it and men were restricted to the home, locked in a male version of a harem? For an answer to this question, we have no examples. None. Except in fiction and fantasy, such a matriarchy has never existed anywhere in human history.

But my gut instinct is that with the passage of time, such a world would be stultifying. We'd be strangled by an unchecked female inclination for social stability, subjected unrelentingly to the deeply seated desire to avoid rocking the boat. We would lose the excitement that comes with innovation, restlessness, exploration, striving.

All of these can be motivated by curiosity or the desire to benefit others, but are also frequently fired by aggression and status-seeking. I use the broad definition of aggression that includes assertiveness and ambition. Aggression is the urge to assert oneself at the expense (however slight) of others, to push one's own agenda, or to achieve one's desires by a variety of means. At low levels it equates with assertiveness, ambition, forcefulness, and in extreme form it involves physical violence.

No one questions that males have aggressive tendencies, or that they bring an abundance of positive things to the human equation, small things as well as great ones. It would be a great mistake to lock males away at home. What we think of as male energy has impelled us to venture out to explore the unknown, climb the highest peak, create the grandest building, push beyond just one more horizon, to invent the newest, most amazing gizmo.

We may one day find ways to eliminate the proximate causes of war and redirect aggressive urges entirely into positive endeavors (exploration on earth and in space, invention, sports, business), but the capacity for aggression is not going to disappear.

Nor would we want it to! My use of aggression is similar to that used by Konrad Lorenz, a founding father of the study of animal behavior (ethology). His book *On Aggression* is in some respects outdated, but it remains an impressive review of animal behavior and its relationship to all forms of aggression.[117] In Lorenz's last chapter, "Avowal of Optimism," he writes that without aggression "the tackling of a task or problem, the self-respect without which everything a man does from morning till evening, from the morning shave to the sublimest artistic or scientific creations, would lose impetus; everything associated with ambition, ranking order, and countless other equally indispensable behavior patterns would probably also disappear....In the same way, a very important and specifically human faculty would probably disappear too: laughter." Any comedian understands at once how much of humor depends on a subtle, and sometimes not too subtle, expression of aggression.

Again from Lorenz: "The bonds of love and friendship, from which all kindness and charity springs and which represent the great antithesis to aggression" are, in fact, dependent on aggression. Psychologists have studied the tension of give and take, the conflicts and resolutions that are inseparable from the formation of loving bonds. No marriage, no relationship between parents and children, no deeply rooted friendship is ever without conflict—*or the reconciliation after conflict that cements the bond.* We cannot afford to lose our aggressive instinct. We'd lose too many good things that are expressive of being human.

When women exhibit traits of daring and exploration—as they frequently do—we value those traits as something men in general bring to the dance of life. These women could be said to be in touch with their "masculine side." Balance is what we need, not one-dimensionality, in our personal lives and in our societies.

We revere those of either sex whose aggression (ambition) leads them to stretch the limits. It's just important that those who push the boundaries be restrained so that, in their enthusiasm, they don't step on or crush others or provoke turmoil, riots, or wars.

The Outer Boundaries of Human Nature

The extraordinary flexibility of human behavior and the critical importance of culture in shaping our behavior are undeniable. It is also critical to note that we cannot live contrary to our nature.

For example, we have inherited from our primate ancestors the urge to form dominance hierarchies. Primate species are quite diverse in the way dominance is expressed: for example, their hierarchies can be strictly linear and rigid, or they can be fluid, and composed of alliances. But the use of dominance and submission to resolve conflicts is found in some form. And that includes humans. Short of some sort of genetic engineering, we cannot eliminate the human penchant for creating dominance hierarchies and for being keenly aware of status. To propose such a thing is pointless folly. There are no human societies where the sense of rank or status is entirely absent, even if it is found only within families.

Societies have found ways to curb both dominance hierarchies and aggression. They build traditions, laws, and customs to shape and limit a range of actions they deem undesirable. One of the main goals of liberal democracies, for example, is to moderate the urge to rise in status to the point of dominating all others.

Consider another example of how our nature constrains us. With the best of intentions, we have created governments or societies designed to improve the people's lives. Communism was one such experiment. It was based on the notion that each person would work, but the greater portion of the profit from his or her labor—say 60-70%—would be given to other people who might work little but have greater need. Wealth would be redistributed according to need. Now, unless the laborers in such a system get something back that they value very highly, the system may persist for a time, but is ultimately doomed. Witness the many tax revolts in history, the stunning demise of Russian communism, and the evolution of Chinese communism to capitalism. Humans are not geared to work so that others (e.g., a wealthy elite) may benefit…we are fundamentally selfish about the relationship between our labor and our benefits.

In some countries like the Nordic ones, wealth is taxed highly, but the benefits in free health care and education and high quality of living are deemed worth the taxes…the people do get back benefits they very much enjoy in return. Time will tell whether that system, social democracy, can persist, but it seems hopeful because of the high standard of living and personal satisfaction among residents of Nordic countries it has so far produced. In his book *The Political Economy of Human Happiness: How Voters' Choices Determine the Quality of Life*, political scientist Benjamin Radcliff presents results of his studies of "happiness" across many countries. They reveal that higher levels of social programs (rather than rugged individualism) does correlate with higher levels of public sense of well being and fulfillment.[118] The World Happiness Report of 2013 listed the top five happiest populations as Denmark, Norway, Switzerland, the Netherlands, and Sweden. Evidently these citizens feel they are "getting their money's worth," a sense that certainly is in harmony with our nature.

Another example of how our nature constrains our social choices: You might convince many members of a society to allow children from impoverished, dangerous neighborhoods to be bussed into their own, safe neighborhood to attend school—providing you convince the adults that such an effort serves some very great good. For example, that it will reduce crime rates in the city itself while also lowering future financial costs of incarceration of children who grow up to be criminals. But you would never convince any significant number of people to bus their children into an unsafe neighborhood, no matter how hard you might try or how worthy your cause. Humans are not geared to allow their own children to be put into dangerous situations.

To attempt any of the above or anything else that is contrary to our nature, perhaps thinking we can bring it off through education or some sort of social engineering, is to spit into the wind. If it is contrary to our fundamental nature, it will ultimately be unstable. Turmoil will result, and the arrangement will ultimately collapse or be supplanted. At some point we reach an outer boundary where our innate nature absolutely limits what is possible.

Short of some future form of genetic engineering, we cannot eliminate the penchant to band together in an aggressive mood that has the potential to escalate into battle. Nor can we eliminate the penchant to make nice and make peace. Yet if we could learn how to control and benefit from both tendencies, to learn how to make the best of what we are by nature, surely more communities would thrive and the planet's resources would be more sustainable.

Much as many of us continue to cling to the emotionally satisfying myth that we are a highly rational, complicated animal, one that has transcended our biological nature, that just isn't so. Our biologically built-in male and female tendencies shape our behavioral choices far more than we like to admit, including how we feel about using physical aggression.

I stress again that I'm not talking about individual differences: some women are very physically aggressive, even violent, and some men are gentle as lambs. It's also true that rare cultures exist that allow women to be physically aggressive while simultaneously suppressing physical aggression in men. The issue is statistical differences between men and women acting over long periods of time in a great many environments and cultures. We're talking numbers: in this case a general male biology operating with respect to war virtually unrestrained for millennia by meaningful female input.

The trick is to know the outer boundaries of our nature. Then anything that lies within that wide scope is possible if we choose it and foster it. The challenge becomes a matter of creating the conditions that favor what we desire.

Summary on Genetics, Biology, and Aggression

My view, shared by many others, is that the tendency for males to band together and be easily roused to an aggressive group effort is greatly magnified in warrior cultures, while in more peaceful societies, it is suppressed and controlled—*but is still there.*

Males encouraged to behave aggressively, including fighting or making war, do so because the behavior is reinforcing: exciting, thrilling, challenging, riveting. At least in the heat of the moment, it feels right or creates an emotional high. Chris Hedges, in *War Is a Force That Gives Us Meaning*, powerfully describes this effect in war, likening it to drug addiction.[119] Evolution enhances survival strategies, so martial bonding and expressions of ferocity have become a source of pleasure because in the world of our ancestral nomadic hunter-gatherers they facilitated group protection and some forms of hunting, and the acts satisfied emotional and social needs as well. Note, however, that this martial bonding does not include indiscriminate killing of other human beings; humans have a built-in aversion to killing another human who is not guilty of doing some specific wrong. The important significance of this with respect to creating warriors and waging war is obvious and will be mentioned again.

The other half of the picture is that females, sometimes even many females, can be roused to aggression, and they can also find bonding together for a common cause exciting and thrilling. They can even be so roused by anger that they become frighteningly aggressive, even vicious. But it is much harder to rouse great numbers of women to this state of aggression and harder still to keep them there because, on average, women find greater reinforcement in an environment that is not in turmoil. A community that is at peace, that is secure and where relationships are stable, just feels right. Because of genetic inclinations that are as deeply rooted as the bonding-for-aggression inclinations of men, most women would prefer to make or keep the peace, the sooner the better.

> *None of us realized how much more powerful is instinct compared to intelligence. We would do well to bear this in mind or the tragic errors of the past may be repeated.*
> Albert Einstein
> Otto Nathan and Heinz Norden.
> *Einstein on peace.* 26.

CHAPTER 5 – BONOBOS, CHIMPANZEES, AND ARDI

There can, consequently, hardly be a doubt that man is an off-shoot of the Old World simian stem…the Simiadae then branched off into two great stems, the New World and Old World monkeys, and from the latter, at a remote period, Man, the wonder and glory of the universe, proceeded.

> Charles Darwin
> *Descent of Man*, Chapter VI, p. 181.

What Can Be Learned about War from Our Close Primate Relatives?

Through the ages the thoughtful among us have struggled to understand why we suffer under the tyranny of war. One reason for our considerable limitation in trying to figure ourselves out was that we had no other species to which we might compare ourselves, no other examples of how primates like us might organize their social world.

Then in the 17th and 18th centuries, Western explorers of Africa, a continent that to them seemed hidden and mysterious, returned to their centers of knowledge with tales of man-like apes. We learned about chimpanzees, and the extraordinarily massive ape, the gorilla. Eventually, intrepid scientists ventured into the heart of these animals' worlds to see how they lived. Notable among the first of these was Jane Goodall, a young woman who, accompanied by her mother, ventured into the world of chimpanzees.[120]

At first it seemed that these forest dwellers lived quite peaceable lives. Further study over time led to more disturbing observations, among them that, on occasion, a group of chimpanzees—overwhelmingly but not always exclusively males—would band together and enter an adjacent territory and kill a lone member of the adjacent group. Some scientists were quick to label this a kind of primitive warfare. We now had a close relative to study, and more researchers—anthropologists and primatologists—took off for Africa.

When bonobos first came to the attention of western scientists, they were thought to be a subspecies of chimpanzee. They do resemble chimpanzees physically, at least to the untrained eye, but bonobos and chimpanzees are different species of ape. An introduction to bonobos is given by Frans de Waal in *Bonobo, The Forgotten Ape* and by Takayoshi Kano in *The Last Ape*.[121] While chimpanzees can be found in a variety of forest habitats in Africa, bonobos live in a rather restricted forest area in a part of Africa formerly known as the Congo, one of the reasons why it took so long to discover them. The ranges of these two apes do not overlap.

The DNA of both species has been compared to ours. Rather surprisingly, they both are more closely related to humans than they are to gorillas. So now we had two primate species closely related to us to study. What, if anything, might they tell us about our capacity for violence in general and war in particular?

In the wild, chimpanzee social structure, like patriarchal cultures, is based on a hierarchy of dominance, with males at the top. They settle their disputes and social disagreements with aggressive displays of dominance and submission. Males wrangling over dominance can engage in spectacular fights. What's more, chimpanzees practice infanticide (killing of infants or very young offspring) as well as the aforementioned killing of members of another troop.

Bonobos, on the other hand, live in the wild in a social world where females, especially female alliances, are the central focus of a troop's life. Male bonobos are slightly larger than females, and in one-on-one interactions, males dominate females. But female bonobos have high status, with the dominant female and dominant male generally being co-equal. Dominance hierarchies are more flexible than those of chimpanzees. Male dominance hierarchies roughly parallel those of female hierarchies. Whenever tensions erupt within the group, bonobos often find resolution when members of the group engage in sex. All kinds of sex. Male/female, male/

male, female/female, young/old. Even, most astonishingly when first observed, frontal sex, unknown among chimpanzees.

Bonobos are not flower children. When different bonobo groups meet at territory boundaries, agitation can occur. Clashes can erupt. Occasionally these lead to bloody wounds. Bonobo groups are not without conflict, and the males are not without aggressive tendencies: for example, they form hierarchies. But so far among them there are no recorded instances of either murder or infanticide.

In one experiment, Takayoshi Kano set out sugarcane as bait to attract bonobos for observation, and he inadvertently placed the bait on the border of the ranges of two foraging groups. By chance the two groups arrived simultaneously. Tensions flared. While males on both sides avoided each other, females from the two groups engaged in sex with each other and sometimes with males from the other group. This is a fairly typical bonobo response when different groups encounter each other. Bonobos use sex as both a bonding mechanism and in this case, a mechanism for diffusing social tension.

Richard Wrangham and Dale Peterson wrote a long exploration of the origins of aggressive human behavior called *Demonic Males: Apes and the Origins of Human Violence.*[122] In two chapters, they compare human anatomy and behavior with the anatomy and behavior of chimpanzees and bonobos. They suggest an interesting evolutionary scenario that might explain why chimpanzees are so demonic and bonobos so peaceable. The essence is that female bonobos are able to restrain male bonobo aggression against them or domination over food because bonobos eat foods that allow them to travel in slightly larger groups than chimpanzee females. A chimpanzee female tends to forage alone or with an infant and perhaps one of her older offspring. As a result, Wrangham and Peterson suggest, female bonobos can spend enough time together to form critical alliances that allow them to act together to prevent male domination. Unable to spend much time together, female chimpanzees aren't able to form strong female alliances. Consequently, according to this hypothesis, in the wild, female chimpanzees are not able to check male aggression against them.

Based on the abundant historical evidence of human wars and other expressions of human male dominance and aggression,

Wrangham and Peterson concluded that when students of human evolution consider our deep past, they should use a chimpanzee model as a starting point. Christopher Boehm has studied the origins of egalitarian human behavior. In his book *Hierarchy in the Forest: the Evolution of Egalitarian Behavior*, he also accepted the chimpanzee model.[123] He says he did so for the pragmatic reason that science knows more about chimpanzees and because he was also personally familiar with them. He also noted that chimpanzees are tool-using generalists that appear in a wide-variety of habitats, as do humans, while bonobos are not.

By accepting this assumption, however, an investigator is primed to accept that extreme male dominance and male aggression are fundamental characteristics of human ancestors and that females in our lineage have been kept in their place from the time of our pre-human past. But both apes are equally closely related to us genetically. So it is equally possible, given that humans are astonishingly flexible when it comes to social and sexual behavior, that humans may have the genetic capacity to organize themselves in a more bonobo-like than chimpanzee-like fashion.

In fact, as discussed in *Women, Power, and the Biology of Peace*, we share three traits with bonobos, one physical and two physiological, that appear to relate to female empowerment in ways that would imply that human social organization does share more with bonobos than with chimpanzees, or at least did so in our deep past:[124]

- hidden ovulation
- positioning of the vagina and clitoris in a more ventral and forward position so that frontal sex is both possible and pleasurable (reinforcing)
- continuous female receptivity (being willing to mate during all stages of the reproductive cycle).

Hidden ovulation makes it impossible for males to know when a female is fertile since the female shows no outward signs of her reproductive condition. This makes it totally impractical for bonobo males to try to keep other males away from a female during her most fertile period since males cannot know the appropriate time to do female guarding. Since guarding is rendered essentially useless, male bonobos don't do it. This gives bonobo females greater flexibility and freedom to mate with males of their choice. Wrangham and Peterson recognize this and even point out how it empowers female bonobos.

It's also reasonable to assume that face-to-face sharing of pleasure serves to facilitate personal bonding. (Wrangham and Peterson vividly describe how this works to facilitate bonding between female bonobos.) The shifting of the female sexual structures to a more ventral/forward position in humans and bonobos very likely facilitates the use of sex by both species as a bonding mechanism rather than as simply a mechanism for fertilization.

Further, it has been theorized that continuous female receptivity facilitates a female's ability to bond with one or more males that can serve her interests beyond fertilization, perhaps giving her protection or sharing food (such as animal kills) during non-fertile parts of her cycle.

To the extent that these exceptional shared physical and physiological traits of human and bonobo females suggest a more egalitarian social world, students of human evolution need to shift their view of our deep past to allow for a more bonobo-like model of our hominid ancestors. After our lineage's separation from the common ancestor we shared with these two apes, the chimpanzees may just have proceeded ever further down their path to the demonic aggression described by Wrangham and Peterson while the bonobos proceeded down the path to the peaceableness we see now.

When we consider what these close relatives have to say about the origins of war based on war-like behavior, a chimpanzee model certainly does not appear from this evidence to be an appropriate starting place.

The Discovery of Ardi

In an October 2009 issue of *Science*, a number of specialists (Tim D. White et. al) reported on the discovery of a new fossil primate, affectionately known as Ardi. They make the case that this is the oldest known primate ancestor of *Homo sapiens*, the official handle for her being *Ardipithecus ramidus*. She lived roughly 4.4

million years ago, a time well after the separation of the human lineage from that of chimpanzees and bonobos (somewhere between 5-7 million years ago).[125]

What is so remarkable about Ardi when trying to reconstruct the origins of war is that at least two traits in this fossil hominid are quite unlike chimpanzees. The canine teeth (eye teeth) of *Ardipithecus* males are small and blunt, clearly not the long and sharp fighting weapons of male chimpanzees. Given that Ardi lived before the use of even stone tools, let alone other weapons, the idea of warfare resembling the skirmishes of chimpanzees in which canine teeth are the killing weapons, seems highly unlikely given those reduced teeth. And in body size, male *Ardipithecus* are not much larger than females…there is very little size dimorphism. Chimpanzee males are significantly larger than females, and chimpanzee males fight forcefully for access to and to dominate females.

The relatively small degree of body size dimorphism and those small male eye teeth suggest that male *Ardipithecus* did not gain access to females by fighting with each other. It also hints that perhaps female *Ardipithcus*, like living female bonobos, were either equal in dominance status to the males or perhaps even dominated the males.

While certainly not proving that ancestors in our deep deep past did not make war, Ardi should put to rest the notion that chimpanzees are acceptable models. The truth for human ancestors probably lies somewhere in between the chimpanzee and bonobo models, with the human specialization being flexibility.

The social structure that developed for early hominid groups may have depended heavily on the availability and nature of local resources, as we will explore subsequently in a section entitled Features Associated with Settled Living. And given even more creativity than species like the male Laughing Gulls which adjusted their behavior to their new situation, ancient *Homo sapiens*, with bigger brains and presumably profoundly greater behavioral flexibility, were likely able to readily adjust their social structures to suit their environment in ways that fostered survival and reproductive success. A more bonobo-like model for early humans certainly fits better with Christopher Boehm's examples of behavior among nomadic hunter-gatherers where social status is egalitarian and both sexes take lovers. (Taking lovers is, by the way, the major cause of disharmony and even murder within human egalitarian communities. Murder has clearly been with us a very long time.)

Though controversial, as I'll pursue below, it is likely that it wasn't until the Agricultural Revolution—which is a very recent occurrence in human history—that humans began to shift strongly in the direction of a more chimpanzee-like social structure and behavior, characterized by strong male dominance, warfare, and extreme female subordination. Chimpanzee-like behavior is what scientific establishment thinking considers to be a good model for basic human nature; that assumption is what feeds the conclusion that war is, therefore, a long-evolved trait and thus inevitable. To even suggest that this notion is a serious error is still treated by much of the scientific establishment as seriously mistaken.

The response from skeptics when I say that war is not an evolved adaptation and that we can end it if we so choose is most often a benign, indulgent smile. Try introducing these ideas at a friendly gathering, and you're likely to hear something like, "You're just naive if you think humanity's warlike nature can ever change." The issue actually can evoke passion among lay people and academics with invested egos. Even the origins of human cooperation arose out of our aggressive tactics, they assert. "It takes cooperation to make war and it is the warlike groups in our past that survived." I've had this view expressed to me accompanied by an elevated voice and slightly red face. I've had "hate" e-mails to the effect that I'm a deluded and entirely unscientific idiot. But this assumption of a chimpanzee-like aggressive nature is in need of reassessment and the setting aside of invested ego? Did we, in fact, evolve our extraordinary capacities for cooperation so that we might better wage war? We consider that possibility in the next chapter.

CHAPTER 6 —MAN THE WARRIOR OR HUMANS THE COOPERATORS?

Origins of Empathy and Cooperation

Far from being a nagging exception to the rule of evolution, cooperation has been one of its primary architects.

Martin A Nowak
"Scientific American," July 2012

In this and the next chapter we look not to other apes to understand when we might have started making war, but into the deep past of the human lineage. If we know when, it may help us to understand why.

The anthropologist Sarah Hrdy's most recent major synthesis is entitled *Mothers and Others: on the Origins of Mutual Understanding.*[126] Here is a compelling explanation of why humans are cooperative, altruistic, and capable of empathy, and she also makes some cogent comments on the contention made by others that our paleo-ancestors made war.

Empathy allows us to identify with others, in some sense to feel what they are feeling and understand emotionally "where they are coming from." Hrdy points out that no other ape is "nearly so good at guessing what others want, or as eager to understand why they want it. We exhibit spontaneous impulses to share with others, and are routinely eager to help."[127] According to Hrdy, to care and to share—for humans—is to survive.

This work is cutting edge because her fresh explanation for how cooperation evolved differs from the two most widely accepted previous explanations: the man-the-hunter and the man-the-warrior models. Those models that argue that the need for men to hunt big game or to make war to acquire food or other essential resources required cooperation. This created sufficient pressure on our species, so the argument goes, that we became ever more cooperative. Hrdy questions the evolutionary logic, pointing out that if ever-better cooperation was good for either hunting or war, it begs the question, where did the capacity for the level of cooperation required to hunt and kill big game or to make war on other humans come from in the first place?

Is the origin of our capacity for cooperation inextricably linked to war? If so—and assuming that humans have been cooperating with each other from the time we became human—that would place war very deep indeed into our past, which goes back roughly 200,000 years, the time of the appearance of anatomically modern humans.

Can we ever know the truth from that long ago Pleistocene age? In *Blood Rites*, essayist Barbara Ehrenreich makes a stab at reconstructing our evolutionary path to war.[128] In his books, anthropologist Douglas Fry also attempts to describe how ancestors from our ancient past may have lived and how that may have involved making war.[129] Another writer seeking to illuminate the deep past when it comes to the issue of war is Lawrence Keeley whose book, *War Before Civilization: the Myth of the Peaceful Savage*, has been extremely influential. All such efforts are simply best guesses. Short of riding a time machine back hundreds of thousands of years, we can never know for certain. I present Hrdy's new exploration because I find it the most compelling explanation for the origins of human cooperation, and it does not depend on making war.

Cooperative Breeding

Hrdy surveys the animal kingdom, looking for "cooperative breeders." These are "species with alloparental assistance in both the care and provisioning of young."[130] In laymen's terms, *alloparental care* means individuals other than the parental mother and father share in caring for offspring that aren't their own. Those "alloparents" are the "others" referred to in her book's title. The care provided can include guarding, carrying, or just general babysitting. Adults of some cooperative breeders supply food to young.

Examples of cooperative breeding species are honey bees, Superb Starlings, Florida Scrub Jays, meerkats, lions, wild dogs, and hyenas.

What cooperative breeding does *not* mean is that relationships within the group are necessarily harmonious...far from it. For example, in some groups, only the dominant female breeds...she may kill the young of any other female who tries to breed.[131] What is key is that these species live in groups and share in care of the young.

As already noted, we are primates, closely related to other Great Apes: the orangutans, gorillas, chimpanzees, and bonobos. Other primates less closely related to us are baboons and other monkeys, lemurs, and even more distantly, tiny cousins called marmosets and tamarins. Among some 276 living primate species, types of offspring care can be described on a continuum from strictly maternal care of offspring to genuine cooperative breeding.

About 50% of living primate species show some alloparental care, but in only 20% does that include food provisioning. And the only full-fledged cooperative breeding primates besides ourselves are from a family called the Callitrichidae, in which food provisioning by individuals other than parents is characteristic. These are the little squirrel-like marmosets and tamarins.[132]

In a chapter entitled "Why it takes a village," Hrdy starts building her case that we actually evolved from a previous species, probably *Homo erectus*, that was already a cooperative breeder. She develops the argument from several angles. First, she points out ways in which our infant care is very unlike that of our close Great Ape relatives (gorillas, chimpanzees, bonobos, orangutans). Two differences are particularly striking.

First, human mothers will let someone other than themselves hold and care for their child. Even right in the hours after childbirth, she'll let others—the midwife, the grandmother, and so on—hold her child. No other great ape mother will let anyone other than herself touch, let alone hold, her infant.[133]

And second, human alloparents may regularly give food to babies and children. Cross-cultural studies show that adults like aunts or grandmothers often masticate food and then feed it to a baby or child. Food sharing of such a systematic nature is never seen in the other great apes.[134] These big differences in child-rearing behavior strongly suggest that our ancestors might have been very different from what we see in our close primate relatives in their relationships to their young. So if different, how and why?

Hrdy continues making her case that we likely are descended from a cooperative breeding species by comparing traits shared by the little Callitrichid cooperative breeders and humans:

1. Mothers may abandon or kill their infants.
2. Members of the group other than the parents feed or care for infants.
3. Cooperative breeders tend to breed faster than other species within their biological taxon.
4. Cooperative breeders are faster colonizers than other species within their biological taxon.

Consider point #1. A really striking trait shared by humans and our tiny relatives is that females of some Callitrichids and human females will sometimes abandon or even kill their infants. Killing an infant is not that unusual for an unrelated individual (across primates, more often an unrelated male, but could be an unrelated female), but it is extremely unusual—"vanishingly rare" says Hrdy— for a primate mother to injure her own infants or for a mother not in dire straits to abandon her infant. The only chronic exceptions are found in humans and in species belonging to the Callitrichidae.[135]

When you look for some possible explanation for what seems an astonishingly inexplicable behavior, the commonality that emerges is that they do this, often within the first 72 hours of birth, when they detect that sufficient resources, including alloparental care, are not available.[136] Putting it rather coldly, natural selection shaped these females to cut their losses quickly because for them, alloparental care is an essential for successful child rearing. This is another human trait we share with Callitrichid females that strongly suggests that we evolved from a cooperatively breeding species.

Regarding point #2, food provisioning by group members other than the parents has already been mentioned.

This brings us to points #3 and #4. According to Hrdy, something we share with virtually all cooperative breeders is that, compared to other species in a particular biological group, cooperative breeders breed faster, and they are faster colonizers.[137] Both are major reproductive advantages. Under natural conditions, humans breed faster than other apes. Orangutan birth intervals are about 8 years. The average across the Great Apes is 6 years. Humans, who of all the apes produce the largest, slowest-maturing, and most costly babies, nevertheless breed the fastest, roughly every 3-4 years in hunter-gatherer societies.[138] And we have relatively rapidly colonized the entire planet. Hrdy points out that cooperative breeders in other taxa (e.g., wolves, elephants, and lions, all of which were once much more widely spread around the world than today, and cooperatively breeding members of the crow and jay family) also benefit from the advantages of alloparental care.[139]

Human babies have traits that are crucial to their ability to attract care from group members who are not their biological parents. For example, when touched or spoken to, our babies smile. Many studies show how smiling babies bond better with their mothers and positively attract attention of other adults. Our babies also, very early on, look for eyes, follow gazes, seek out faces.[140]

Hrdy convincingly argues in *Mothers and Others* that development of bonds between helpless babies and their mother and other critical caregivers would have put major adaptive pressure on ever more sophisticated cooperation and empathy between babies and caregivers. To enable survival, the babies and caregivers would need to know when an interaction or relationship is in good shape, and when it's not. Survival of toddlers would likewise benefit from empathy. Learning how to please others becomes critical to survival. This essential need for care-giving of such helpless young would have provided a major adaptive push toward any latent empathetic or cooperation tendencies, and the roots of the behavior, she argues, were likely already established in a cooperatively breeding ancestor to humans.

So, why did we initially evolve to cooperate? Was it to facilitate the planning and coordination needed for group hunting? Or to make war on each other? Or was it to provide essential care to helpless offspring within a group while speeding up our rate of reproduction and ability to colonize? We may not be able to prove that the origins of cooperation and empathy do not lie in making war, but at the very least, Hrdy's hypothesis is a compelling explanation of the origins and subsequent elaboration of cooperation that does not depend on killing each other.

What About War?

Hrdy also describes the likely environmental and social conditions our ancestors in the Pleistocene would have faced, given that our primate ancestors were living at low population density in highly variable habitats. She writes:

> "Small bands of hunter-gatherers, numbering 25 or so individuals, under conditions of chronic climate fluctuations, widely dispersed over large areas, unable to fall back on staple foods like sweet potatoes or manioc…would have suffered high rates of mortality, particularly child mortality, due to starvation as well as predation and disease. Recurring population crashes and bottlenecks were likely, resulting in difficulty recruiting sufficient numbers. Far from being competitors for resources, nearby members of their own species would have been more valuable as potential sharing partners. When conflicts did loom, moving on would have been more practical as well as less risky than fighting."[141]

Hrdy's assessment agrees with my hypothesis, mentioned earlier, that the first choice of early humans confronted with serious conflicts—Plan A if you will—was not war but dispersal whenever that choice was available. In their empty world, of course, that possibility would have been their norm. Later, in a discussion of the fascinating case of hunter-gatherers living on the Andaman Islands, where dispersal is not an option, I propose that plan B for human competitors who could not avoid conflicts was the development of ritual fighting and other peacekeeping and peacemaking behavior to avoid war whenever possible. War, far from being Plan A for *Homo sapiens*, appears to be at most Plan C, and to have emerged very late in our history, long after our fundamental nature had been wrought in our genes.

CHAPTER 7 – UNINTENDED CONSEQUENCES OF SETTLED LIVING

Males were potentially persons of great leisure. Or, put another way, males were potentially all but useless. Given these circumstances, it is small wonder that they developed warfare to a high degree. It was a way they could maintain their dignity as human beings.

C. B. Kroeber and B. L. Fontana
Massacre on the Gila – 173.

Nomadic Cultures are Not Peaceful Utopias

In this chapter we explore several theories to explain war's origins, beginning with athropologists Douglas Fry[142] and Raymond Kelly.[143] Together these works provide a major review of cross-cultural literature on violence with an emphasis on the nature of traditional and nomadic cultures (also called hunter-gatherers, nomadic foragers, or mobile foraging band societies).

Current data indicates that anatomically modern, big-brained humans were present extending back 200,000 years from the present, and during that vast extent of time, these early humans were likely nomadic foragers.[144] Based on what we know about living traditional and nomadic cultures, we can dismiss immediately any idea that simple (non-stratified) nomadic cultures are utterly peaceful. They are not all warlike, but they have conflicts and experience violence. As described earlier, ethnographers record instances of male/male, male/female, and female/female fighting. It's not unreasonable to assume that our ancient ancestors also had conflicts which resulted in violence. In a 2013 article in the journal *Science*, Fry and Patrik

Söderberg report another reanalysis of data on nomadic hunter-gatherers (what they call mobile forager band societies) which confirms that even these cultures experience conflicts and violence, the majority of which are interpersonal grievances. The article makes a strong case against war being characteristic of cultures like these that are our best insight into our long evolutionary history.[145]

Under rare environmental conditions, hunter-gatherers may exist in a constant state of armed conflict—which is often Exhibit A for those who favor the man-the-warrior concept. On the Andaman Islands, for example, live several distinct social societies, described by Raymond Kelly in *Warless Societies and the Origin of War*. If men from these markedly different linguistic Andaman groups encounter each other when they are hunting, they may engage in spontaneous killings. Or they may make a surprise raid on the other group, make a surprise kill, and then retreat. These people might seem to prove a proclivity for constant warfare.[146]

A close look offers a different conclusion. The tropical Andaman Islands are an archipelago located in the Indian Ocean, 177 miles from the nearest mainland in Burma. According to Kelly, humans are thought to have lived on the islands for about 2,200 years. Before outside contact, they used hunter-gatherer technology. They also lived at uncharacteristically high population density for nomadic foragers. Furthermore, as Kelly points out, the islands at some point became so isolated there was no way for people to emigrate to the distant mainland to escape conflicts. This means that the option to disperse rather than fight—so critical to ancient nomadic people as one way to deal with conflicts and one reason why humans have so rapidly colonized the planet—this dispersal option has not been available to Andaman Islanders for at least a couple of thousand years.

Kelly describes peacemaking tactics these groups have developed to deal with conflicts and fights, what I earlier called Plan B. Especially interesting is a unique case involving two groups where efforts at peacemaking are entirely absent. It is noteworthy that these two populations do not speak the same language. One speaks a dialect sufficiently different from languages of all other groups on the islands that Kelly hypothesizes that at some time in the past they invaded from a smaller island to the south. Communication has not been reported between these two groups and unlike the island's other groups, they have not developed peacemaking or peacekeeping agreements. A general pattern found cross-culturally is that people who share a common language are less likely to make war on each other than groups that do not share the same language.

Does this example of constant warfare confirm the man-the-warrior hypothesis? Recall now the male Silver Gulls described earlier, and that evolved nervous systems can produce behavior that is not an evolved trait. That is, behavior that while based on genetics and evolved behavior patterns, is not itself the result of natural selection in the past.

Kelly notes that environmental conditions on the Andaman Islands that severely restrict dispersal would rarely have been encountered by human populations of our paleo-past.[147] Moreover, the islanders are living at uncharacteristically high population densities for nomadic foragers, increasing the likelihood of conflicts. Thus it is not surprising that what we see there is uncharacteristic. Like the male Silver Gulls, hunter-gatherers on the Andaman Islands also responded with behavior that arises in response to their unusual environment. This example nicely illustrates the profound impact environmental context has on behavior, in this case, inability to disperse and lack of a shared language.

A recent study by Wiessner and Pupu of the Enga of Papua New Guinea provides a specific illustration of the relationship of a small-scale culture to war.[148] It illustrates how a traditional system of customs and rituals that serve to avoid war if at all possible (Plan B) can be disrupted by introduction of new weaponry. In 1990, shotguns, rifles, M-16s and other semi-automatic rifles replaced bows and arrows in inter-clan conflicts. In response to this new environment, extremely deadly wars led by young men erupted. The Enga are highland horticulturalists who depend on the sweet potato to feed large human and pig populations. These are not nomadic hunter-gatherers without war, nor do they have the option of dispersal into unoccupied land, but the authors note that the underlying background of Enga worldview is that warfare is a last resort for solving problems. For Enga's, war as a means to resolve disputes has not been and is not a preferred choice. It is the very last choice.

The study illustrates how by making a conscious decision to adopt appropriate peacemaking institutions/customs that had been developed in the past, a means for resolving conflicts and avoiding war can be established and in a very short period of time. Beginning around 2006, village court sessions indicated that the Enga people were sick and tired of war. State government institutions were not working to keep peace. The people called on local village courts to solve conflicts through customary institutions developed in their past. The decisions of the local traditional court magistrates relied on "precontact maxims," understood throughout the society, about how group members should behave to each other. The number of deaths and the duration of wars declined steadily. By 2010 and 2012, few wars were fought. The authors write, "Social technology from generations past was adapted to contain the impact of adopted modern technology." We are not helpless. We can devise customs, laws, and conditions that avoid war.

Origin of the Inhibition of Murder

Finally, a word about the innate revulsion humans have against killing another person absent provocation. Fry describes rare instances of murder that occur in otherwise internally peaceful societies. Particularly provocative are cases where murderers were killed (executed) by their own kin[149] or after agreement by the entire group.[150] Kelly also suggests that overly aggressive individuals may actually have been selected against.[151] In our deep past, systematic execution of murderers would have been a strong selective pressure against using lethal violence against others without provocation: murderers would be prevented from having (further) offspring. I'll mention later, under a discussion of our need to foster a sense of human connectedness as one of the battlefronts of our campaign to end war, that our well-documented, evolved aversion to killing others without provocation is an important, positive aspect of human nature. It's a trait we can build on as we do the work to shift our worldview away from using violence (including killing) to dominate other people.

Settled Living: A Radical New Environment

In the *Human Potential for Peace* and *Beyond War,* Fry details what he learned by rereading original fieldwork on hundreds of cultures across the globe. He examined the evidence offered for the existence of war, keeping in mind that if previous anthropologists held the common view of their day, that we have always made war, they might very well have been looking for, and finding, signs of war when, in fact, there was no war.

Focusing on 35 hunter-gatherer cultures, Fry separated the nomadic hunter-gatherers—those living in ways most closely resembling the lives of our most ancient ancestors—from those that had settled down. The classic example of settled hunter-gatherers were tribes along the north-west coast of the United States that depended on massive salmon runs. The fish runs provided both a generous and reliable food supply so that nomadism was not necessary.

Tallied in the table on page 92 are remarkable differences that emerged. Listed on the left are eight variables about these societies. These are compared between the nomadic (simple) hunter-gatherers and the settled, complex hunter-gatherers. All of the cultures were using hunter-gather technology, but complex hunter-gatherers have found a food source sufficiently rich and reliable that they can settle down. For example, they may have taken up some horticulture.

Table 1 – Simple vs. Complex Hunter-Gatherers
Douglas Fry - *Beyond War*[152]
Adapted from Robert Kelly, *The Foraging Spectrum: Diversity*
In Hunter-Gatherer Lifeways - n=35

VARIABLE	SIMPLE HUNTER-GATHERERS	COMPLEX HUNTER-GATHERERS
Primary Food	Terrestrial game (or plants[153])	Marine resources or plants
Food Storage	Very rare	Typical
Mobility	Nomadic or semi-nomadic	Settled or mostly settled
Population	Low population densities	Higher population densities
Political system	Egalitarian	Hierarchical – wealth or heredity
Slavery	Absent	Frequent
Competition	Not accepted	Encouraged
Warfare	Rare	Common

Look at WARFARE on the bottom and note that nomadic, simple hunter-gathers, who arguably most resemble our ancient ancestors, rarely make war while settled ones commonly do. If you don't separate the nomadic from the settled groups, which many reports on warfare among hunter-gatherers fail to do, these patterns are not detectable.

Look at POLITICAL SYSTEM. Another trait key to avoiding war is the egalitarian, non-hierarchical system of nomadic hunter-gatherers. There are no special roles: not even chiefs or shamans. There is no one who can order others to take up weapons to kill other people. And this egalitarian structure includes women: women in these societies are of equal status with men and their opinions influence group decisions. The article by Fry and Söderberg, also lists a number of other characteristics of the lives of nomadic hunter-gatherers that mitigate against the use of war as an adaptive behavior.[154]

Kelly's analysis of the social structure of complex hunger-gatherers (his term for them is "segmented") reveals an important change in the status of women (i.e., in the social structure) that he relates to the origin of war.[155] Keep in mind that humans have a built-in aversion to killing another human being without provocation, meaning killing at random and not in retaliation for some wrong done to them. As a rule, men in *complex* hunter-gatherer cultures are dominant. Moreover, Kelly notes that as you move from simple to complex hunter-gatherer cultures, giving of a woman in marriage functions to create alliances and group identity that are critical to making war – group vs. group. In complex hunter-gather societies, lineages and clans emerge. Marriage is no longer merely a case of husband and wife becoming related to their respective families' kin. Marriage linkages are related to marriage payments and marriage transactions that change the social order. Women become objectified or symbolic of alliances.

Members allied via marriage have a sense of unity that, Kelly argues, creates a situation in which an insult to any individual in a kin group (formed via marriage) becomes an insult to the whole group. There is the origin of what he calls "social substitutability." This allows rationalization for the whole group to seek vengeance for a wrong done to any member of their allied group. And it allows justification for taking out that vengeance on any member of the other group who is allied by marriage to the person who did the wrong, whether they were the wrongdoer or not. In other words, vengeance is not taken out only on the perpetrator, but can legitimately be taken out *indiscriminately* on the perpetrator's group. For the origin of war, this is a change of profound consequence. Use by complex hunter-gatherers of women in marriage as a way to generate alliances is a critical step in moving away from the innate sense that only those who have done a wrong can legitimately be executed (killed). I would also point out that it is also a step to making women something possessed and exchanged rather than individuals equal to all other individuals.

If we accept the assumption that modern nomadic hunter-gatherers are probably our best window into our deep past, then most likely we did **not** always make war. The agricultural revolution, around 10,000 to 11,000 years ago, is the documented time when nomadic hunter-gatherers, most likely cooperative breeders, began a massive switch to settled living. But the key to war's origin would not have been the Agricultural Revolution per se. The key is access to *any* reliable and sufficient resource.

For example, David Dye focused on archeological and ethno-historical data on a variety of indigenous cultures in eastern North America. His research leads him to conclude that changes in social structure were reflected in changes in both the kinds of violence and also, he stresses, in the kinds of conflict resolving, peacemaking behaviors.[156] And with respect to the onset of war, he found essentially the same pattern as Fry in that war emerges whenever key environmental resources are reliable and relatively abundant.

When people using hunter-gatherer technology settle down they increase their susceptibility to war because they posses a valuable resource that can be horded or stolen. By giving up their tendency to disperse, their population densities also increase. In effect, by settling down, our ancestors created a new environment, different from the one that during 190,000-some odd years of natural selection had been theirs. And we settled down in an epic shift at the Agricultural Revolution, some 10,000 YA.

Individuals tried out new behavior, and not all new ways were unalloyed good. Dominance hierarchies emerged, a trait we undoubtedly inherit as part of our primate heritage and which, nicely documented by Christopher Boehm in his book *Hierarchy in the Forest*, nomadic hunter-gatherers find ways to suppress.[157] Group members now were no longer socially equal; some ended up on the bottom. This included women.

And we started making war. Given that the antiquity of our lineage is roughly 200,000 years, settling down roughly 10,000 years ago makes these new behaviors, including war, a very recent thing.

Two More Theories for War's Origins

As is often the case, it's reasonable to imagine that a major change as significant as making war may have its origins in more than one factor. Now we consider two more factors which may also have contributed to our vulnerability to engaging in war. The first is psychological, suggesting that war provides a definition of masculinity that is a substitute for being a "hunter." The second focuses on our relationship to food resources.

Fulfillment of a psychological need - In *Blood Rites*, Barbara Ehrenreich proposes that wars originated in no small part as an emotional substitute for hunting. It's a consequence of the transition of our species from prey to predator.[158] She traces extinction of megafauna in many parts of the world to the arrival of human hunting-gathering bands combined or coincident with other possible factors: climate changes resulting in the retreat of the glaciers, or the spread of forests on formerly grassy plains. Whatever the cause or causes of these extinctions, once humans had reduced or eliminated or no longer had access to big, impressive prey animals, she argues that human males were reduced to having to find some new prey to satisfy their need to define masculinity. Wars served as an outlet for emotions associated with the dangers of hunting and killing.

> "….the rise of war corresponds, roughly, with a global decline in the number of large animals, both 'game' and predators, for humans to fight. Many scholars have attempted to explain war as a function of rising human population density and the attendant competition for resources. But the key factor may be *animal* populations, and these were declining in the Mesolithic on what was, in many settings, a catastrophic scale."[159]

Ehrenreich suggests that extinction of the supply of big animals to hunt may also have encouraged settling down, and also places this in the time period around 10,000 years ago.

> "At some point, inevitably, there were no longer enough wild animals to satisfy either the hunger or the anxiety of the human race. Even at very low human population densities, the productivity of hunting is eventually limited by the supply of animals to hunt. Most human cultures reached this point about 10,000 years ago, immediately following the extinctions of the late Ice Age. There was nothing to do then but turn to agriculture—and to war."[160]

The merits of Ehrenreich's entire hypothesis aside, war itself is seen as a recent human enterprise and not a species-typical result of a long history—tens of thousands of years—of evolution by natural selection that favored a genetically based disposition to make war.

In *Massacre on the Gila*, in a section entitled "To Be Male and To Be Human," Kroeber and Fontana detail their version of the hypothesis that war emerged as a male response to a decline in status as hunters when humans took up agriculture. They point out that in hunter-gatherer societies, men and women share in bringing in sufficient calories for survival, but with the advent of agriculture, women could provide virtually all essentials for survival. No help from men required.

> "With the advent of farming, however, it became evident that women often could perform most or even all essential community chores: tend the hearth, bear and raise children, and plant, cultivate, and harvest the calories needed to stay alive. The worth of males, their dignity as human beings, was challenged to the utmost. A major response appears to have been a shift from man the hunter (and killer) to man the warrior (and killer); from man the physically strong hunter and gatherer…. to man the statesman and world diplomat."[161]

With this shift to agriculture, say Krober and Fontana, "Males were potentially persons of great leisure. Or, put another way, males were potentially all but useless. Given these circumstances, it is small wonder that they developed warfare to a high degree. It was a way they could maintain their dignity as human beings."[162]

The historian Robert McElvaine, in *Eve's Seed*, proposes a similar psychological effect on men, over time, due to a decline in the status associated with being a fierce hunter.[163] McElvaine stresses how this has led men to create male identity by defining it as qualities/traits that are "other than" female, an historical shift in psychology Goldstein also explores in *War and Gender*.

The hazard of dependence on rich and stealable food or other vital resources - Kroeber and Fontana also take the view that farming *per se* is not the key. Nor is settled living. Other possible factors triggering this change they mention are animal husbandry, equestrian nomadism, and intensive fishing.[164] Again our relationship to vital and reliably accessible resources is critical. In the case of animal husbandry and equestrian nomadism the resource is rich and reliable but it is moveable so does not necessarily lead to settled living. But it is stealable. This sets up the need to guard and defend it from outsiders who can use force to take it or displace owners from it. This situation, too, creates a new environment, and one that makes us vulnerable to war. To hold onto your horses or herd of goats, you may need to fight.

Fossil Evidence for War

As mentioned earlier, paleontologist Lawrence Keeley's book, *War Before Civilization*, has been widely influential.[165] It suggests that we have essentially always made war. Steven Pinker, in *The Better Angels of our Nature*, for example, draws heavily on Keeley's interpretation of fossil data to indicate that paleo-human violence was substantial.[166]

In *Beyond War*, Fry reviews fossil evidence and concludes that Keeley intermingles examples of homicides, ambiguous cases of violent death, and even multiple deaths that might have been due to starvation or disease as examples of warfare. He argues that Keeley's work does not provide reliable evidence for warfare anywhere in the world much before 10,000 YA.[167]

Brian Ferguson also critiques Keeley's interpretations of the available data, and asserts that Keeley's assessments aren't verifiable.[168] Ferguson notes that the earliest persuasive evidence for warfare comes from a 12,000 and 14,000 year-old graveyard along the Nile River in Sudan. The site contained 59 well-preserved skeletons in close association with stone pieces that were interpreted as parts of projectiles.

Looking at the issue from yet another perspective, Ferguson argues that the ancient Middle East provides good evidence for the late emergence of war by what has *not* been found. Some 370 Natufian hunter-gatherer skeletons have been discovered in areas that are now Israel, the West Bank, Jordan, Lebanon and Syria. Only two showed any sign of trauma, and nothing to suggest a military action. The famous walls of Jericho (dating from 10,500 to 9300) were originally said to be defensive and evidence for war, but according to Ferguson, they are now thought to have been built to control floods.[169]

Kelly similarly presents a reanalysis of fossil finds and concludes that there is no reliable evidence for human warfare going back into our deep past.[170] In short, this is another area of thinking that requires updating. The archeological evidence suggesting that war goes into our deep past is under assault from several directions and may not hold up under continued scrutiny. Data is converging on the view that making war is a recent cultural phenomenon.

Agricultural Revolution and a Further Decrease in Women's Influence

Resources influence power relations between people and nations in critical ways, a subject explored by Jared Diamond in his masterful book, *Guns, Germs, and Steel*. Referring to the onset of massive changes in the history of human societies, he points out that only within the last 11,000 years or so did some of our ancestors turn to food production: domesticating wild animals and plants and eating the resulting livestock and crops. From this pivotal resource change of the Agricultural Revolution, he explores the subsequent history of the conquest of nations.[171]

Resources also influence power relations between the sexes.[172] In most hunter-gatherer societies, women bring in and control vital food supplies for their families. They may even gather sufficient material to share within the group at large, but families are, generally speaking, independent food-consuming units. Women's importance to the families' food supply is in part what gives hunter-gatherer women impressive influence.

Marjorie Shostak provides an example in *Nisa. The Life and Words of a !Kung Woman*.[173] The !Kung of the African Kalahari desert are the people of the diminutive hero of the movie *The Gods Must Be Crazy*. Typical of nomadic hunter-gatherers, !Kung men and women have essentially equal status.[174] The women, gatherers of mostly plant materials, are recognized as being the group's primary economic providers.[175]

In societies where the men are hunters and occasionally bring in the prized delicacy of protein-rich meat, there is special appreciation for this valuable hunting skill. But anthropologist Christopher Boehm, in *Hierarchy in the Forest: the Evolution of Egalitarian Behavior*, makes clear the many ways, including ridicule, the !Kung make sure no "upstart" hunter uses this ability to gain higher status than any other group member. Should a hunter bring in a gazelle and brag about it, a woman might laugh and offer a sharp put-down. If ridicule is insufficient to keep potential upstarts in place, egalitarian societies will use shunning and in severe cases, ostracism.

In present-day agricultural societies, women are typically the primary laborers in the fields, which could well have been the case from the time we took up agriculture. The fossil record indicates that with the advent of the Agricultural Revolution, birth intervals shortened and group sizes increased. It seems reasonable that women—whose birth intervals dropped from an average of roughly four-years characteristic of hunter-gather women to roughly 2.5 or 3 year intervals in modern developed countries—would have had less time for a "public" life. They would have been consumed by the duties of child bearing, child rearing, and food gathering and processing. This would likely result in a decline in influence on the community's social life, including a decline in women's influence as a pleader for avoiding physical violence or war.

Another factor might also work against public expression of, and public acceptance of, women's preferences. As already noted, settling down is associated with emergence of dominance hierarchies and lowered status of women (Table 1). It seems reasonable to suppose that males being no longer engaged in the time-consuming pursuit of game would have time to turn to other behavior, including scrambling for dominance (politics) as well as war. Kroeber and Fontana, Goldstein, and McElvaine all suggest that having lost the status that hunting game provided, men were led to create a new male identity that involved elevating the status of warrior while simultaneously equating everything feminine with being other than, and lesser than, male.[176] To the extent that the status of women decreased, so would the worth of their opinions. Women's aversion to violence and war would have been of increasingly less value.

Did the Agricultural Revolution Seal Our Fate?

The blossoming of war, it seems, is one of many unfortunate, unintended consequences of the Agricultural Revolution. Other similar unintended consequences were shortened stature and more dental cavities, a change that clearly shows up in the fossil record when bones from hunter-gatherers are compared to those from early agricultural settlements. In our time in the United States, we suffer obesity from ingesting easily acquired fat and sugar and sitting for hours of the day, all ultimately made possible by the Agricultural Revolution.

No one intended this tragic shift in the status of women or the rise of war. No one could foresee what the result over centuries and millennia would be. In our time, however, we have an urgent need to halt the insanity. If war resulted from the profound change in our environment that was a consequence of making the choice to settle down, then we are immediately led to ask, is a retreat to a hunter-gatherer lifestyle required to keep us from exterminating ourselves through ever more ghastly means of modern warfare? Since such a return is unrealistic, is the hope to end war a tragic fantasy? Fortunately as we explore in the second half of *Shift*, there is excellent evidence that we are fully capable of creating yet another new environment. We can, within two generations or less, consciously fashion a "new normal" in which war is never a tolerated option. This change will move us into another era of the human story.

CHAPTER 8 – MATRIARCHY?

*So it will come to pass that when women participate fully and
equally in the affairs of the world, when they enter confidently
and capably the great arena of law and politics, war will cease;
for women will be the obstacle and hindrance to it.*

'Abdu'l-Bahá, son of the founder of Baha'i
The Promulgation of Universal Peace, 2nd Ed., 135.

Social Structure and Power Relationships

With respect to the ability of women to influence decisions about war or peace—and thereby end wars—misconceptions and misinformation abound, often accompanied by heated controversy. A closer look at the dynamics of women and power cross-culturally can inform, reassure, and inspire a positive new social direction, an exciting shift.

Matrilineality – To begin, social relationships reflected in social structure has major implications. Who your relatives are and where you live out your adult life are critical. To understand how social structure and power (social influence) are related, we begin with a generalized overview of how social structure, specifically aspects of residence, influences power relationships.

Keeping track of kinship is a pervasive (and often mind-boggling) human preoccupation in virtually every culture, especially when family ties are critical to social success.[177] In simplest terms, if parentage is traced through fathers, the social structure is patrilineal. If traced through mothers, it is matrilineal. Even in patriarchal societies, lineage may be traced through the mother's line due to the straightforward biological fact that at birth, we always know who is the mother of a child.

From a biological perspective, an individual's resources should be given to his or her own offspring. One can gain status by controlling resources and doling them out to others. But one's highest evolutionary priority is to one's own children—which is no problem for a mother. But it can be a huge problem for fathers. For a father to ensure that his resources go to his offspring, it is important to know which of a woman's children are his—a problem that has inspired literature on the theme of adultery from ancient Greeks to modern soap operas.

In the past, when modern medical testing did not exist, paternity determination was virtually impossible for men because of the potential for adultery or the acceptance within some societies of the legitimacy of having more than one sex partner. The prime reason males have had great difficulty determining whether they fathered a particular child has to do with that odd feature of human biology mentioned earlier—"hidden ovulation." For example, sexual parts of a female chimpanzee in heat swell, prominently announcing her fertile condition. Human females do not outwardly signal the time of their greatest fertility. Men cannot reliably know when a woman is able to conceive, and so they cannot precisely time sexual activity to correspond to a woman's fertile period of the month. If a male chimpanzee remains with a female at this time and allows no other males but himself to have mating access to her, it is fairly biologically assured that her offspring are his. (He must, of course, occasionally sleep, or he may at some moment become distracted even in this situation, so guarding does not guarantee 100% assurance.) But in humans, (perhaps even in *Homo erectus*) evolution favored hiding a female's fertile period.

Mentioned earlier as well is that human females are unusual among primates in that they will engage in sex at any time they choose during their menstrual cycle—they are "continually receptive" (with the exception of bonobos, most other female primates are like most mammals and will not mate unless in "heat").

Hidden ovulation and continuous receptivity mean that only in extremely strong patriarchies, where the lives of women are tightly regulated, can males be assured that they have fathered a given child. Indeed, such practices as female sequestration (restriction to a harem or the home) and infibulation (removal of the clitoris then sewing together the labia to minimize the opening to the vagina thus preventing sexual pleasure) are radical attempts in some patriarchal societies to ensure that the mother's child actually belongs to her husband (despite whatever social or cultural reasons are offered to explain the behavior).

So how, if at all, does matrilineality relate to power relationships; specifically how does it relate to the influence women may have outside their homes within their culture? In societies where women have considerable power, matrilineality is sometimes found. If we look across many cultures, however, matrilineality is not strongly correlated with women's empowerment. In patriarchal cultures, it's merely a way to keep track of parentage through the mother's line, but sons are the offspring that inherit wealth and power. So the answer is that for women there is no correlation of matrilineality and social power outside the home.

Matrilocality –The term matrilocal, however, often is associated with female empowerment. It applies to marriage customs. Specifically, it describes one way of resolving the question of residence after couples complete wedding vows.

In societies living at low densities and widely spread out, the pair may move away from both families to begin their own "homestead." In most societies, though, one member of the couple must leave his or her family and go to the home, village, or town of the other spouse. They move to where that spouse's family holds its resources—perhaps a farm, or plot of garden, or fishing rights. And the spouse that moves loses power.

They leave behind their relatives and friends—their allies. When the woman joins her husband and his kin, the system is patrilocal, and when he leaves his family and moves in with hers, it is matrilocal. The anthropologist George Murdock analyzed ethnographic information on 862 representative cultures. The vast majority are patrilocal. Examples of matrilocal societies are North American Hopi and Iroquois Indians, the Karen of Burma, and the Jaintia of India.

In a matrilocal society—some experts call them women-centered cultures—family property is handed down through the mother's line, from mothers to daughters. (In a minority of cases, a woman's brother makes all property decisions, so the woman owns the resources in name only). A husband typically comes into a situation where the matriarch—and here the word is very appropriate—runs the family, and he contributes his labor to the efforts of his wife's family. If the marriage doesn't go well, there may be a divorce—he usually returns to his family. He is the one who leaves while the wife stays with her family, still supported and assured of resources for herself and her children.

In societies where women actually control the resources, matrilocality does strongly correlates with women being powerful not only in the home but within the community because women are in control of vital resources. In biology—in life—resources are the most pivotal key in the power game. For humans there are many paths to power—one can climb the status ladder by being a great shaman or artist, warrior or hunter—but he or she who controls vital resources always has power.

Cultural anthropologists Ember and Ember describe a fascinating pattern detected cross-culturally relating to war. From the type of warfare practiced, we can often predict whether residence will be matrilocal or patrilocal.[178] How does this work? Neighboring communities are often enemies. If the wars that break out between such groups are between people who speak the same language, it's called "internal warfare." If the wars are at least sometimes internal, residence is almost always patrilocal.

In other societies, warfare is with speakers of other languages and never within the same society. This is "external warfare." When warfare is *purely external*, residence is almost always matrilocal.

Undoubtedly, numerous environmental and historical conditions underlie the development of patrilocal and matrilocal societies. But whatever may be the causes of matrilocality or patrilocality, a key factor affecting decisions about how to settle disputes appears to be whether the disputes are resolved "between us" or "between us and them." Female-centered cultures appear strongly inclined to accommodation (using nonviolent forms of conflict resolution) instead of making war among "us."[179] This has powerful implications. To the extent that we can foster a global sense of "usness," a global sense of oneness of belonging to one family of humanity, and to the extent that our cultures might become more "female-centered" in our approach to war, we may benefit from this apparent reluctance of female-centered cultures to make war among "us."

Bilocal/Opportunistic – In *Mothers and Others*, Hrdy reviews residence patterns of the Great Apes and living nomadic hunter-gatherers.[180] [She considers forager-hunters as a more appropriate term than hunter-gatherers since the majority of their calories typically come from foraging, not hunting. I use hunter-gatherers since it is a more widely familiar term]. Hrdy critiques a commonly held assumption about the residence patterns of hunger-gatherers. Based primarily on early observations of chimpanzees and gorillas where females typically leave their natal group (the group into which they are born), the assumption had been that females in our deep past would likewise have left their kin behind. They would have joined a group in which males were living out their lives surrounded by allies and their kin. Lacking related allies, this assumption suggests strongly that females would have been handicapped when it came to power (social influence). And Hrdy stresses, if this were so, they would not have had available to them trusted relatives they knew to be reliable caregivers (alloparents). They would have had no close ally to rely on for assistance raising their own extremely dependent young. This, she stresses, would put them in an extremely non-adaptive situation reproductively.

When the residence patterns of nomadic hunter-gatherers are studied as opposed to being assumed to resemble chimpanzees, however, reality is far more complex, interesting, and evolutionarily sensible. By the late 1980s, some human behavioral ecologists began to puzzle over why post-menopausal women lived so long. If the end-game of biology is reproducing, and if these women were no longer reproducing, why should they be around? Kristen Hawkes and colleagues suggested a "grandmother hypothesis:" that the continued presence of these older but not reproducing women was critical to the survival of their grandchildren.[181] The researchers marshaled human data indicating that indeed, the presence especially of a grandmother, but also other close kin, tended to result in better reproductive success for the family. But if cooperatively breeding women in our deep past were leaving their natal groups,

Hrdy asked, how could they get vitally needed help from their mothers?

It turns out that the actual residence pattern for nomadic hunter-gatherers is one in which "couples move between the woman's natal group and the man's. Furthermore, various customs increase the likelihood women will have matrilineal kin nearby when they first give birth."[182] The residence pattern of hunter-gatherers is not typically patrilocal or matrilocal. It is commonly bilocal/opportunistic. If something is not going well in one group, a couple may pick up their few belongings and move to join another group that usually has some of their kin, say a sister or aunt or uncle. It may be hard to tease out cause and effect, but probably not coincidentally, these societies tend to be sexually egalitarian, the kind of society in which women's opinions carry weight.

Matriarchy?

We've had patriarchies. We've had oligarchies. But there is no documented case in history of a matriarchy—a society in which women ruled and men were ruled over. Not one example where women controlled all of their society's levers of social power. This apparently is simply not what happens when women are socially empowered.

We have examples of cultures where women are highly important, but in such societies, men characteristically share in community decisions. Such cultures can only be called matriarchal by redefining (weakening) the word, which undermines its usefulness. History records many extraordinary women who, in patriarchal state-level societies, rose against the odds to positions of high power, but those women stand as exceptions that prove the rule. In a true matriarchy there might be a rare, extraordinary man now and then who would gain a position of public power, but such men would be exceptions. Women would run or head virtually everything, the reverse of a patriarchy.

In hunter-gatherer cultures, where women share in community decisions, or in community-based societies where women enjoy critical social influence, community power is usually spread out so there is an approach to male/female balance. One sex does not make all decisions. Very typically men decide some issues, women others.

Consider the Goba of the Zambezi. According to Chet Lancaster, they are a "women-centered" culture; some call them matriarchal. Nevertheless, men hold most political offices and men make decisions about care of and commerce in cattle. Women make decisions about care of the critical gardens and whether grain resources can be spared for making much-valued beer.[183]

In small-scale societies where women's views carry weight, decisions on important issues may require consultation and agreement within the entire group, including all the women. In some cultures, the shaman may be a man for example, and he may decide matters of belief, while the decision about when the group should break camp to move to a summer or winter quarter may be left to a women's council. In some larger communities, two groups, a men's council and a women's council, may consult separately and then negotiate together and reach agreement before any major group action is taken.

While patriarchy in some form is characteristic of many tribal cultures, in *Hierarchy in the Forest*, Christopher Boehm focuses particularly on egalitarian tribes and bands. He describes how, by virtue of women's strong exercise of what he calls "moral authority," women in these egalitarian hunter-gatherer cultures share forcefully in regulating male behavior.[184]

Ember and Ember describe the Iroquois as follows:

"Among the Iroquois of North America, women had control over resources and a great deal of influence. But men held political office, not women. The highest political body among the League of the Iroquois (comprised of five different tribal groups) was a council of fifty male chiefs. The women could not serve on the council, but they could nominate, elect, and impeach their male representatives. Women also could decide between life or death for prisoners of war, they could forbid the men of their households to go to war, and they could intervene to bring about peace." [185]

Again, the pattern in this culture with power-holding women was that social power was not highly centralized nor entirely in the hands of one sex.

During the height of the Women's Liberation Movement in the US, I more than once heard the fear expressed that if we were to empower women, women would probably try to take over everything. That we might end up with matriarchy, in which men were somehow of no consequence. I'm not sure precisely where this fear comes from, but it is not founded in fact. In societies where women are powerful, the two sexes share power or wield influence in different spheres of life. One of the key arguments in *Shift* is that this sort of balancing and sharing of power will be essential to ending war. That if we want to build socially stable and war-free societies, we need to foster balance of power and utilize the best traits of the two sexes.

How Women Use Power

There should be no doubt that women are interested in power, clearly explored by Hrdy in *Mother Nature*. But there are notable differences from men in how women who acquire power exercise it and for what goals. Hrdy argues that females compete for resources and social status, and with the status comes the ability to impact the behavior of others ("local clout"); they seem more interested in this ability to influence others than competing for positions in linear hierarchies. In *The First Sex*, biological anthropologist Helen Fisher argues that when possessing power and confronted with choices, women *in general* are more inclined to network and listen to many voices to find a win-win solution, a term which originated in game theory.[186]

Win-win resolution requires cooperation between parties in disagreement rather than a heads-on competition, winner-take-all mentality. A comparable term for win-win conflict resolution is "mutual gains bargaining."[187] The essence of the process lies in keeping all parties reasonably satisfied. Each may not get everything desired, but they get much of what they want and in fact need. This avoids the pitfall of slipping into conflicts and retaliations where, in the end, no one wins (lose-lose). In this way, win-win tends to foster social stability.

Debra Tannen's chapter "Boys Will Be Boys, Gender and Opposition" in her book *The Argument Culture* highlights many of the same points. Tannen sums up studies as showing that girls seem less forceful than boys only if the boy's behavior is considered the norm. Girls are forceful and assertive in their own, but less overtly physical way. The girls " . . . use the force of their wills to balance their needs *with the needs of others*."[188] (emphasis mine).

How *individual* men or women use power is not in question here. There are always individuals who don't fit the expected "pattern" for their sex: in Western cultures, a woman who is extremely assertive, a man who is painfully retiring, women who may be more competitive than any of the men in their group, and a few men in a group who may be uninterested in competition in any form. Nevertheless, the *general* difference in male and female ways of exercising power whether by persuasion and negotiation or by threats and force makes biological sense. This is because over the long run, when individuals must interact repeatedly, win-win conflict resolution tends to facilitate the important female priority of a more stable social milieu. A win-lose approach tends to produce winners and losers, a dominant and a subordinate—and a retaliatory mentality. The only way the loser will have his or her essential priorities met is by defeating the winner, setting up conditions for yet another battle. Both sides expend considerable resources perpetuating the fight rather than on a productive agenda.

A Recent Trend Toward Decline in Violence – The Influence of Feminization

In *The Better Angels of our Nature*, Steven Pinker marshals an impressive body of material to support an argument that we are experiencing a decline in violence.[189] *Shift's* Appendix II summarizes the five key factors he considers most responsible for that decline. This includes "feminization," which I address shortly.

Joshua Goldstein, in *Winning the War on War*, also provides a major historical review of levels of violence in wars. He makes a compelling case that, rather than the jerky but steady decline presented by Pinker, the reality is one of fluctuation and cycles; violent and brutal killing of the kind associated with the Mongol warlord Genghis Khan erupts for a time and then decreases.[190]

What does appear to be the case as documented by both Goldstein and Pinker is that our time does seem to be a time of decrease. Clearly we want is to hasten this decline and figure out how to make it last. To do that, we need to understand why levels of mortality (number of deaths *per capita*) and the numbers of wars have dropped over the last several hundred years.

One explanation many scholars attribute it to is the introduction of democracy. It certainly is noteworthy that, in general, democracies do not declare war on each other (democratic Germany under Hitler being a notable exception). Democracy is not essential to avoid war; an enlightened king (or queen) may choose to reign without launching a war. But history teaches that enlightened monarchs may be, virtually always are, replaced eventually by ones not so enlightened.

Pinker stresses the 18th century Enlightenment as being critical to the decline. This was, he points out, a time when human thinking began substantial evolution away from a love of violence. In an essay, "How Far We Have Already Come," when describing why our time in history is beautifully poised to end war, I extend the beginning of this shift back a bit further, to the Renaissance and Reformation, but certainly the Enlightenment that followed is equally important.[191] Indeed, many Middle-Eastern cultures seem to be in desperate need of their own version of those major kinds of social transformation.

To return to Pinker's point, the Enlightenment as described by him was one of the strongest factors responsible for the general pacific social trend because of a "humanitarian revolution" which began to criticize torture, political imprisonment, and religious persecution. He stresses that Enlightenment thinkers emphasized the primacy of reason, and he ranks reason high as an explanation for the trend away from violence. Note, however, that the end of the 18th century also witnessed the rise of Romanticism. Romanticism brought us the values of intuition, imagination, and feeling. These are traits we associate with the feminine side of our natures. Other highly valued Romantic values were originality and creativity.

Intuition and feeling are arguably more emotionally tied to empathy than is reason. Pinker stresses the rise of reason, but a case, perhaps even stronger, can be made for the impact on violence of the rise of respect for emotion and feeling in our dealings with others. Although Pinker includes "feminization" as one of the five keys to the decline in violence, he fails to tie it to the humanitarian revolution.

It was also out of Romanticism that a respect for women slowly emerged. Women began writing and expressing themselves through poetry, novels, and other literary works. Mary Wollstonecraft—mother of Mary Shelly who would give us *Frankenstein*—wrote for example, *A Vindication of the Rights of Women*. England's Mary Robinson wrote *The Widow's Home*, and *The Savage of Aveyron*. Charlotte Smith was a poet who gave us *Elegiac Sonnets*. Dorothy Wordsworth, the sister of the poet William Wordsworth, was an author, poet, and diarist who gave us *Grasmere Journal*. There began a sea change in how Western societies regard women; they were not to be considered chattel or simply as a helpmate to be ignored. Rather, in the Romantic ideal, women became an object of adoration and love, to be admired for gentle and nurturing traits, to be protected.

Although women had little (or no) social power, this emerging regard for them would, I suggest, have subtly persuaded men to listen more to them. In public, women's voices may not have been persuasive, and were in fact continuously ignored. But what about behind the scenes? Abigail Adams, wife of the United States president, John Adams, famously wrote to him in 1787, when he was at the Continental Congress trying to decide what to do about independence, "Don't forget the ladies." It was lightly written, not a somber demand, but surely his subconscious mind registered from his intelligent wife the sense that the "ladies" were worth attention. The Adams' correspondence indicates that they were much in love. What other feelings and ideas might she have regularly shared with him? To what extent would "pillow talk" have shaped the ideas and sentiments of many prominent men?

The Baroness Bertha Sophie Felicita von Suttner, an author and pacifist in the late 1800s, was the voice that convinced Alfred Nobel to create a Nobel Prize for Peace. In 1920, when the time came for the final vote to ratify the 19ᵗʰ Amendment to the U.S. Constitution and enfranchise women throughout the United States, Harry Burn, the Senator from Tennessee, responded at the very last moment to a note sent to him by his mother. He changed his pivotal, deciding vote from no to yes. Eleanor Roosevelt was a strong supporter of women and of peace. In President Roosevelt's last term she arguably was running the government because of his infirmities. She was critical to composing the Universal Declaration of Human Rights during the founding of the United Nations. Since the Romantic era, the feminine preference to avoid violence, to avoid sending sons off to war, to find other ways to solve conflicts has likely been seeping ever more persuasively into men's views of life.

Thus not only has the power of reason over dogma and the reintroduction of democracy encouraged a decline in wars, it seems reasonable to suggest another factor fostering the notable recent decline: the change in the status of women. As Pinker himself points out, the increasing influence of "feminine" values and the input of women into intellectual thinking needs to be included in any consideration of a present trend away from violence. Recall also, as we begin to move further away from direct discussion of biology, that these female proclivities rest on a firm biological foundation. As a consequence, when women are included in decision making about war and peace, their built-in preferences for social stability (peace) will be strongly and consistently expressed.

Which brings us to a fundamental puzzle about women. It is not uncommon for someone wearing a frown to ask, "What about women in the military? What about women who take up prize fighting? Doesn't that prove that women aren't so peace-loving?" The next chapter tackles this seriously perplexing, seeming contradiction.

CHAPTER 9 – WOMEN AS WARRIORS

Battle life has swallowed me completely. I can't seem to think of anything but the fighting. I'm burning to chase the Germans from our country so we can lead a normal happy life together again.

Lily Litvak - Russian flying ace, WW II
Quoted in Kate Muir's *Arms and the Woman*

To say that women, in general, have an innate preference to avoid physical fighting doesn't mean that women won't fight—history makes clear they will. If the situation calls for it, women are quite able to get in touch with their "masculine side." In this chapter we explore this apparent paradox.

Most people believe wars have to be fought. For Americans and many others, the Second World War is a prime example. Women, it turns out, are often just as convinced as men about the perceived "reality" that it is sometimes necessary to fight and win. Karla Cunningham outlines, in an article entitled "Terror's 'Invisible Women,'" the increasing participation of women in terrorist actions by jihadist organizations. She also points out that the participation of women in the United States armed forces continues to expand into areas involving combat.

A number of books explore the subject of women who were warriors. In *Arms and the Woman*, for example, Kate Muir focuses principally on modern combat, from the WW II Special Operations Executive (SOE) organized by the British as resistance fighters and behind-the-lines saboteurs in France to such battles as the Gulf War of 1991.[193]

Muir describes the success of women in the Gulf war. They served on ships. They served as pilots and as ground troop support. They loaded the ammunitions and set the computer coordinates for the Patriot anti-missile batteries that took on Saddam Hussein's Scuds.

Muir also assesses the significant difficulties women encountered while serving, from dealing with resentful males to having menstrual periods under trying circumstances to becoming pregnant. She describes the significant difficulties the services had, and still experience, in trying to integrate women into what has been an all-male world. Recent scandals have revealed an alarming, high incidence of rape by fellow soldiers.

Despite these difficulties and barriers, Muir's conclusion is that under the conditions of modern warfare, there is no reason to exclude women as a group from any tasks. Lucinda Peace comes to a similar conclusion in an essay, "Gender and War," reviewing whether women are "tough enough" for military combat.[194] If women's influence is to be felt in the military, something that would be critical to the ultimate goal of achieving social balance and stability and a permanent end to war, logically they must serve or else have limited ability to speak with authority in matters involving security.

Only in the infantry, says Muir, where size and strength continue to be all-important, are women unlikely to be qualified in great numbers. Demi Moore and the film G.I. Jane aside, this is likely also true for Special Forces. But, Muir argues, women who can meet identical physical requirements for men and want to serve on the front lines should be allowed to.

Muir also describes, as does Jessica Amanda Salmonson in the *Encyclopedia of Amazons*, women warriors of the past. We learn of the record of Hippocrates in the fifth century BCE concerning the Sauromatian women who "ride, shoot, and throw javelins while mounted."[195] We learn about archeological discoveries from this same geographic region dating to the third and fourth century BCE where women are buried with what are clearly a warrior's belongings.

Traditionally this region north of the Black Sea, in the Ukraine and Southern Russia, has been associated with the Amazons of Greek fame, and these burials have revitalized the idea that Amazons were something more than mythological creatures. Jeannine Davis-Kimball has published studies undertaken in this region and has a book, *Warrior Women: An Archaeologist's Search for History's Hidden Heroines*.[196] Muir, citing Davis-Kimball's work, tells us about the burial of one of these women. Those who laid her to rest gave her such feminine objects as bronze and silver bracelets, a necklace of glass beds, a bronze mirror, and a Greek amphora, but in addition, two iron lance blades lay by her head and she had a quiver of twenty arrows and a woman-sized suit of iron-scale armor.

Defense vs. Offense

One comes away from these books, and others like them, knowing that women have fought bravely and successfully throughout history. Less clear, or at least not explicitly explored, is whether these women warriors fought in what they perceived to be wars of aggression or wars of defense. Whether they fought because they had no choice or because they enjoyed it. Were they the instigators and leaders of these enterprises, or merely swept up into the conflict?

In the Kingdom of Dahomey in West Africa during the 1800s there supposedly lived genuine Amazons. The impression usually given was that these were fierce women, in charge of their own lives, who had chosen a life of war.

Muir looked a bit deeper. The Dahomey were ruled by a king who was, indeed, surrounded by a bodyguard of fierce women warriors, at its height a group of around 4,000 women. These women had status equal to the male warriors. According to Salmonson, some had multiple husbands. They apparently often went barechested and would train by leaping over burning barriers and running barefoot through thorn thickets.

Muir notes that these women were recruited every three years when the king's subjects had to bring their teenage daughters to the king for selection. The strongest and most intelligent girls were chosen as officers. The rest were rejected or became foot soldiers. This was conscription, not voluntary service. And the organizer and instigator of these Amazons was a king, not a queen. This was not a way-of-life choice led and freely chosen by women with other options.

Muir also tells the compelling tale of Lily Litvak, a Russian ace pilot. In the Second World War, the Russians were so desperate for troops that they took some 800,000 women into the military. These women learned to be snipers, fighter pilots, drivers in tank battalions, submachine gunners in the infantry, and medical orderlies. In 1942, Lily Litvak joined the 73rd Fighter Regiment. She brought down ten German aircraft. A day before she died in an air battle she wrote home, "Battle life has swallowed me completely. I can't seem to think of anything but the fighting. I'm burning to chase the Germans from our country so we can lead a normal happy life together again." Great courage, lots of fighting spirit, but marshaled in the cause of defense!

Female mammals, including female primates, are typically, within their physical and behavioral limits, fierce fighters in defense of their young. With humans it seems quite likely this strong inclination to defend one's young could be extended to include defense of the community where one is raising those young. Or even to the defense of one's society or culture if the prospect of that society's or culture's falling creates underlying fear that the security in which one will raise one's young is threatened.

History certainly shows that women sufficiently roused to take up arms can be determined and in some cases brutal, vicious, and vengeful fighters. But what moves them to these actions? How often are women not defenders but active instigators in wars of aggression or expansion? How often do women use aggression, including killing, to take the territory or property of others?

One objection often raised to the proposition that women are less likely to be roused to war is, "What about Margaret Thatcher?" For example, the caption beside a picture in a recent *Science* article, "Gender and Violence," reads, "Many scholars contend that women are not innately more peaceful. Margaret Thatcher led the United Kingdom into war."[197] This reflects the pivotal misconception about *why* women differ from men with respect to war. These scholars correctly argue that women are not innately more peace-loving. But like Lily Litvak, who yearned to once again lead "a normal happy life," women generally are innately adapted to prefer social stability. If women are convinced, by whatever means (e.g., their own experience of what will follow if they don't act, by lies of their leaders about potential dangers from an enemy, or by being attacked), that using physical violence is the only way to achieve social stability, they will embrace physical violence. England's Maggie Thatcher did not invade Argentina. Argentina had invaded the Falklands, an island with people of British origins and culture who begged assistance from the homeland. To maintain her subject's security—to maintain their social order and way of life—Thatcher took steps she deemed necessary to accomplish that goal.

Are women aggressors or defenders? Salmonson's book, *The Encyclopedia of Amazons*, lists female warriors from the present going back into the ancient past. For each entry, an information snippet tells a bit about the woman and usually explains the context in which she fought, affording a further exploration of the Amazon archetype.

Women's Motivations to Fight in Wars

Salmonson's encyclopedia and the book *The 110* by Gary Hart provide individual cases of women and men to sample. A simple exercise using these two sources allows us to make a rough assessment of women's motivations when they take up weapons and compare them with men's.

Salmonson's A-Z listing is impressive, although the inclusion of goddesses and mythical women gives it a weight not entirely based in reality. She defines an Amazon as a woman who is a "duelist or soldier, by design or circumstances, whether chivalrous or cruel, and who engages others in direct combat, preferably with some semblance of skill and honorability." She adds that spies, assassins, modern frontline technicians, famous criminals, modern athletes, explorers, orators, big-game hunters and mothers saving their children from wild beasts would not be included. Still, the remaining list is impressively long.

To narrow the sample, all mythological women were excluded and only women in the A—B and the T—Z sections of the alphabet were included. This provided a randomly selected list of 110 total names. The reason Salmonson gives as the motivating factors or contexts in which these women fought was noted to put their reason for fighting into a context.

Salmonson says, "I have given special consideration to active defenders of castles." She says she does this because some critics argue that castle defense isn't sufficiently active and so shouldn't count as making a woman a warrior. They argue that such a woman is simply waiting for besiegers to tire and go home. She replies that defense against siege *is* active participation, and so she includes such women, so long as they took up arms and directed operations. She did note *several instances* of women venturing out to take castles and found them especially thrilling moments in history (emphasis mine).

Only several instances among hundreds throughout history (not including mythology)!? This was a tantalizing hint that there might not be many examples of female acts of conquest.

She includes heroines of a "chivalrous or warlike nature." Those of chivalrous nature are perhaps freedom fighters or defenders of one sort or another. Women born into high status in a warrior culture may, not surprisingly, take up arms to defend the right of their young, their lineage, to inherit this same high status. Defense of one's high rank by female primates (not uncommonly for humans, by poisoning one's rivals) is well known. But it is those women of true "warlike nature" who would be relevant here: women warmongers in the grip of a lust for power, lust for territory—in other words, the generators of war. These would be women who, in order to *achieve* high status or to make their status rise to even greater heights, started wars of conquest or continued a husband's campaigns.

MOTIVATION	NUMBER	EXAMPLES
Defense of castle, country, or throne	58	Agrippina the Younger Tamara of Georgia
Overthrow oppressive regime/rebellion	19	Boadicea Harriet Tubman
Fighting against captors, personal revenge, or to be with a lover or husband	8	Sofie Vansa Princess Wolonsky

Pirates/Raiders	6	Anne Bonney Nancy Walker
Adventurers	6	Eliza Allen Loreta Velasquez
Conquest	12	Agrippina the Elder Xenobia
Because of religious visions	1	Caterina Benincasa

Table 2   Reasons Women Took Up Arms

If the "chivalrous" categories of Defense of Castle, Country, or Throne, Overthrow of Oppressive Regime, and Resisting Captors/Avenging a Loved One/Or To Be With a Lover are combined, they total 85 cases or 77.3% of the reasons why women took up arms (Table 2). This quick sampling is suggestive evidence that defense of one sort or another and not offense is the chief reason women take up arms.

Pirates and Raiders seems to be a category of women on their society's fringes who found status and made a living by questionable, not particularly honorable means, but they did not instigate war. They are roughly 5.5% of the sample. The same is true for the Adventurers, another 5.5%. These were virtually all women who apparently lusted for something other than the humdrum and enlisted in wars started by others. It would be interesting to know why they picked a particular side. Was the nature of the cause at all relevant to their choices?

Those women involved in wars of conquest (12) are 10.9% of the cases, even though a number of them simply accompanied their husbands into battles being waged in a foreign territory. The women themselves were often not the instigators of the original conflict, but because they actively took up arms and went to a foreign field, they are included. This makes the percentage in the female Conquerors category actually higher than the reality.

To measure the extent to which men and women differ in taking up arms, we would need to do a similar examination of the motives of equally prominent warriors in history. Curiously, no lists of males equivalent to Salmonson's volume were available, no books with a title like *1000 Most Famous Warriors in History*. There are books on famous battles, biographies of famous warriors, lists with brief descriptions of the top 10 most famous, but no handy listing of history's most famous male warriors through time giving the reason they took up arms.

So we turn to Michael Hart's *The 100: A Ranking of the Most Influential Persons in History*. It, too, gives thumbnail sketches of people, in this case not selected as warriors but as individuals the author considers as having had the greatest impact on history. He listed them in his estimated order of most significant to least significant. The book makes fascinating reading in part because of his ranking.[198] We can use his list to compare with Salmonson's.

The Hart list includes some remarkably obscure names, for example ranked at #7 is Ts'ai Lun, the man who invented paper. There are 98 men in the top 100—and two women: Isabella I and Elizabeth I. Most of the men are great men of ideas (Newton, Einstein, Darwin, Copernicus, Edison, Plato, etc.), or religious thinkers (Mohammad, Jesus, Buddha, Confucius, Lao Tzu, Mahavira), or artists (Beethoven, Michelangelo, Bach, Picasso), and others whose contributions did not include war.

When the short biographies are examined, a rather ugly picture emerges in which men and one woman who were not themselves warriors, chivalrous or otherwise, created or promoted ideas that brought war or suffering as enormous as any war: Stalin, Hitler, Machiavelli, Umar ibn al-Khattab (leader of the most important Arab conquests), and Isabella I (the Inquisition).

Nevertheless, Hart chose 21 men who at some point took up arms.
5 (23.81%) were Revolutionaries (Lenin, Mao Tse-tung, George Washington, Simon Bolivar, Oliver Cromwell).
16 (76.2%) were Conquerors who launched wars into territories not their own. Most are well known: Augustus Caesar, Genghis Khan, Alexander the Great, Napoleon Bonaparte, and so forth.

None of the men was a Defender, for the obvious reason that the list was drawn up not just to indicate that men could and had fought, abundantly self-evident for men. Rather, the list was selected to represent people who made the greatest historical impact. Merely defending something (one's castle or even one's throne or country) is clearly less likely to have a major impact than launching a war.

Although we can't make a direct comparison from these two very different lists, we can restrict the sample of women to revolutionaries versus conquerors, the same two categories we have for men. A revealing difference emerges.

	Conquerors	Revolutionaries
Men	76.19%	23.81%
Women	38.7%	61.3%

Table 3   Conquerors vs. Revolutionaries

12 out of 31 such women (38.7%) were conquerors while 19 of the 31 (61.3%) were revolutionaries.

This compares to the 76.19 percent of the males who were conquerors and the 23.81 percent who were revolutionaries. The pattern is clearly reversed.

Salmonson and Hart set their own standards of selection for their lists and made the judgments about motivations or conditions affecting each listed individual. It's certain that some historians would disagree with some of their assessments. Nevertheless, this exercise throws light on three points.

First, the principle of the overlapping, albeit offset, bell curve with respect to gender differences holds here in the matter of conquest. It's not that there are NO women motivated by conquest. Rather, that their numbers are small, actually tiny, both historically and as a percentage of notable women who have taken up arms for any reason. Second, when we look at history, at who has made the greatest impact for good or ill, all of the conquerors who took up arms and made the top 100 are male. And third, the overwhelming majority of women who take up arms are not motivated by the desire to gain personal power by controlling or dominating other people. A frequent reason motivating women is some aspect of defense.

So what of the famous Cleopatra (a women in "C" of the alphabetical list, which was not in my sample)? Salmonson indicates that Cleopatra is a genuine example of female lust for power. At least as described by Salmonson, Cleopatra appears to fit the profile of Conqueror, along with Catherine the Great and Semiramis (if she was real, not mythological). These are additional women on the female bell curve who, along with Agrippina the Elder and Xenobia, overlap the bell curve for men when it comes to initiating wars. The principle clearly is that while it is not uncommon for women to be fierce defenders, they are rarely initiators of conquests.

What of Elizabeth I, one of the two women who made Hart's 100? According to Salmonson, Elizabeth never led her troops in battle, and so she doesn't qualify to be a warrior. But could she qualify as a warmonger, one who drags a country into war even though they may not fight themselves? According to Hart, the great Elizabeth not only did not involve herself personally in campaigns of conquest, she avoided involving her people in battle whenever possible. Her diplomatic and political skills brought a long period of stability, a Golden Age, during which literature and exploration flourished. Elizabeth I wisely built the island's navy into a formidable force, one able to defend England from threats, most notably the Spanish threat in the battle with the Spanish Armada. But in contrast to Isabella of Spain, Elizabeth did not attempt to use her impressive military force for armed aggression and violent conquest of other nations. The expansion of England into empire using military might came well after her enlightened reign.

It's important to remember to look beyond the specific individual. There are always individuals who don't fit the general pattern of their sex, but we are discussing statistically significant differences in inclinations of males and females as groups. Any woman who could in a patriarchal society fight her way to the top and remain there and from that platform launch a war of aggression is going to have what we would call strongly masculine inclinations. She will be very in touch with her masculine side, and also be an uncommon find.

Women, Cycles of Defense (Revenge), Raids for Resources

Recall that what characterizes women is not that they oppose war *per se*. Biologically (evolutionarily) what women want is social stability and sufficient resources to raise their children. What follows are examples of two situations where women, even in (complex) hunter-gatherer conditions, may support war: revenge cycles and raids for resources.

The first case is revenge cycles. A well-known example of revenge cycles are raids of patriarchal Yanomamö groups studied in South America by the anthropologist Napoleon Chagnon.[199] Heated debate at one time raged over Chagnon's work and his conclusion that the principle resource gained by the warriors is access to women in the other group as mating partners.[200] The women are either taken in the raids or are raped. And particularly fierce warriors (those known to have killed other men) turned out to have more wives and more offspring than other men in their group. Controversy as to Chagnon's evolutionary explanation for these raids aside,[201] there is little doubt that these tribal people, and many others like them, find themselves in vicious cycles of attack and counter-attack where revenge is an important psychological motivating ingredient.

Tribal cultures aren't the only ones to find themselves in a revenge quagmire. We're reminded of this almost daily when we contemplate the mess of the Israeli-Palestinian conflict. Once these violent patterns are set in motion, they are extraordinarily difficult to stop. In part, this is because each side feels, and can assert, that it is defending itself. Each side recites previous examples of violence by the other side as it prepares to retaliate. The logic is that if their side doesn't demonstrate its strength, the enemy will grow bolder, and their side will ultimately lose ground if not be entirely eliminated. For this reason, women, disposed to defense of children and community, may provide support for and encourage the men's counter-attacks.

All too often neither side can bring off a definitive win, nor can they get enough psychological distance from the situation to find a way out. The cycle continues with both sides losing people and squandering resources, a situation experts in negotiation call lose-lose.

It's striking to note that cycles of attack and counter-attack occur even when the social milieu *within* a group may be egalitarian and nonviolent. Once the process of demonizing the enemy has been established, treatment of and behavior toward "them" is often quite different from and much more violent than behavior practiced among "ourselves." As described earlier, women can be fierce defenders. Consequently, they are vulnerable to the appeal of defense against implacable, evil "others" and may even staunchly support a preemptive war.

On the other hand, if, as described by Fisher in *The First Sex*, women are more inclined to habitually think forward to anticipate problems (and surely this would include problems that might lead to future deadly retaliatory conflicts), we should see a difference between egalitarian and patriarchal societies as women's priorities temper male ones. No societies, however, are ever identical except for the degree to which they are egalitarian or patriarchal. So it becomes difficult to make legitimate comparisons. In theory, if my hypothesis about a female preference for stability providing a brake on male inclinations for head-to-head fighting is true, all other factors being equal, egalitarian societies would find ways to terminate (or mitigate) such feuds sooner than would otherwise be the case, or they would have fewer feuds than patriarchal societies.

A second case where women have frequently supported war occurs when raiding allows warriors to bring back needed resources. This sets up a dilemma for the women who must choose between the value of the resource and the costs the women may have to pay when their enemies in turn attack them. One can imagine super-heated debates in egalitarian communities as the men and women struggle to determine where their true, long-term best interests lie. Again, if my hypothesis is correct and all other factors were equal, egalitarian groups would more frequently (but not necessarily always) reject the war option than would patriarchal groups.

Theory aside, it is clear that the relationship of women to conflicts and the use of physical aggression is complex, but not an unsolvable mystery. Women throughout humanity's evolutionary history have been under great reproductive pressures to bear and care for helpless, slow-developing offspring. The hypothesis put forth in *Shift* is that natural selection in response has produced inclinations that foster social stability and these are more characteristic of women than men. And when the lives of their children or the existence of the community in which they are raising those children is threatened and no other option is available to them, women can and will fight. The key is the need to produce living, successful offspring.

Breaking Free

Peace won't just happen. Certainly these two critical elements must be mastered: breaking and preventing revenge cycles and distributing the earth's resources equitably. And our most pressing need with respect to both of these two problems is not for new information or further studies. We've had experts studying these issues for years. The second half of William Ury's book *Getting To Peace,* for example, lays out detailed steps to facilitate more win-win and less lose-lose conflict resolution.[202] As for how the earth's resources can be best preserved and more equitably distributed, we've created mountains of books and scholarly papers with equally compelling insights and plans that can set us in the right direction.

No, our most pressing need is the will to act in accordance with what we claim to desire. Peace is being made and kept daily by millions of people. We can study how they do it, we can learn from them. Then we need to do the work necessary to create conditions globally that foster peace. So in the next section, we shift gears. We move from our understanding of the biology of war to ask what can be done to move the global community from where we are to where we would like to be.

PART II - HOW WE CAN END WAR

There is no compromise possible between preparation for war, on the one hand, and preparation of a world society based on law and order on the other.... The United Nations now and world Government eventually must serve one single goal, the guarantee of the security, tranquillity, and the welfare of all mankind.

Albert Einstein
Open Letter to UN General
Assembly, October 1947

CHAPTER 10 – CORNERSTONES OF A CAMPAIGN TO END WAR

I think we should commit ourselves to fighting for something that is so big that we may never live to see it because otherwise we're not fighting for something big enough.

Abigail Disney
Joan B. Kroc Institute for Peace and
Justice, March, 2011

Having established the roles of the two sexes as these relate to making war and that war is not a genetically evolved adaptation but a relatively recent cultural creation, we explore now how we end it. The quest will be founded on what we know about psychological, proximate, and ultimate causes of war and male/female differences with respect to physical aggression and a preference for social stability.

War is an insidious, pernicious, and deeply-entrenched foe. But we are capable of greatness. Were we to succeed, putting a permanent end to war would certainly qualify as one of our greatest achievements. It certainly qualifies as something big to fight for, something so big that many reading this book will not live to see it.

The perspective that follows is mine. I know other individuals won't agree with everything. But I hope these assessments, speculations, and proposals will stimulate discussion—even contention in the best sense of the word—by individuals who are able to step back to see the big picture rather than focus on differences, and by uniting us in common cause, move us forward.

Shifting Our Worldview by Ending War

It is crucial to note something before we proceed: ending war is about much more than just ending war. *The challenges to be explored in this chapter are fundamental to creating more just, egalitarian, and ecologically sustainable communities.* And ending war is foundational to success in mastering those challenges. Ending war is the horse needed to pull our cart of enduring peace.

Consider this example. In *Winning the War on War*, Joshua Goldstein has a chapter on "Peace Movements." He poses a strategy debate between whether a movement should work first to establish justice before you can have peace, or whether a movement should work directly for peace, and justice would follow.[203] A similar debate can be had about how to pursue other goals. For example, whether we should work first on creating ecologically sustainable communities and then work on ending war, or the reverse. In a section about gender justice, Goldstein writes:

> "The evidence in this book suggests that .... war is not a product of capitalism, imperialism, gender, innate aggression, or any other single cause, although all of these influence wars' outbreaks and outcomes. Rather, war has in part fueled and sustained these and other injustices. So, 'if you want peace, work for peace.' Indeed, if you want justice (gender and others), work for peace. Causality does not run just upward through the levels of analysis....it runs downward too. Enloe suggests that changes in attitudes towards war and the military may be the most important to 'reverse women's oppression.'"[204]

Goldstein is in essence making the case that acceptance of the legitimacy of war and of the values and assumptions supporting war is the prime cause of many other evils. The perspective presented in *Shift* is the same: that ending war will set up conditions, social and psychological, within which justice can be introduced and prevail. A campaign to end war that simultaneously addresses all nine of the cornerstones to be described shortly will create a massive world shift that will have extensive, ramifying, positive effects. Justice. Equality. Issues of environmental sustainability. All will be simultaneously affected. While we work to end war we will be creating an altered environment, a new worldview, a new normal. It is from these effects—creating a necessary shift in worldview while simultaneously dealing with the proximate causes of war—that a campaign to end war is foundational to other highly desired positive goals.

Enormity of The Challenge

The remarkable anthropologist Margaret Mead said that war is an "invention." There is danger, however, in thinking or assuming that ending this obsolete perilous invention will be in any way easy. John Horgan, for example, implies in *The End of War* that ending war is simply a matter of realizing that it isn't innate and then resolving to end it.[205] Barbara Ehrenreich shares my view. About Horgan's book she writes, "In the service of optimism, Horgan ends up making one of the oldest military mistakes that there is—underestimating the enemy."[206] Resolve is not going to be nearly enough.

People have looked in vain for some single cause of war, or even two things or maybe just three things we could fix that would end it. The list in Chapter 3 of war's multiple proximate causes, however, makes clear the improbability of any simple fix. But that doesn't mean that abolition is impossible. The nine sections that follow outline challenges to be met to end war and, most importantly, to prevent backsliding. I call them cornerstones of an ending war campaign. They are also the foundations of enduring peace. These challenges deal with war's proximate causes and more. Think of them as analogous to battle fronts, like the Russian, European, and Pacific fronts of World War II. Stated in military terms, we need warriors to do battle, we need a battle plan, and the effort to wage a war against war will be fought on these many fronts and battlegrounds.

I arrange the cornerstones in a circle, not a list, to indicate that they must be addressed simultaneously, not one after the other.[207] None of them alone has the power to end the slaughter; dealing with each is necessary but not sufficient to achieve an enduring peace. More detailed essays for each cornerstone can be found at the website A Future Without War.org.

Embrace the Goal

Spread Liberal Democracy   Empower Women

Shift Our Economies

Provide Security and Order   Enlist Young Men

Promote Nonviolent   Ensure Essential Resources
Conflict Resolution

Foster Connectedness

These efforts can be grouped differently. For example, Robert Hinde and Joseph Rotblat, in their book *War No More*, touch on virtually all the same problem areas and proposed solutions, just in a different arrangement and with different emphasis.[208] This is also true of other books on how to end war such as Robert A. Irwin's *Building a Peace System: Exploratory Project on the Conditions of Peace*, and Winslow Myers' *Living Beyond War: A Citizen's Guide*.[209] Two notable differences I *explicitly stress* that to my knowledge no other authors stress or, in many cases, even mention, are the need to empower women, and to enlist young men. What is most important is that when we see how all are interrelated, individuals and organizations will be better equipped to address these issues synergistically.

For each cornerstone, Appendix I lists a few organizations for which that cornerstone is their *principal* focus. These groups are already at work. Their members have the expertise in their field of interest needed to advance our cause. In *Shift* you will find only a few practical steps to tackling cornerstone issues, as illustrations. For the most part I simply describe the battlefronts because I do not presume to have the required expertise: no one person does.

Chapter 12, "Pulling Elements of the Plan Together," introduces an action plan for uniting these separate efforts. A united global community sharing in directed action can eliminate war in two generations or less.

The Nine Cornerstones

1 - Embrace the Goal

Determine that the thing can and shall be done, and then we shall find the way.

Abraham Lincoln

The single greatest barrier to ending war is the near universal belief that ending war is impossible. If you ask 100 people if they believe it would be possible to create a future without war, what do you think you would discover? I posed this question to hundreds in the United States, noted their responses by counting raised hands, and kept records of the results. If you think we can end war, you may be surprised, even saddened, to learn that the vast majority of Americans said, No. It's not possible. If you also believe it is impossible, your belief would be nicely reinforced by overwhelming agreement with you. This is likely to be the general view in other countries as well.

This lack of belief is of profound consequence. We cannot achieve any goal unless we believe it is achievable. Success and belief in the possibility of success hang together when undertaking even a modest goal to say nothing of one as monumental as abolishing war. If we believe we must settle for just reducing the damages or incidence of war, disbelief becomes a self-fulfilling prophecy. We will not even think about how we might abolish it, let alone take up the effort.

Believing something is possible, however, is not the same as embracing it as a goal for which people will vote, donate money and time, pay taxes, possibly risk jail, prison, or their life. So the first cornerstone of any campaign to end war is to spread the knowledge to powerful and common people alike that the goal is achievable, and spread that knowledge in such a way that they embrace the challenge. To that end, John Horgan's book, *The End of War*, Joshua Goldstein's *Winning the War on War*, and Douglas Fry's books and others like them are important contributions.

In their book *Opting out of War*, Mary Anderson and Marshall Wallace offer examples of thirteen different communities around the world that opted out of the violence surrounding them. These non-war communities predicted the cost of violence on themselves and their families and found options to prevent their community from being drawn in. They embraced the goal of rejecting war; what is needed is for the global community to do the same.[210]

2 - Provide Security and Order

Our government has kept us in a perpetual state of fear -- kept us in a continuous stampede of patriotic fervor -- with the cry of grave national emergency. Always there has been some terrible evil at home or some monstrous foreign power that was going to gobble us up if we did not blindly rally behind it.

> General Douglas MacArthur
> Address to the Annual Stockholders
> Sperry Rand Corporation 30 July 1957

2.1 General Principles Concerning Security – Enforcement by Enlightened Leaders - It is self-evident that where there is no security and no order, countries entangled in internal or external battles are not going to make much progress on any of the many challenges to be met to create a lasting peace. These challenges include issues like ending poverty, advancing the concept that we are all one people, empowering women, teaching and demonstrating nonviolence for our children, and building liberal democracies. Building lasting peace also includes doing what is necessary to put an end to what students of peace call structural violence—the situation in which specific organizations, practices, or conditions within a society such as racism, sexism, elitism, nationalism, and poverty injure or harm individuals or masses of individuals.

But tackling these and other critical issues depends upon the world community's ability to maintain a reasonable level of social order. When a community or nation is in chaos, available resources will of necessity be spent on dealing with the violence and destruction first, and only what's left over—often a tiny sum—may be put to the good works that would undergird a future wholly without war.

In Joseph Rotblat's 2006 article, *A world without war. Is it desirable? Is it feasible?* he addressed this security issue.

> "One of the main functions of the nation-state is to ensure the security of its citizens against threats from other states, which is taken to mean possessing the ability to wage war. A change will be called for in this respect: sovereignty will need to be separated from, and replaced by, autonomy. In particular, the right of the state to make war will have to be curtailed. This means no national military forces, and the only legal coercive power on the world scale to be vested in some kind of police force responsible to a global authority. Some form of world governance seems a necessary outcome of the evolution of the United Nations. As a way towards this we have to acquire a loyalty to humankind."[211]

We need a critical mass of global leaders from powerful countries who embrace a loyalty to humankind. We need leaders who understand that embracing the concept and practice of nonviolent conflict resolution is ultimately the *only* path to end war. Not fewer wars. Or fewer dreadful wars. Or nuclear wars. We need leaders who commit themselves, their lives, their resources, and their ingenuity to building a future without any wars whatsoever. Leaders who make clear through policy and actions—positive ones such as providing aid and negative ones such as applying sanctions and boycotts—that they will not tolerate the killing solution by other leaders. Not between nations and not within any nation. And we will need an overarching body to foster and enforce this commitment to peace.

Sadly, if all nonviolent means (sanctions, boycotts, incentives) have failed to halt an aggressor determined to maintain or expand his (or her) power by killing—killing people within his (or her) own country or people from other nations—military intervention may be an unavoidable necessity.

Agitated skeptics of the idea of global peace often protest, "What about Hitler? We can't end war. There will always be a Hitler!" In 2014 we might just as well ask, "What about Assad?"

To build a global community at peace, a means of enforcement necessarily stands as a bottom line. But it will be critical that use of force is seen by the global community as an act of policing ourselves, not an act of conquest and domination. Before military action is taken, for example, the world community should agree. And of course, this sounds fine, but if the global citizenry is to live by law and order, not violence, what is the best way to achieve agreement? How should the people of Earth police our warless future? For that matter, is there any reason to think we can?

In *The Better Angels of Our Nature*, Pinker searches back through history and proposes five factors that were (and presumably can be) the most consistent reducers of violence.[212] [In Appendix II, I describe all five and indicate where they are similar to factors proposed in *Shift* as keys to ending war.] Pinker called the chief among these five factors "Leviathan." Leviathan is the condition in which a state with a monopoly on force uses that force to protect its citizens from other groups. Potential warring parties come under the control of this power with overwhelming military force and it imposes penalties for violence and when necessary enforces penalties with physical punishment. Think of *Pax Romana*, the power of Rome. Or the power of a dictator like Marshal Tito of Yugoslavia or Iraq's Saddam Hussein. And think of the chaos that results when such overarching powers fall. At this time in history, the United States of America is such a state.

This historically documented fact does illustrate the positive effect of having an overarching authority with the power to enforce peace. It is not, however, likely to be a model that can be realistically applied "as is" to the hundreds of nations and cultures that compose the global community of our time: they will virtually unanimously reject the notion of a single nation as dictator of order over them. And in the less violent future we hope to create, using physical force to enforce stability will (hopefully) be contrary to our way of life. So, is there a way to modify the Leviathan approach that might be acceptable and useful now?

In an article in *Science*, "Life Without War," Douglas Fry proposes a model of a "global peace system."[213] He explores this concept using examples from three cultures on different continents.

[Appendix III compares the shared key characteristics of these peace systems with the *Shift* cornerstones.] The three peace systems Fry highlights are ten tribes of the Upper Xingu River basin of Brazil, the Iroquois Confederacy of Upper New York State, and the European Union.

His analysis leads him to suggest six essentials of a successful peace system, and among them is something he calls "superordinate institutions for conflict management." As described in the article, it should be noted that peace is not maintained by using force but by shared values, shared rituals that promote unity, shared commerce, and so on. Think of the formation of the United States from thirteen separate colonies "by creating a kind of higher level of governance in which people with differences do not take up weapons and battle it out; they take their case to the Supreme Court." In these three peace systems we see some models for a future without war that are likely to be willingly adopted by the world community…once the vision of the possibility of abandoning violence, including war, exists as a conscious and realistic choice.

Goldstein, in *Winning the War on War*, explores many possibilities for the not-so-peaceful world of now and makes a number of specific recommendations for maintaining the social order and enforcing peace. Chief among them that we need to revamp the United Nations and then strengthen it.[214]

In contrast for example, Robert Hinde and Joseph Rotblat, expressd in 2003 the sense that the United Nations may be beyond restructuring, and that we need some other "supranational forum" to settle disputes and authorize intervention by an international police force.[215]

J. J. English is one of many proponents of ending war and writes, "There can be no question that the United Nations system needs reform, but the basic principles as outlined in the original charter are a beacon of hope for future generations."[216] Former U.S. Senator Gary Hart is another expert who writes that old ideas of National Sovereignty upon which the United Nations was originally founded need to be reexamined in the light of new realities.[217]

Peacekeeping—doing what is required to maintain a peaceful condition within a society—is fine. But so long as the world has warmongers who reject the vision of peace, the United Nations (or some similar organization) must be given peacemaking ability—given the means to prevent or stop a war. Until that happens, the world community's option appears to be negotiating and agreeing upon Resolutions and building military coalitions that rely primarily on the massive military might of the United States. Simply put, most people who wrestle with this thorny problem agree that to bring war to an end, we'll need a global approach and means of enforcement. The United Nations is an established, globally oriented organization whose founding mission was to prevent war. Fixing rather than replacing it seems to be the most workable choice.

2.2 A Glimpse of the Future Without War, R2P – A historic step on our path to global policing has recently been taken. From it we can see how the global community can develop its peacemaking and peacekeeping muscles.

In 2006, the United Nations Security Council formalized its support for an initiative called the Responsibility to Protect (R2P). In 2009, the UN General Assembly also adopted the resolution. It establishes a set of principles based on the idea that National Sovereignty isn't a right, it's a privilege. It provides a mechanism for member nations to reach agreement to intervene in severe crisis situations. All means are to be used to persuade the involved parties to stop the violence, military intervention being a last resort.

R2P is the first challenge to the founding principle that the UN's mandate is to prevent war between nations, but that whatever a dictator, tyrant, or government chooses to do within the country's borders is strictly its, his, or her business. R2P says it is the responsibility of a sovereign nation to protect its citizens…and if there is a failure to do so in four specific cases—genocide, war crimes, crimes against humanity, and ethnic cleansing—*the international community is obligated to step in and use all means necessary to bring an end to these four behaviors targeted by R2P.*

Predictably, and understandably, R2P is controversial. For example, developing nations can argue that the Security Council (which has the final say on the use of force) is a biased tool of power interests of Western states. Others question the criteria upon which decisions about whether military intervention is warranted are based.

Consider the case of Libya. On March 19, 2011, the UN Security Council approved a resolution, based on the R2P mandate, that directed Libyan authorities to protect the Libyan population. It called for an immediate ceasefire, including attacks on civilian populations which, if carried out, would constitute a "crime against humanity." There would be a no-fly zone imposed over the country, and sanctions against the Libyan dictator Muammar Kadafi's regime were tightened. The resolution passed with 10 votes for, 0 against, and five abstains that included Germany, China and Russia.

Media reports said that Kadafi had made a strategic blunder by announcing that his forces would invade the city of Benghazi and destroy it and its people for their rebellion. The naked threat to kill all the civilians gave Kadafi's opponents at the United Nations the argument they needed to convince that body, based on R2P, to act. The arrangement for implementation was to have NATO forces carry most of the burden, although they would be heavily assisted initially by technical and military resources only the United States could provide.

On 21 October, 2011, Kadafi was found and killed without trial—essentially on the spot. His regime was ended. On 8 July, 2012, the freed people of Libya voted to elect a 200-member provisional National Congress. The process of preventing a massacre in Libya illustrates how the United Nations, acting in concert, can enforce desired behavior.

In September of 2013 the UN Security Council voted to sanction Syrian dictator Bashar al-Assad for his use of the chemical weapon sarin gas on his people. The result of global pressure was an agreement to have experts destroy his chemical arsenal. This sanction was the world community's alternative to a credible threat of military attack on Syria by the United States as punishment for use of the gas in defiance of the global treaty against such use. Use of negotiations backed by this credible threat of overwhelming force appears to have achieved a desired end, and done so without having to use violence. If the chemical weapons are in fact destroyed this would serve as an example of the outcome when some entity can challenge bad actors with a credible threat of punishment or non-compliance with globally agreed upon rules of law.

When global consensus can be agreed upon, the United Nations can likewise enforce the cessation of war. If all parties that start killing their subjects or that launch a war were aware that the united global community would promptly act to begin the process of removing them from power, arguably the frequency of such acts would decrease….eventually to zero.

Lest we lose touch with reality, however, we need to look behind the curtain at how the decision to intervene in Libya came about. The independent blogger Andrew Garvin Marshall offers a critique illustrating how complex, and often devious, the reality of human decision-making is. His lengthy review takes strong exception to the version of history most people heard or read from mainstream media about the use of R2P in this case.[218] He presents evidence that elements desiring to be rid of Kadafi manufactured the case used to rouse the UN Security Council to intervene. He questions, for example, media claims that Kadafi had threatened to destroy Benghazi.

Whether or not this is actually true, R2P is a significant step toward normalizing the worldview that war crimes by a state against its people are not acceptable. Its significance is definitely not that its implementation is, or ever will be, an example of flawless human decision-making. Humans are not perfect. Our decision-making will never be perfect. Our goal will always be to achieve the best outcome of which we, in our imperfection, are capable. What we seek is not the unrealistic or utopian "perfect." We seek to fashion a new "normal." A culture with values and institutions that foster a less violent reality within which we live our not-perfect but immeasurably precious lives. We start from where we are. We can change our worldview using the means described in what follows. Politics at all levels is complicated and often ugly. People of good faith can and will, nevertheless, navigate us forward on a positive course.

2.3 Practical Issues –It is generally understood that the first responsibility of any government is to provide security and order for its people, which includes:

- security from external threats, and
- order along with justice within the society.

Another commonly understood principle is that to win a battle, you should act from a position of strength. The same principle holds when negotiating to resolve differences so that your side secures a favorable outcome. This is why stakeholders in an ending-war campaign will likewise need to stand on a sufficiently high ground of strength that enables the imposition of order.

What is certain right now, as we take initial steps to provide for a secure global community, in whatever form it ultimately takes, is that a society that cannot resist threats from without or resolve disorder within is not a strong society. Therefore, stakeholder nations in a campaign to end war at this time need to:

- Protect their borders
- Secure their infrastructure (e.g., dams, roads, ports, power plants, water supply, food supply, communications, financial institutions)
- Maintain internal social order
- And until the United Nations or some similar body has sufficient enforcement authority and power, the United States, her democratic allies, and peace-preferring nations must maintain sufficient military force to mount a defense against any entity considering a war that would destabilize the global community. A powerful military capacity clearly does not guarantee peace, but if properly led, the historical record shows that it can be a significant deterrence to mass outbreaks of violence.

Political strategists might include other essentials as fundamental to a position of strength, but these are certainly the basics. And a collateral benefit to maintaining adequate national security is that it can provide jobs for young men and women (e.g., soldiers, police, border guards, airport inspectors, shipping yard inspectors, infrastructure inspectors, military and peacekeeping strategists, linguists, et. cetera).

2.4 Allocating Financial Resources to Achieve Security – What about money? Stakeholders in creating a war-free future should not allow expenditure of resources—money or human-power—foolishly or thoughtlessly. For example:

- Stop spending, in the United States, on non-workable weapons systems like Star Wars (SDI) or its smaller cousin the Medium Extended Air Defense System (MEADS). Everyone should finally admit that the SDI program will not work and, therefore, is a financial extravagance that makes no one more secure,[219] and that MEADS is ill designed to provide protection from threats that are likely to emerge.

- Stop funding obsolete or unnecessary weapons systems solely to generate employment or to allow politicians to give their constituents pork-barrel rewards (e.g., the U.S. Marine Expeditionary Fighting Vehicle – EFV). Instead, shift funds to projects that contribute to ending war (e.g., using creative resources to provide water to all communities, inventing and distributing technology to enable farmers on unproductive lands to utilize that land, finding new ways to combat diseases). Richly reward politicians who support ending war goals by funding projects from their districts that serve that mission.

- Stop funding the development of exotic weapons, dreams of how to kill by agencies like the United State's DARPA (Defense Advanced Research Projects Agency). These dream projects consume resources to plan for wars that *might* begin with any possible, *but not actual*, enemy. Hypothetical war, hypothetical enemies. Spending money on fascinating theoretical ideas is an absurd waste. Robot warriors will not win the war on terrorism; arguably they may only prolong it. Why are we inventing robot warriors? We don't need faster and stealthier jets to protect the free world from North Korea or Iran or any other nation. Not only do we not need to put lasers or any other potentially offensive weapons into space, treaties should be adopted immediately to prevent such a disastrous, short-sighted, wasteful and immoral crossing of the Rubicon, no matter how much money contractors stand to make. A strong case can be made that planning for yet a new kind of war, no matter how entertaining and intellectually challenging that may be, is in fact the first step to manifesting that new kind of war. At some point we need to lay to rest the fallacy (propagated by the war business machine) that spending money on more and bigger weapons is a path to peace.

A people living under the perpetual menace of war and invasion is very easy to govern. It demands no social reforms. It does not haggle over expenditures on armaments and military equipment. It pays without discussion, it ruins itself, and that is an excellent thing for the syndicates of financiers and manufacturers for whom patriotic terrors are an abundant source of gain.
Attributed to Anatole France, 1844-1924

Not only do we need to avoid foolish spending, for security's sake we need to engage in smart spending. For example:

- The level of support for international peacekeepers and peacemakers, under the auspices of the United Nations (or some similar entity or entities), should be vastly increased.[220] Nonpartisan unarmed peacekeeping organizations like Nonviolent Peaceforce and Peace Brigades International can be supported. These non-governmental efforts use trained teams to apply proven strategies to protect individuals in communities in turmoil. They deter violence and create a space where local civil society people can build and sustain peace. These teams can also provide secure environments within which reconciliation, reconstruction, and building or rebuilding the social institutions that provide for law and order can occur after a war.

- To encourage combatants in countries in the throes of wars to lay down their weapons, we can provide negotiators and mediators, and assure all parties there will be generous financial support for rebuilding when compromise is reached. This can be done via a body like the United Nations, which already does it but needs greater resources. Member states seeking to end war must provide sufficient funding.

The support should be so generous that dictators or warlords find it hard to say no for fear of triggering mass insurrection. Aid must be well planned and the results carefully monitored by independent, outside agencies specialized to do so, as well as appropriately equipped civil society organizations. The aid should demonstrate to everyone that negotiation and compromise are superior to battle.

The reconstruction taking place in Liberia is, at this time, an inspiring example of what can be done when a people support peace and the nation's leadership is enlightened. The mess of Afghanistan, at this time, is a perfect example of how money and resources can be grossly wasted when the people do not demand that their fighters cease fighting, the leadership is corrupt, and monitoring of aid isn't sufficient or transparent.

• Ultimately, security depends not just on providing adequate means to deter anyone thinking of starting a war and in enforcing peace agreements and laws that foster peace. It depends also on eliminating institutions, practices, and attitudes of structural violence. The global community must resolve to devote financial resources (taxes) to the works of these nine *Shift* cornerstones. Global citizens should demand that apportionment of tax dollars to their Defense (or War) Departments are matched by the amount devoted to their State Department's programs of aid and educational programs that advance peace. Governments should set up Departments of Peace that are given the same status and funding as War (Defense) Departments. If we spend more on preparing for and waging war than on building and sustaining peace, history and life experience teaches that we will reap what we sow.

No one nation can do all this. But in concert, the world's democracies with other willing allies have sufficient resources to fund the United Nations' missions for peacemaking, peacekeeping, and a wide array of programs dealing with *Shift* cornerstones: health, education, the advancement of women, ending poverty, economic sustainability and more.

Finally, we need to financially starve the war machine. Leaders and politicians around the globe who represent corporate entities of the war industry—corporations that fund their campaigns and essentially buy their votes—will do what power hungry individuals have done through the ages: they will use scare tactics about unsubstantiated threats to keep the war business alive, they may invent threats, they may even invent a war.[221] Free citizens, if they choose, can embrace the duty to curb such ambitions by putting those polititians out of office and boycotting the corporations.

2.6 Conclusion - Imagine that in the near future the possibility of ending war is universally acknowledged, the United Nations (or some similar, global entity representing the world's people) has declared that war is illegal, and this entity, empowered by universal (or near universal) agreement, rapidly and firmly enforces any breach of the law. We will be in good position to rapidly pursue the work of moving us from our current warring state to this condition of a future of mutually embraced peace.

To move us to that future, a third key challenge will be to ensure that the world's citizens have access to essential resources.

3 - Ensure Essential Resources

True individual freedom cannot exist without economic security and independence. 'Necessitous men are not free men.' People who are hungry and out of a job are the stuff of which dictatorships are made.

Franklin D. Roosevelt, 32nd U.S. President
State of the Union Address, 1944.

3.1 Resource Basics - It is self-evident, or should be, why any effort to end war must include giving the world's teeming millions access to life's three essential resources: fresh water, food, and shelter. Without these, personal survival isn't possible. Natural selection built into us an unrelenting drive to acquire these things. Arguably, adequate health care should also be included as a survival essential. When people don't have the three basics in some at least minimal amount, at some point they will do whatever they can, including fighting if they are able, to acquire them; revolution occurs. Only a repressive government willing to use all the tools at its command, including military force, can keep a citizenry deprived of these essentials under control for any extended length of time.

A means to make a living to support one's offspring is "essential" as well to successful reproduction. In an ever more technically complicated and globally connected world, education sufficient to make a living is also an essential, and it generally must include some basics: reading, writing, basic arithmetic—and for a real chance at success, often much more.

Fortunately, legions of organizations are already devoted to the work of this cornerstone. There are hundreds of thousands of small, local projects in villages and towns on every continent. There are massive efforts by international organizations based at the United Nations and elsewhere. There are personality based efforts like the Jimmy Carter Foundation, the rock star Bono's ONE, the Bill and Melinda Gates Foundation, and the Clinton Global Initiative (see Ensure Essential Resources, Appendix I).

People laboring for these causes often do it simply to relieve suffering. They follow their moral compass. They don't want to live in a world where some people enjoy fabulous plenty while others live and die in squalor, pain, and the absence of hope. And most especially, a driving motivation behind this tireless work stems from the desire to create something better for the world's children. This alone can be sufficient motivation. But whether they are aware of it or not, their work contributes fundamentally to the quest to end war.

Unfortunately, providing access to these needs alone will not end war, not even if we succeed in doing so, as has been the case in many developed countries. For example, the highly developed United States of America, where such basics are available, launched a preemptive war on the country of Iraq. As our exploration of proximate causes of war indicates, other motivations having nothing whatsoever to do with resources may move leaders to make war. It's significant, and hopeful, to note that to make the launch of that Iraq war palatable to the democratic U.S. citizenry at large—people in possession of life's essential resources—it had to be duplicitously marketed as a defensive act.

3.2 Living Sustainably in Harmony with The Environment – We also need to change the behavior of millennia in how we relate to our natural environment, the source of our essential resources. In the article in the September 2005 issue of *Scientific American*, "Economics in a Full World," ecological economist Herman Daly discusses implications of extraordinary changes in our environment.[222] As noted previously, he points out that we evolved in an "empty world,"[223] and we are now confronted with a radically altered "full world." This astounding terraforming change, which we ourselves have brought about, confronts us with potential global ecological disaster.

The global community, Daly argues, cannot continue to rely on growth as the cure for our economic ills. He describes "economic growth" and "uneconomic growth." Economic growth occurs when increases in production generate corresponding increase in personal well-being, and the cost to environmental resources is outweighed by improvements in lives and the accumulation of man-made capital (such as roads, factories, and appliances). Uneconomic growth occurs when production increases at the expense of well-being and the resources that are depleted are worth more than the items created or built.

According to Daly, most developed countries have probably already made the transition from economic to uneconomic growth: developed nations are using up natural resources at an alarming rate and not becoming all that much personally happier or healthier for it.

Many experts dealing with resource issues are, for example, questioning the wisdom of massive globalization when it comes to the basics. Sharing art, music, scientific advances, sports, sharing the cultural advancements that can link us together as humans facing a shared future is to be valued. But when it comes to what most of us now consider life's essentials—food, water, shelter, good health care, and education—people and organizations with foresight are exploring the importance of local self-reliance.

Although it is gaining momentum, this concept certainly isn't new. For example, the great social transformer Mohandas Gandhi spent much effort on teaching local villagers how to be independent and self-reliant. This grew out of Gandhi's understanding of human nature and his own belief that no man who depends on others for his life's essentials can be totally free. Experimental communities that use "green" principles to guide their development are springing up across the globe, growing their own foods, making efficient use of water, adopting renewable sources of power that they can manage themselves.[224] The issue of access to fresh water grows more critical every year.

Heedless exploitation and then "moving on" can no longer be a successful strategy for *Homo sapiens*. The quality of our survival will depend on how we do, or do not, learn to live in balance with Mother Earth.

3.3 Global Climate Change - Global climate change, first called global warming, is also a phenomenon critical to having access to essential resources. How we respond to this climate shift will affect our susceptibility to or possibility of ending war. Beginning roughly 30 years ago, some scientists began to warn that Earth's climate seemed to be entering an unnaturally rapid warming period. They also felt it was the result of humans putting too much carbon dioxide into the atmosphere. In the intervening decades, scientists from a variety of disciplines continued to collect data and argue about what it all meant. Was the trend to global warming even a real trend? And if the global atmosphere was warming, did it have anything at all to do with human activity, or was it just one of earth's normal climate change cycles?

In 2007, the IPCC, the Intergovernmental Panel on Climate Change, issued a definitive report in four parts.[225] The central debate is now over. The overwhelming majority of knowledgeable experts agree that we are warming at an uncommonly rapid, very unsettling, rate, and that this warming was triggered by increased human industrial and agricultural activity.

The warming of the atmosphere and its effects on our global environment may, probably has, already taken on a life of its own. For example, the ice caps at the top and bottom of the world are melting. Less ice means that less heat from the sun is reflected back into the atmosphere and more heat is captured by the water. This makes the ice melt even faster. A cycle of melting has been set up and we aren't in control of it.

Now debates among experts are about exactly how much the climate will warm, how fast, and what exactly will be the consequences for our societies and countries. The effects will be felt unevenly across the globe, but the general outlook is pretty clear, and not good: more and stronger hurricanes, more and longer droughts, uncommonly heavy rainfalls that bring on flooding, snow storms that dump huge amounts of snow, a rise in sea-water level that will wipe out some countries and a lot of shoreline real estate, disease-bearing insects moving into formerly disease free locations, the extinction of plants and animals that can't move fast enough to reach a new location that can support their lives. Agricultural productivity as seasonal changes shift will be dramatically affected, challenging farmers to accommodate to new conditions.

There is going to be a lot of death and destruction. One can legitimately argue that we are already seeing increased deaths from storms intensified by this climate shift. Just how bad it will ultimately be, nobody knows.

So how does this massive global climate shift relate to a campaign to end war? There are numerous possibilities. Here are two.

First, imagine that we continue to deny that the phenomenon is real or act as though it isn't, thus proving that we are incapable of responding to it. We do nothing meaningful enough to blunt the effects of the now inevitable change, and the resulting massive assault on our affected populations causes social disruption and migration on a massive scale. To secure those required essentials, we end up at each other's throats on an equally immense scale. We fall into a kind of perpetual "Road Warrior" future brought on, not by a war, but by the collapse of order in the face of economic, social, and physical chaos.

Or, suppose we take this lemon and make lemon meringue pie. Perhaps the magnitude of this onrushing catastrophe will bring out the best in us, specifically our ability to survive through cooperation—not fighting. A number of experts on human evolution are turning away from the "man-the-warrior" hypothesis for why we survived and became human and filled the globe. They suggest instead that what enabled us to be so enormously successful is our ability to cooperate: the "humans-as-cooperators" hypothesis mentioned in the chapter on "Mothers and Others." [226]

If what our survival instinct brings out is a massive global move toward cooperation, one of the things we might seriously agree on is to stop wasting critically needed resources on wars and use them instead to blunt the worst effects of global warming. We could recognize global warming as our common enemy. [227]

3.4 Population Growth - No discussion of the relationship of essential resources to a campaign to abolish war can avoid the issue of population growth, or as some would call it, population explosion. Simply put, given the limited amount of habitable land and fresh water now at our disposal, and that our planet is now "full" of us, we cannot continue to produce more humans with longer life spans without seriously depressing our quality of life, creating toxic environments, and exhausting vital resources. Global warming, apparently created by increased production of greenhouse gasses, seems to be an obvious example of this toxic waste phenomenon. Already vast millions of us live in conditions ranging from bare subsistence levels to abject poverty.

This complicated issue forces us to look deeply into our future. It forces us to address questions about our reproductive lives, and so it hits strong emotional chords and religious views. We are forced to think about the fact that some scholars, most notably Catholics, argue that our problem isn't over-population, but unequal resource distribution. If so, what exactly can we do to make distribution equitable? This in turn forces us to think about quality of life issues such as how densely populated we want our cities to be; assuming that we can provide essential resources for even more teeming millions, just how much crowding are we willing to tolerate. And beyond the bare essentials, how much comfort do we want at our disposal; what level of pleasures will we sacrifice to allow us to support vast numbers of people at the bare essentials level?

What is thus evident in any serious consideration of ending wars over essential resources—or over resources that provide comforts and technological advances we don't wish to give up—is that our numbers must be kept in balance with our natural resources. In the immediate future that requires a reduction in the overall rate of population growth. It will be a tricky challenge to do so in a balanced approach so that national economies don't crash when they reach a point of having too few young people to maintain a stable economy, but it must be done.

We desirably reduce growth by providing women with knowledge about and access to family planning (not through infanticide, plague, or war). Many organizations listed in Appendix I under

"Empower Women" include this reproductive aspect of empowering women. Given access to the means to regulate pregnancy, women voluntarily tend to have fewer children. This is part of a shift, including lower death rates, that is called the Demographic Transition. The result is a lower rate of population growth, and it brings us back to biology. This female response is a consequence of a somewhat surprising aspect of human female biology.[228]

From a biological perspective women might be expected to bear, over their lifetimes, as many offspring as they possibly can. But they don't. Here's how noted biologist E. O. Wilson describes this remarkable, unanticipated phenomenon:

> "Reduced reproduction by female choice can be thought a fortunate, indeed almost miraculous, gift of human nature to future generations. It could have gone the other way: women, more prosperous and less shackled, could have chosen the satisfactions of a larger brood. They did the opposite. They opted for a smaller number of quality children, who can be raised with better health and education ... [H]umanity was saved (from an increasing population explosion) by this one quirk in the maternal instinct."[229]

This profound transformation, the Demographic Transition, occurred first in the developed countries and eventually reached into the developing world. Most significantly, the change was largely the result of voluntary choices made by millions of women who had only minimal information and minimal access to reproductive control. Moreover, these women frequently acted in the face of powerful, sometimes threatening, religious prohibitions against reducing births and/or over the protests of their spouses.

The single most effective tool at our disposal to reduce population growth and bring our reproductive output into harmony with resource availability is education and empowerment of women and giving them access to family planning.[230] Obviously the results will spread faster when their spouses and their religious communities support their choices.

3.5 Essential Resources, Happiness, and Ending War - Finally, it is critical for our campaign that we understand the relationship between resources and happiness. Happy people are reluctant to go to war themselves or to send loved ones into battle. Consider that convincing comfortable, middle class citizens to go to war is a tough sell, although it can be done. Pearl Harbor made middle class Americans willing to enter WW II. The hunt for weapons of mass destruction was the rationale for starting the second Iraq war. In both instances, only fear of encroaching attack or subjugation by demonized enemies or of death itself was sufficient to rally the necessary support of democratic citizens. In a liberal democracy, where citizens are free and basic needs are met, leaders must virtually always rattle some dire threat posed by an enemy, real or concocted, to shake happy citizens from their profound reluctance to go to war.

When people everywhere are asked if they are happy, a remarkable, almost counterintuitive conclusion emerges. There is no correlation between "happiness" or "life satisfaction" and absolute level of affluence.[231] If they have access to the basic resources— adequate life-sustaining food, reasonably clean water, adequate shelter, education and health care for their children—even people from poor villages in India may say they are happy and their lives are fulfilling, often even more so than the happiness reports of CEO's of major international corporations sitting comfortably on one-hundred-foot luxury yachts.

Financial resources are an ingredient of happiness, but by no means are they the most important. As most of us feel intuitively and as studies have supported, a chief, if not *the* chief, fundamental of human happiness is satisfactory relations with family and friends and satisfying work, not things bought with wealth.[232]

Critics of the idea that we could end wars over resources sometimes woefully bemoan that there is no way to make all the people in the world happy because the globe simply cannot sustain worldwide consumption at the level that developed countries enjoy. The latter half of that statement is indisputably true: the globe cannot sustain all of humanity at developed country levels. But to eliminate dissatisfactions that lead to violent conflicts, it isn't necessary or even desirable to raise all societies to Scandinavian, American, European, or wealthy Gulf State levels of affluence.[233] In fact, great wealth has the potential to be a burden. Suggesting that we need to do the impossible—raise the whole world to fabulous levels of affluence—in order to foster the happiness that leads to social stability is simply an excuse to do nothing. People can lead happy and fulfilled lives with far less than extravagant wealth.

3.6 Democracy, Middle Classes, Happiness, Avoidance of War - Another way to look at the issue of providing essential resources is a less altruistic, more economically oriented view. As discussed later, liberal democracy is important to constrain warmongers, but it is also important because it produces a middle class.

Studies of what causes people to feel happy reported by experts such as British economist Richard Layard have shown that we compare ourselves to the people around us.[234]

- We tend to feel happy about ourselves and our circumstances if we are at the norm (in money or goods) or above.
- We tend to feel happy about ourselves and our circumstances if we feel we have a chance to rise in status, or our children do.
- We tend to feel bad if everyone around us seems to be better off or our status is sinking.

In a liberal democracy, with a large middle class, people can always feel good when they look around and see others who are not quite as well off as they are. In a liberal democracy, the great numbers of people in the lower and middle class also feel that they or their children have a future in which their status may rise.

By setting the goal of creating a global middle class—in other words, by creating the means for people to feel that their basic needs are well met—we not only create buyers of the goods we need to sell to each other, we also create people less inclined to make war with each other.

We create a global middle class by assisting those living in poverty to help themselves—not by giving one-time or permanent handouts that create dependency. To end war permanently, we must ensure that essential resources, not massive wealth, reach all of the world's citizens and do so in ways that foster the dignity and self-reliance that is characteristic of a middle class.

Every gun that is made, every warship launched, every rocket fired, signifies in the final sense a theft from those who hunger and are not fed, those who are cold and are not clothed. This world in arms

*is not spending money alone. It is spending the sweat of its labor-
ers, the genius of its scientists, the hopes of its children. This is not a
way of life at all in any true sense. Under the cloud of threatening
war, it is humanity hanging from a cross of iron.*

> Dwight D. Eisenhower, 34th US President
> Speech to the American Society of Newspaper
> Editors, 1953.

4 - Promote Nonviolent Conflict Resolution

*When it comes down to having to use violence, then you're playing
the system's game. The establishment will irritate you—pull your
beard, flick your face—to make you fight. Because once they've got
you violent, then they know how to handle you. The only thing they
don't know how to handle is nonviolence and humor.*

> John Lennon
> TV Interview – Montreal, 1969

4.1 The Addictive Nature of War - War has addictive properties
compellingly described by Chris Hedges' in *War is a Force that Gives
Us Meaning.*[235] The warrior's experience is profound. It includes
great emotions at their highest peaks: comradeship, the sense of
sacrifice for something greater than self, and the opportunity to
prove manhood. And above all, it includes excitement. Combat is
the biggest adrenalin rush most men will ever experience, and if
they survive, the biggest high of relief. War provides all of us with
entertainment, as the genre of war movies and books attests.

This is the stuff of addictions, and war is a cultural addiction:
its negative consequences inevitably outweigh the positive. This is
certainly true for the defeated. But even victors pay what many feel
is an unacceptable price in debt, waste, and personal loss.

So how do we wean ourselves, men especially, from war's exciting, addictive allure?

In the next section (4.2), we begin by understanding that a
future without war will provide a satisfactory role for manhood that
does not depend on killing other people.

4.2 A Warless Future Will Not Be A Future Without Heroic Service or Heroic Deeds – A warless future won't be a bland, unexciting place with no challenges, dangers, or perils… a place with no need for heroes. Though the role of the police and military would be refocused, something discussed later (section 9.1), the tasks we require of them will compel many acts of heroism. Crime won't stop, and societies will continue to require law enforcement. For some time, international extremists will continue to create havoc. And emergency rescue personnel will continue to deal with dangers—car crashes, hurricanes, floods, tornados, fires, landslides, volcanic eruptions, natural gas explosions, miners trapped hundreds of feet underground. When natural disasters strike and "first responders" are nowhere to be seen, ordinary people will rise to the occasion as they have always done. The challenges of exploration present endless opportunities for daring, courage, and self-sacrifice. We don't require war to build character or bond us together in the face of disaster or lift us into the sacrifice and daring of heroism.

4.3 A Warless Future Will Not Be A Future Without Aggression – Nor will a warless future be a saccharine place filled with flower children and saints, loving and sharing without complaint—a place that would eventually bore most of us silly. We're social animals. Most of us not only enjoy living with others, few of us could survive without community. Living together guarantees that we'll always have conflicts, large and small, whenever the needs or wants of one person conflict with the needs or wants of others. We thrive on social interaction, including social conflict.

Indeed, social conflict is one of the spices of life. Conflict is an expression of and is the result of the aggressive component of our biology. Aggression is a motivating inclination. It moves us to heightened blood pressure and harsh words when two individuals who have different wants assert themselves. It underlies fighting. But as described earlier, aggression is also essential for desirable human qualities such as achievement, friendship, love, and laughter.[236]

No great feat is accomplished without push by someone with an aggressive drive. Much great art, from books to paintings, thrives on the study of conflicts. We need our aggressive drive, but we don't need wars.

4.4 Nonviolent means of conflict resolution and why we don't use them – Another component of weaning ourselves from war requires us to promote nonviolent means of resolving our inevitable social conflicts. Fortunately, we don't have to start from scratch: organizations listed in Appendix I under "Promote Nonviolent Conflict Resolution" are hard at work promoting nonviolence. We already know and successfully use nonviolent methods for resolving conflicts without fighting: negotiation, mediation, compromise. Readers of this book who want to get involved in the struggle to end war can seek out, join, and work within any one of these groups.

The phrase "win-win" is a pithy description of the result when essentially no one side in a conflict gets everything they want, but everyone gets what they need and honor is saved. No one is a loser.[237] Game Theory provides insights into why and how win-win methods lead to outcomes that are more inclined to last—that is, to provide for social stability. Game theorists examine the results of various strategies in games of competition or war. For example, two basic strategies players can adopt are "Hawks" and "Doves."

The most stability-producing strategy over the long haul for players who interact repeatedly and who remember, as humans do, their opponent's previous moves has been called "Tit-for-tat with forgiveness." 1) The players all use some form of win-win resolution whenever possible, 2) they deliver quick punishment to offenders/cheaters (there must be policing), and 3) they forgive (reconcile) when offenders shape up. Wars, with their win-lose outcomes, are an invitation to future retaliation: human communities have been known to carry grudges not only for one lifetime but for centuries.

The tools of diplomacy have had plenty of practical use. So the question immediately arises as to why the world hasn't long since settled upon the unwavering use of nonviolent conflict resolution. The difficulty is that these approaches, while they can clearly be used by men, are not always the ones to which men, in general when left entirely to their own devices, are frequently drawn. And they certainly are not the orientation of a warmonger, who does not want compromise but full control.

Until very recently, women have never wielded significant power at nation-state level. With the exception of a rare queen, throughout recorded history men have set the rules for group-level conflict resolution. Unless specific customs or social constraints are in place, men tend to approach conflicts in ways that emphasize dominance. Individually and at state level, this is often achieved through armed combat. Seeking dominance (I win, you loose) is part of their biology.

4.5 Teaching an Ethos of Nonviolence by Example – Another essential to making this great change to nonviolence in our psychological and practical approach to conflict is to be aware of what we are doing. Children learn how to live by observing what they see modeled. Currently the prevailing global ethos is that of the "warrior culture." Violence or threats of violence—the raised fist or the parent's paddle—are used as a fairly early choice when conflicts are brewing, not the very last choice, adopted with enormous reluctance, even grief. The tales we tell our young often glorify the warrior (the "kick-ass" guy or gal) over the peacemaker (if the peacemaker is mentioned at all). Our leaders, writers, artists, and our educational and entertainment media ought to model nonviolent ways and honor them highly. Art reflects culture, but also reinforces it. Consequently, we should honor *most* highly—with our money at the box office, video checkout stand, Internet downloads, and our attention to them in the media—those artists who give us visions of a nonviolent future. Stories told where cleverness, humor, reason and expressions of love are the means a hero uses to solve a dispute or guide a child.

Individuals who currently gain or hold power using the-way-things-have-always-been-done may tenaciously resist the campaign to end war if it will cut off their income source or rob them of status. Even if they simply think it will. Others may resist because change can be frightening. To end war we must be savvy users of all possible media, every bit as savvy and committed as individuals and groups determined to cling to the past.

For example, we can seek out and honor *our* heroes, individuals like the Nobel Laureate Aung Sang Suu Kyi of Burma, heroes who are using nonviolence to create positive change today. No great revolution has ever been bloodless: we continue to honor Mohandas Gandhi and Martin Luther King Jr. But martyrdom is not always necessary. Our biggest heroes in this campaign may be masters of nonviolent techniques who achieve positive shifts in the direction we desire to move and do so without bloodshed of others or their own.

How about a film about the demonstrators in Egypt's Tahrir Square who practiced nonviolence. A biography of Lech Walesa? How about interviews on major talk shows with protestors like Medea Benjamin, thrown into jail for a variety of protests and author of a compelling book, *Drone Warfare: Killing by Remote Control*.[238] How about showing peace activists in a positive light, as dedicated visionaries rather than unrealistic dreamers? What about a major, flashy T.V. documentary series featuring heroes who by dint of hard work are moving us away from war? We need to make heroes of and celebrate people like the co-founders of Nonviolent Peaceforce Mel Duncan and David Hartsough, and Jody Williams, architect of the treaty banning Land Mines. The the organizers of Global Zero, dedicated to eradicating nuclear weapons.

We continue, rightly, to honor those who fight and die in physical battles because they believe their sacrifice is necessary to protect freedom, the social order, and perhaps most realistically their comrads. To end war, however, equal honor should be bestowed, even if it must be posthumously, on nonviolent protesters who die, unarmed, in the battle to end armed conflicts.

Finally, we must think about how *we* respond to violence and conflict in front of our children. What do they see us do to resolve conflicts with the people we know? What do they see modeled by characters they respect in TV shows and movies, and how do we respond to those situations? Do our children hear us laugh at patently slap-stick violence but hear sadness in our voices when we talk about gratuitous violence in a film? What do they see in school from their teachers? What do the adults around them find amusing, entertaining, exciting to watch, and what do those adults find disgusting?

We need to be aware of what we do personally. Gandhi said it famously. We must "be the change we want to see in the world." People who revere war and tolerate violence will never live in peace.

4.6 Cultural Norms Can Change - Is it possible to embrace a culture of nonviolence? Don't all human cultures regularly use striking, spanking, and beatings to teach their children and regulate their interactions? Do not all cultures engage in wars?

The answer is Yes to the first question and No to the other two. Raymond Kelly summarizes ethnographic literature on child rearing practices of nonwarring cultures, and many of them characteristically use "permissive" socialization; they do not use physical punishment on children.[239] As described earlier, many human groups do not make war. There may even have been state-level cultures that rejected war (see Minoan, Caral, Harappa in Chapter 11).

The Romans enjoyed watching slaughter of animals and people in their arenas. A recent film based on a young adult novel, *The Hunger Games*, allows millions to vicariously enjoy a gladiatorial slaughter while patting themselves on the back that we do not entertain ourselves with real slaughter any more.[240] This is true, and it is a step in the right, less violent direction. But we are many hundreds of years past the fall of Rome and we still make war. If we rely on that rate of progress, we may likely miss this historical opportunity to make the Great Shift.

Shift's Introduction reminded readers that for thousands of years slavery was assumed to be normal and natural and that now it is at least officially outlawed. Most of the world no longer considers burning at the stake or stoning acceptable for a civilized people. We considered earlier social changes brought about by various nonviolent, direct action campaigns by people seeking democratic reforms around the globe. Cultural norms have been and can be changed.

A warrior culture that embraces violence may be deeply rooted in today's dominant societies, but nothing prevents us from changing *if we choose*. We live, and our young die, in violence so long as we accept it. Thus this cornerstone, Promote Nonviolent Conflict Resolution."

5 - Spread Mature Liberal Democracy

Man's capacity for justice makes democracy possible, but his inclination to injustice makes democracy necessary.

Reinhold Niebuhr
The Children of Light and the Children of Darkness, 1944

An observation mentioned earlier is that, to date, rarely have democracies declared war on each other. Some thinkers, noting this fact, embrace the idea of democracy as a panacea able to eliminate armed conflicts.

For example, in *The End of History and the Last Man*, political scientist Francis Fukuyama calls men driven by a passionate desire to dominate or conquer others *"megalothymic* males." [241]The names of the most famous such men are well-known: for example Alexander, Caesar, Attila, Saladin, Napoleon, Hitler. Simpler terms I prefer are *hyper-alpha male* or *warmonger*. And to date, democracy has proved to be our most effective cultural mechanism to prevent any one individual's ability to initiate conquests whenever he, or she, might please.

Other theorists and politicians arguing for the spread of democracy often emphasize freedom. Freedom, after all, is a highly attractive state—we all long to be free. But the potential for democracy to constrain hyper-alpha males/warmongers is what makes it a cornerstone here. Democracy diffuses power. Heads of democratic states cannot launch a war without the permission of others. Therefore, spreading democracy throughout the world is a cornerstone of a future without war.

5.1 Liberal Democracy, not just Democracy - A warning, however, is required. Looking back to biology, we understand that a democratic/republican form of government cannot eliminate the innate male inclination to seek dominance. What democracies can do is restrain excesses of dominance-seeking behavior. But democracies are not all the same. Immature democracies may not be up to that challenge.

Journalist and author Fareed Zakaria, in *The Future of Freedom: Illiberal Democracy at Home and Abroad,* suggests that what we need are "liberal democracies." Giving people a vote is only the beginning. A "liberal democracy" must include the rule of law protected by a constitution, independent and impartial courts, separation of state from religions, equality for all under the law, freedom of speech, and protection of property rights.[242] I stress, although he does not, that to be a fully *mature* liberal democracy, equality must translate to equal participation of women in governing bodies.

Length of existence is not the defining criterion for maturity: it is the extent to which these essentials are in place and enforced. As of 2014, none of the world's democracies, with the exception of some Nordic countries and the Netherlands, come close to being fully mature. For example, only in Rwanda does the number of women in national government exceed 50%. This has been attributed to the fact that the Rwandan civil war killed so many men it created a severe need for women to serve. In Rwanda, however, many other aspects of a fully mature liberal democracy are not yet in place. Nevertheless, perhaps not coincidentally this African country is making impressive gains in economic growth and stability.

The Nordic countries in 2012 ranked high on a variety of tests of maturity and were in the 40% range of female participation in governing (Sweden #4, 44.7%; Finland #6, 42.5%). The rest of the world lagged behind, usually pitifully behind. For example, Uganda #19, 35%; Canada #40, 24.7%; Sudan #41, 24.6; United Kingdom #54, 22.3%; China #60, 21.3%; United States #78, 16.9% (see data at the website of the Inter-parliamentary Union and follow the links for Women in Parliaments in world governments).[243]

Furthermore, if powerbrokers in immature democracies can manipulate the information on which citizens base decisions, by controlling information sources or the media that broadcasts it, those at the top can still persuade a sufficient number of decision-makers to accept the "need" to make war.

Even democracies can turn on each other when serious conflicts erupt over essential resources—as they will continue to do especially in light of world population growth and global climate change which disrupts agriculture. The world holds its breath whenever immature democracies like India and Pakistan lock horns. Immature democratic Russia and the moderately mature democratic United States of America, given their current governments, could conceivably take up arms or engage in proxy wars over oil, water, or some other "essential" need, such as rare earth metals.

If the world community settles for less than fully matured, liberal democracies, history will surely record that we failed—as Athens and Rome failed before us—to achieve long-term stability with peace. As extraordinarily powerful and innovative in the invention of democracy and the rule of law as Athens and Rome were, it may be no coincidence that neither gave women or women's priorities significant influence in political life.[244] The absence of women's input is also a likely contributing factor in the disappointing failure of modern attempts to end war, such as with the League of Nations and the United Nations.

5.2 Non-democracies and the Ending War Campaign – What about China, Saudi Arabia, North Korea and numerous other non-democracies? Must they all undergo sociopolitical conversions for us to end war?

No, is the short answer. So long as their leadership finds that peace serves the goal to maintain their hold on power, they can be campaign allies, at least in the immediate future. China's elite, for example, are likely to find more wealth and power in commerce with the rest of the world than in war. They may do the required saber rattling and keep some of their enormous population employed in a war industry, but at least for now they show no signs of wanting to dominate the world through war. If the global community at large, at least its most developed nations whatever their form of government, is fully committed to diplomacy rather than killing, they can find the means to contain even a nuclear power like North Korea.

But can we make permanent a warless future if our current kingships, dictatorships, oligarchies, and tyrannies remain in power? Permanency! That is an entirely different challenge. Economic struggles will certainly continue, and if we fail to resolve them with peacekeeping tools to be discussed later, a tyrant, dictator or group of oligarchs can readily declare war. The old cycle of indiscriminate killing would begin again. Fukuyama makes the case that

all other forms of government we have tried (kingships, communism, socialism, totalitarianism, and so on) have within them the
seeds of their own demise. Collapse, not stability, has been and
is the inevitable end result, and this often involves violence and
war. Only democracy, he argues, can end the political shifts typical
of recorded history.[245] I agree that democracy, specifically mature
liberal democracy, will be a key—although not the only one. There
are other necessary elements of a shifted worldview that rejects war,
the elements outlined by the *Shift* cornerstones.

5.3 Our Situation Now – A united global community,
drawn into the unity of a peace system like those described by
Fry (Appendix III), would have the leverage and resources to win
this ethical struggle and police any actors violating the global will.
A united global peace system committed to nonviolence can use
the carrots of trade and aid and the stick of a global police force,
boycotts, and sanctions to make war an undesirable option. And
spreading liberal democracy and nurturing existing democracies to
full maturity is one of these nine critical cornerstones in the overall
long-term goal: zero war, permanently.

6 – Empower Women

*If women around the world in the twenty-first century would
get their act together they could, partnered with men of like mind,
shift the direction of world history to create a future without war.*

Judith Hand
Women, Power, and the Biology of Peace

6.1 Historical Background -Thousands of years of human history demonstrate conclusively that complex, state-level societies
governed by men alone are unable to avoid war as an instrument
of policy. This is true no matter what the political organization.[246]
Which brings us to this cornerstone dealing with women.

The framers of the U.S. Constitution recognized how easily
sovereigns or small groups of determined men could be tempted
to unleash the dogs of war.

> *In no part of the constitution is more wisdom to be found, than in the clause which confides the question of war or peace to the legislature, and not to the executive department. Beside the objection to such a mixture to heterogeneous powers, the trust and the temptation would be too great for any one man.*

James Madison, 4th U.S. President
Letters of Helvidius, No. IV, 1793

U.S. history since Madison's time shows that giving war-making decisions to the (usually all male) legislature also could not prevent the country from going to war. Far from it. The United States, including the legislature, has devolved to the point of effectively accepting a policy of massive preemptive war at the behest of the executive, as in the case of the 2003 invasion of Iraq.

We've already explored the biological explanation for why women, more than men, are inclined to avoid direct physical aggression in their dominance interactions, why during social conflicts they more typically prefer to engage in negotiation, mediation, conciliation, and compromise, and why they have a strongly evolved preference to avoid war.

We've already explored the biological explanation for why men are much more willing to use physical aggression to overturn the social order and thereby rise in rank. We've also seen how in egalitarian societies, such urges can be successfully suppressed by a variety of social norms; in other words, when it comes to war it is quite possible for culture to trump nature.

So how do contemporary women view war and what are they already trying to do about it? Consider just two examples. First, Code Pink founders Medea Benjamin and Jodie Evans edited a book entitled *Stop the Next War Now*.[247] Benjamin and Evans present essays by 74 women of influence, from former President of Ireland Mary Robinson to author, poet, activist, and Pulitzer Prize winner Alice Walker. What is clearly expressed in these women's essays is the passionate desire of them all to end war permanently.

Second, in 2007 the Joan B. Kroc Institute's Women PeaceMakers Program hosted an international conference with the theme, "Is Peace Possible?" The final report can be found online.[248] Its focus was to highlight the actions of scores of women peacemakers from around the globe and draw conclusions about the possibility for sustained peace and how to achieve it. The final report features inspiring biographies of the work and conclusions of twenty women working on major peace issues from their countries, from the Israeli-Palestinian conflict, to Serbia, to Cameroon, to Nepal. Director of the Women PeaceMakers Program Dee Aker summed up the answer to the question posed as the conference's theme by saying, "…it is the application of justice, rule of law, economic development, and gender equity that can prevent the damage that gives rise to further confrontation."[249] Note the important inclusion of "gender equity." Conference speaker Sanam Naraghi Anderlini was influential in the creation of U.N. Security Council Resolution 1325 which calls for the inclusion of women at all levels of decision-making and peace processes. She bridges the gap between civil society and the international framework by sharing stories of on-the-ground efforts in her book *Women Building Peace: What They Do, Why It Matters*.[250]

6.2 *The Effect of Male/Female Differences on Governing Bodies* – Study of the relationship between women in decision-making positions and violence and war is essentially in its infancy, but research from a variety of approaches is starting to accumulate. Because of differences in male and female biology, a congress or other decision-making body approaching gender parity would be much less likely to vote to go to war.

In a cross-cultural study sponsored by the World Bank, David Dollar, Raymond Fisman, and Roberta Gatti found that governments with more women in power had less corruption.[251] Comparing a matrilineal culture and two patriarchal cultures in India, Steffen Andersen and colleagues found greater giving to public goods in the matrilineal culture; interestingly enough, because men in this matrilineal culture gave more than did men in the patriarchal cultures.[252] Swedes, who had a legislature as of 2012 that was nearly 45% women, grant paternity leave for fathers, and they lead the world in fighting sex trafficking. Theodora-Ismene Gizelis looked at 124 civil wars in a variety of nations from 1945 to 2000. She found that United Nations peacekeeping operations were more likely to be successful if the social status of women before the conflict was relatively equal to that of men.[253]

A 2012 issue of *Science* presented several articles on human conflict. Mara Hvistendahl's "Gender and Violence" offered a brief introduction to literature with which she was familiar.[254] She cited political scientist Mary Caprioli and the Deputy Director of the Uppsala Conflict Data Program at Uppsala University in Sweden, Erik Melander.

Caprioli published a series of statistical analyses linking the low status of women to a number of negative phenomena.[255] Among Caprioli's findings was that states where women are treated poorly are more likely to initiate conflicts with other states, the disputes are more likely to turn violent, and there is more likely to be civil war. Intrigued by Caprioli's work, Melander looked directly at the effect of the status of women, including women in government, on rates of intra-state war.[256] He used three measures of gender equality: the sex of the country's highest leader, the proportion of women in the legislature, and the ratio of women to men who had received higher education. He found that more equal societies—measured in terms of female representation in Parliament or the ratio of women to men in achievement of higher education—are associated with lower levels of intrastate armed conflict. He also found that the more democratic the state, the stronger will be the pacifying effect of female representation in parliament. He concludes that his study, together with Caprioli's (2005), shows that gender equality may confer other important indirect benefits to a society as well as reducing the risk of armed, intrastate conflict.

In an important 2012 book, *Sex and World Peace*, professor Valerie Hudson and her colleagues used a large database on the status of women in the world in a major synthesis that reveals that the "best predictor of a state's peacefulness is how well its women are treated." Also, democracies in which women experience a high level of violence are as unstable as non-democracies.[257]

A clear correlation is emerging between the empowerment of women and social stability, but correlation does not prove causation. The causation of the female effect resides in funda-mental, evolved proclivities of women. The biologically based female-preference-for-social-stability hypothesis presented in *Shift* provides the link to explain why this woman effect is not just a correlation. It is causative. When built-in female proclivities are expressed in these contexts there occurs a shift in outcomes in directions that foster social stability.

How might the women operate to produce these differences? Perhaps women representatives would not be nearly so pressured to avoid appearing weak in the eyes of their peers as would the men and so be able to vote their preferences for avoiding fighting. As a group, women might be inclined to negotiate longer.[258] In a parity government, the votes of most women combined with the votes of the many men similarly inclined to avoid physical conflict would create majority blocks with a more stability-seeking orientation about many issues, including making war. More research is called for, but accumulating data strongly suggests that the power of democracies to rein in hyper-alpha men would be greatly strengthened by addition of many women as decision-makers, and that the reverse is what we currently experience.

6.3 Empowered women as a catalyzing force - The exact percentage of women required to reach a critical mass that tips the balance in decision-making bodies in favor of nonviolence is unknown. Melander tested the hypothesis that female representation in a parliament might not affect the rate of intrastate conflict until the level of female representation exceeds one third. This 33% critical mass indicator was not significant and he rejected the hypothesis. Further research might establish whether some other consistent percentage of women participants is needed to hasten a shift to nonviolence in international affairs, or if no consistent percentage would affect all governing bodies. There may be cultural differences: perhaps more women might be required in societies that have historically been extremely aggressive.

6.4 Why Male/Female Partnership Is Necessary – While history teaches that men alone cannot end war, women alone also cannot end war. Success will require male/female partnership. Why?

There is a flip-side to women's greater preference for social stability that must inform our thinking about how to bring about the enormous paradigm shift we want. Consider that shifting our economies away from war will involve wrenching changes socially and emotionally. Just the process of empowering women essentially requires us to turn much of the social order upside down. This kind of social instability is exactly something women, in general, prefer to avoid.

A willingness to embrace change to the extent that it creates serious turmoil is something men who share the desire to end war will bring to the campaign. My blog entitled "Sarah Palin and Why All Women Are Not Progressives" explores the reasons why many women reject changes that would presumably empower them or make raising their children safer and easier—women who are belligerently conservative.[259] For example, why do many conservative women, by opposing abortion of unintended pregnancies, even very early abortion, hinder the ability of a woman to regulate the size of her family or space birth intervals between her children? Why did many women oppose giving the vote to women? Why will women with sons vulnerable to a draft nevertheless support their country going to war? The answer from the *Shift* perspective of underlying biology is that women make those choices because to do otherwise would require them to accept a significant change from the past, from the familiar, or from the religious or cultural norm she has grown up with. In short, the choices are made because making big social change is something women, in general, are primed to avoid. Women, in general, prefer social stability, not social change, and certainly not radical social change.

Fear of change is, of course, not limited to women. Many people, men as well as women, who are made uncomfortable by the changes necessary to end war will resist. Some will fight back. Engagements may turn violent. Rosa Parks, an African-American woman in the segregated American south, had been trained in the use of nonviolent protest. She courageously bucked the norm and refused to give up her seat in a public bus to a white man. The ensuing social disruption of the civil rights movement eventually cost many lives before segregation was officially ended.

Nor were nonviolent campaigns of Mohandas Gandhi and Martin Luther King, Jr. free of bloodshed, something women are biologically primed to avoid if at all possible. Chapter 11 describes six social changes that have made our time in history uniquely poised to make the Great Shift of ending war.[260] Sadly, with the possible exception of the development of the Internet, not one of them has been achieved without bloodshed, including, in some cultures, the beating of women who practice birth control.

So it is that men who have grasped the vision of ending war will be needed to drive the campaign forward. No compromise. Even if for a time it means serious turmoil, maybe even loss of life. There has to be a willingness to engage in struggle, to rebel. Once the campaign is underway and women understand the ultimate vision of peace and stability, however, women will flock to the campaign in great numbers and support it with unflagging courage and determination.

Male/female partnership is critical. For success, we'll need the kick-ass, no-holds-barred, give-me-liberty-or-give-me-death spirit characteristic of men tempered by the we-all-need-to-find-a-way-to-get-along-and-play-nice spirit more characteristic of women. We will need to find balance and work in partnership.

6.5 Women and Long-term Global Stability - Once our goal is achieved, the preference of fully empowered women for social stability, expressed in the halls of government, will be one of several essentials that prevent backsliding. This change will make our future different from past efforts to curtail war in democracies and republics which were not liberal or fully mature (e.g., Athens and Rome). We could justify empowering women because it's the morally right thing to do. A civilized thing to do. A humane thing to do. Part of human rights since women are humans and deserve the same rights as men. From the practical view, however, it is the necessary thing to do. *The question is not so much what the global community can and should do for women, but what women will be able to do for the global community.*

And of course, it is critical that we begin with young people, girls and boys, but certainly girls, the hands that rock the cradles. They need to learn, so they can pass along to their sons and daughters, why having women as full partners in governing bodies was a necessary condition to propel the Great Shift from dream to reality, and remains essential to their continued peace.

7 - Foster Connectedness

Imagine all the people living life in peace. You may say I'm a dreamer, but I'm not the only one. I hope someday you'll join us, and the world will be as one.

John Lennon
Imagine

Connectedness—to family, community, and the planet—is the bedrock of long-term social stability. This cornerstone embraces the labor of anyone who builds bridges between individuals and groups, or who fosters our sense of connectedness to the planet that sustains us.

7.1 The Importance of Family, Community, and Happiness - We deeply social creatures find our greatest fulfillment and happiness when connected in positive ways to family, friends, and community. To be entirely isolated socially—to be alone—is for most people an emotional disaster. In our evolutionary past, to be alone, separated from one's support group, was extremely dangerous, and to be permanently separated was essentially a death sentence.

In *The End of History and the Last Man*, Fukuyama put forth the idea that history is moving, albeit in fits and starts, toward universal liberal democracy, and that when the entire world is filled with said democracies, metaphorically speaking, history would stop.[261] People would have arrived at a political system that meets what he considered their most basic psychological need: the need for recognition. Essentially what he means by recognition is status, a place in the pecking order. He is describing the striving associated with the innate human proclivity to create dominance hierarchies, and says that when people find themselves (or feel themselves) at the bottom of the heap or without a secure place in the hierarchy, they are not happy. If there are too many such people, the social system becomes unstable.

In *Women, Power, and the Biology of Peace* I presented a counter view, namely that the most fundamental psychological need to be met is the need for connectedness. "Until social systems function to ensure that most members satisfy their need for connectedness in positive ways, discontent will persist and the end of history will remain unachieved."[262]

As already noted, happy people are extraordinarily reluctant to march off to war or send a loved one into war. Happy and satisfied young men and women also aren't inclined to become terrorists.[263] With respect to violence and aggression, discontented older teen males are the ones ripe for recruitment into disruptive groups. They become the boys in city gangs, the recruits in service to rogue warlords, the candidates for suicide bombing.

Although it is sometimes the case, it is not always money or education that young terrorists lack.[264] It is happiness in the broadest sense. External reasons they offer for their actions may be varied, but beneath surface circumstances, they ache with dissatisfaction, an ache that is exploited to stir them, in the name of some cause, to kill other people. This makes the study of happiness—learning what make people feel good about their lives—a part of the campaign.[265] Perhaps this is really the ultimate goal: to go beyond ending war and create maximum happiness.

> *We hold these truths to be self-evident, that all men are created equal, that they are endowed by their Creator with certain unalienable Rights, that among these are Life, Liberty and the pursuit of Happiness. That to secure these rights, Governments are instituted among Men.*

United States Declaration of Independence

7.2 Reconciliation and Connectedness - When a war has ended, future stability depends on healing and reconciliation. Connectedness must be reestablished if there is to be any pursuit of happiness. Individuals and groups that labor on post-conflict healing are essential to our campaign. Research on chimpanzees by primatologist Frans de Waal illustrates the power of and necessity for reconciliation.[266] Chimpanzee males, for example, devote considerable energy and effort to issues of dominance/status, and as previously described, this can involve highly charged threats and fights. De Waal reveals how after these fights it is important to restoring group stability that the males engage in grooming behavior that serves the function of reconciliation. Other investigations with both primates and children similarly reveal the importance of reconciliation.[267]

We too have the ability to reconcile and it is likewise essential to restoring a peaceful sense to post-conflict communities. Appendix I lists, under "Promote Nonviolent Conflict Resolution," organizations working around the globe in post-conflict regions to bring communities back together. Only when a sense of connectedness is created or restored can people who have harmed each other look to the future and begin their search for happiness.

7.3 Religion and Connectedness – The relationship of religion to fostering connectedness needs to be mentioned here. Although religious differences may not be the main cause of war, warmongers typically—perhaps always—harness people's religious fervor to support war. Therefore, everyone who works to teach tolerance of religious differences and diversity (Appendix I, "Foster Connectedness"), who strives to look behind superficialities to find commonalities in the human search for connection with the divine, is working to promote connectedness. And a religion that teaches that war against another group of humans is never to be sanctioned also labors in this cause to facilitate connectedness.

7.4 Connected to Planet Earth – Finally, happiness can also be found in nature. Consider people who live close to the land or escape the steel and cement of a city by retreating to the country or even a park. There is profound pleasure in a feeling of connectedness to the earth, its landforms, plants, and creatures. Organizations that teach us, especially our children, a reverence and love of nature are part of this Great Shift effort as this relates to creating happiness.

Another reason why we need to teach our children a sense of connectedness to the planet is that if we don't, we may soon alter the physical environment so drastically that civilization, as we think of it, can't survive. We have so radically altered the planet, with, among other things, dams, ten-mile deep mines, carbon dioxide and methane production, deforestation and extinctions of plants and animals, that geologist are proposing that we have created a new geologic era: the Anthropocene.[268] So we shouldn't be shortsighted about teaching connectedness to the planet lest we discover, too late, that some chemical pollutant, environmental shift, or loss of a critical resource spins us once more into destruction of life and the creative labors of our hands.

7.5 Summary of Foster Connectedness - The picture of earth taken from space—an exquisite gem of blue, white and green against the velvet black of the void—might be the best symbol for this quest to end war. This is our world. We are an enormously successful and dominant life form on it. We need to keep our spirits and wills lifted to ensure that the Earth of the future will be as beautiful and the lives of our descendants on it as satisfying as the potential suggested from that vast, distant view.

The following are all facets of the task to foster connectedness:

- Strengthening families and communities and our sense of being connected to others. We are one human family.
- Building understanding of and joyous appreciation for vast differences in human beliefs and cultures and teaching tolerance of our racial, ethnic, and cultural differences.
- Fostering the sense that, in the most profound way, this place, our home in the cosmos, deserves our respect.

8 - Shift Our Economies
From War-based Economies to Ending-war Economies

A war regarded as inevitable or even probable, and therefore much prepared for, has a very good chance of eventually being fought.

George F. Kennan
The Cloud of Danger 1978

8.1 The Relationship Between Economics and War – Here we look specifically at the relationship of money to war and to ending war. To review, people must have essential resources. For the purposes of this simplified look at economics and war, essential resources in our modern world are considered to be adequate daily food; clean, healthy water; shelter from weather and dangers; basic health care; the means to make a living; and education for children.

People deprived of these must be kept down by force, deception, ignorance, or some combination of the three. By trial and lots of error, we've learned a great deal about what does not work and gained clearer ideas into what will work to meet these needs across the globe. These principles are being ever more systematically applied by organizations like those listed under "Ensure Essential Resources" in Appendix I.

Anyone older than seventy and living in the United States has experienced six major wars: Second World War, Korean War, Vietnamese War, First Iraq War, War in Afghanistan, and Second Iraq War. The world has seen other major killing conflicts: in the Middle East, Cambodia, between India and Pakistan, and in the Balkans. Sadly, the list of our killing conflicts is long, the waste and destruction sad and disgusting. The stupendous amounts of money, time, natural and manufactured resources, and human lives expended in planning for, executing, and cleaning up after wars is beyond comprehension.

The task of a campaign to end war, however, isn't simply to stop spending money on wars. It is to shift our spending purposefully. We need to meet people's needs while promoting all cornerstone objectives. How do we do that? We are talking economics.

We have years of studies to draw on. For example, articles in the September 2005 issue of *Scientific American*, under the overarching title, "Crossroads for Planet Earth," outline how we might proceed.[269] Topics include how we can eliminate extreme global poverty, how businesses can increase profits through efficiency, and how affordable irrigation and market access can enable farmers in the developing world to climb out of poverty.

We have many new ideas to contemplate. Economist and former professor of the Harvard Business School David Korten writes extensively on economic issues. His book *Agenda for a New Economy* makes a case for an economy that works to enrich people's lives and provides suggestions for how to create such an economy.[270]

Social historian Riane Eisler, in *The Real Wealth of Nations: Creating a Caring Economics*, analyzes economies the underpinning philosophy of which is a social model based on domination. She contrasts these (e.g., communism, socialism, and capitalism) with what she proposes as an economic system the underpinning of which is egalitarianism, or her term, *partnerism*.[271] Her argument is that old economic rules and principles are tragically warped because they don't assign financial value to human endeavors that include caring and care-giving, traditionally considered "women's work."

Eric Weiner is Senior Editor and Director of Communications at the Institute for New Economic Thinking. In an article, "Not their Fathers' Economics," he described the sclerotic nature of orthodox economics and what he calls a growing social revolution, fired by younger scholars coming into the field.[272] They reject, in particular, out-of-touch principles of traditional market-oriented theory. For example, the "efficient market" hypothesis makes sweeping generations that, writes Weiner, "render human beings practically unrecognizable. Do people ever have 'perfect information' or a complete understanding of their best interests? Of course not. They're humans." Weiner says these students are "frustrated by a field they believe could provide so much to society but instead is mired in outmoded thinking."

We do need an economics based not only on the realities of human nature, but one that will serve our profound need to shift the global paradigm informing our lives from a dominator model to an egalitarian (partnership) model. How do we make use of our resources to foster the full expression of human creativity and happiness.

In his 2013 book *The Political Economy of Human Happiness: How Voters' Choices Determine the Quality of Life*, political scientist Benjamin Radcliff present an analysis of many economies and makes the intriguing case that countries with the highest levels of social programs (if you will, "nanny states") seem to produce happier populations with high standards of living.[273] The 2013 UN World Happiness Report's top ranked countries were Denmark, Norway Switzerland, the Netherlands, and Sweden. For insights and models we might look to such countries.

8.2 *Gross National Happiness* - A fascinating experiment in this direction comes from the small kingdom of Bhutan. Jigme Singye Wangchuck became king of the Himalayan nation in1972. It was his view that economic growth does not necessarily lead to contentment. In 2005, the tiny kingdom began to design and implement a measurable Gross National Happiness index. *Time Magazine* published articles on this novel approach to economics,

"What about gross national happiness" by Nadia Mustafa and "The pursuit of happiness" by Jyoti Thottam/Thimphu.[274] Another article in *Time Magazine*, the results from the 2010 survey in Bhutan, can be found online.[275]

This index measures wellbeing on things like personal satisfaction with relationships, employment, meaning and purpose in life, as well as the extent to which new drugs and technology improved people's standard of living. It focuses on four pillars of Gross National Happiness: economic self-reliance, a pristine environment, the preservation and promotion of Bhutan's culture, and good governance in the form of a democracy. Economic think tanks from larger nations, such as the independent London-based New Economics Foundation, are starting to explore the utility of looking beyond money in deciding economic theory and policy.

8.3 The Win/Win Nature of Shifting Our Economies - The beauty of our campaign is that its shift in economic priorities creates a win/win outcome because:

- People work in positive, constructive ways, and where possible, in ending-war projects.
- Entrepreneurs make profits, but on positive, constructive, and where possible, war-ending projects.

The goal is not to put anyone out of business—not even companies that currently produce the products and services associated with armed conflicts. Their employees need jobs and their owners and investors need profits. But they need to retool.

We can make this transition. We have the creativity to make it happen. Tax incentives, for example, can be offered for projects that promote human achievement and well-being:

- to correct and prevent environmental damage.
- to develop a means to sequester atmospheric carbon dioxide in a safe manner.
- to bring clean water to every community on the planet.
- to eliminate poverty and provide quality health care and education to underdeveloped countries.

- to retrofit or construct new infrastructures and buildings that can withstand natural disasters such as hurricanes and earthquakes.
- to explore the Moon and Mars (our young people need grand visions) and to explore and create projects and ideas not yet a gleam in anyone's eye.

The list of possible projects is limited only by our imaginations.

8.4 Dealing with Resistance to Economic Change - Governments with economies built around war will not unilaterally cut defense spending (or war efforts) and shift that money to other aspects of the ending-war economy. The pressure will most likely be, if anything, to simply reduce taxes. Tax payers will have to be convinced of the worth of spending the savings on ending war necessities, many of which won't produce immediate, felt payoffs. As the global community's glacially ineffective response to the challenges of global climate shift show us, getting people to invest in delayed gratification projects rather than immediate gratification projects is difficult, but it can be done with sufficient will and powerful marketing. And if citizens demand change that stresses diplomacy in the search for a less violent future, recalcitrant politicians will bend and receptive politicians will be reinforced by their constituents.

Difficult negotiations will be required, but we don't need to invent new processes. We already have international agreements and treaties that further mutual goals between nations.[276] Where humans have the will, and especially if there is necessity, they can always find the way. Continuing reduction in American and Soviet nuclear arsenals is one example. Trade agreements are another. Shifting world economies in an agreed-upon fashion from war-based economies to ending-war economies would be one more set of agreements reached by already known methods of negotiation.

There is also growing understanding that private enterprise is, and must be, a part of the solution to global ecological problems.[277] The same holds true for an effort to end war. Economic incentives like those offered by the United States's Environmental Protection Agency can change the way private enterprise money is spent.[278] Moreover, the industry that makes a great deal of money from war is the war industry. For all others, war is generally bad for business.

Given the right approach by ending war campaign leaders, receptive international corporations can become major allies.

These changes will create profound social disruptions as businesses, organizations, and people retool their economic lives. Nevertheless, constructive projects can provide profits and at the same time employ young men, empower young women, spread democracy, foster connectedness and tolerance, and provide essential resources. Resistance to change will lessen when substantial numbers of people see and feel benefits of decreased war, more stability, and a better business environment globally.

8.5 Ending War Requires a Permanent Financial Commitment - Because of our nature, for some time into our future there will likely continue to be rare individuals—hyper-alpha males/warmongers—so driven by a compulsion to dominate/conquer the world that they are willing to initiate killing to do it. Consequently, every generation must recognize the need to invest financially in maintaining conditions that favor nonviolent conflict resolution and that restrain such individuals.

Perhaps initially the global community will need to invest as much as we have in the past invested in war. Once we define priorities, execute them, and achieve international stability, we will likely discover that we can maintain stability at a fraction of what we now spend on destruction and killing. But this will be a commitment in perpetuity. We will need to fund, for example, structures like the United Nations and the International Criminal Court. Maintaining personal freedom within a democracy requires eternal vigilance. Similarly, maintaining global freedom from war will require eternal vigilance—and financial commitment—with the result that we ultimately save lives and financial, manufactured, and natural resources.

8.6 An Environmental Reason to Shift Our Economies – Finally, there is one more reason to shift our economies before ecological and/or economic disasters of the kind describe by MacArthur Foundation "Genius Award Winner" Jared Diamond in his bestselling, provocative book *Collapse* overtake us.[279] Given that we live on a finite planet and our resources are finite, Daly, in "Economics in a Full World," explains why the global community cannot continue to rely on growth—more people buying more things, more people consuming—as the cure for our major economic ills and outlines the nature of the changes we will have to make. He freely admits that "establishing and maintaining a sustainable economy entails an enormous change of mind and heart by economists, politicians, and voters . . . ."[280]

If we must shift our economies to avoid ecological disaster, why not at the same time shift these economies from their war orientation and provide activities, incentives, subsidies, and treaties that create conditions that can end war. The subtitle on the September 2005 *Scientific American* special issue states: "The human race is at a unique turning point. Will we choose to create the best of all possible worlds?"

Why not? In Chapters 11 and 12, I offer reasons why doing so is well within our grasp. Imagination and will are the primary limits on what we can create en route to freedom from armed killing, a shift that is fundamental to creating that "best of all possible worlds."

9 - Enlist Young Men

Like its politicians and its wars, society has the teenagers it deserves.

Attributed to J.B. Priestley
English critic, dramatist, & novelist (1894 - 1984)

If we do not initiate the boys, they will burn the village down.
African Proverb

This final cornerstone is, in my view, the least appreciated, and is a challenge just as vital as the previous eight. What to do with young men?

Young men join groups for bonding. Aggressive actions are often involved—mild ones like playing competitive games or egging homes on Halloween or violent ones like gang fights. Male bonding that includes an aggressive component is part of their nature, an inherited, genetic tendency that in our deep past served to facilitate hunting and group defense. Culture can modify this predilection and some cultures successfully suppress it, but until we undertake genetic engineering to somehow eliminate it—should we decide to do something so ill-conceived—it will always be with us.[281]

This tendency is not the cause of wars. War is caused by leaders who use a variety of tactics to create and then harness the willingness of young men to kill outside their group or community.[282] Restless young men, however, are the single most disruptive elements in any society. Restlessness and aggressiveness are obvious in little boys more than in little girls at even very early ages, and with the onset of testosterone flow at puberty, the male hunger for status and recognition is fed new fuel. Young men are particularly prone to create social turmoil and crime when they are unmarried or unemployed and before they have children of their own.[283]

Some cultures and subcultures strongly discourage male aggression (for example, the American Quaker subculture, the North American Hopi, or the !Kung of the Kalahari). How this is accomplished differs from culture to culture. Warrior cultures strongly encourage it. In strong warrior cultures, the male preoccupation with aggression, war, and guns seems boundless.

The attraction of young men to violence is often exploited by such a society and by subgroups within it. In the United States, for example, Hollywood tailors the violence of action films to the young male audience it seeks to attract. Or step into a video game parlor and you'll find young, would-be warriors engaged in virtual battles with every imaginable enemy. You won't find many young girls. Entrepreneurs seeking to draw women into computer games have had a hard time, since most games are essentially aggressive shoot-'em-up or smash 'em scenarios.

According to Nyborg, in *Hormones, Sex and Society,* roughly half of America's violent crimes are committed by young men under the age of twenty-four, the age at which male testosterone levels peak.[284] In a 2001 article in *Newsweek,* Fareed Zakaria notes that Arab countries are experiencing a massive youth bulge, with 25 percent of their populations being under the age of 25. Zakaria argues, citing the French and 1979 Iranian revolutions, that "when populations are faced with large numbers of restless young males and this is combined with even slight economic and political change, the society can easily fall prey to revolutionary activities."[285]

If we are serious about permanently ending war, just as we must begin teaching young women the importance of their contribution to the campaign, we must also reach young men.

9.1 Young men and the military - One traditional solution across many cultures to "the problem of young men" has been to put them into military service or to send them off (out of the community) to war. This keeps them occupied during the most volatile stage of their lives. Training under the discipline of older men has an additional advantage: it shapes youthful excesses into behavior acceptable for the culture's adult men.

What will happen when we make war obsolete? How do we keep our young men occupied?

Might we lose the maturing benefits of military life? Not necessarily. Even in a warless future, some military force will be needed for "policing" or "backing up" treaties and other agreements. Some young men will be drawn toward these policing, peacemaking and peacekeeping services.

Several writers cited earlier offer the hypothesis that men took up war when hunting became less important. War was a compensating means to provide a satisfying male identity. If so, it follows that if we ask men to give up war, we need to offer an equally satisfying male role.

The most recent advertisement for the U.S. Navy suggests one: "America's Navy. A Global Force for Good."[286] Many police forces suggest another: "To Protect and Serve." The vast majority of men do not like being drawn into killing other people and will be profoundly glad to be relieved of this burden and to learn that they can, if they choose, be leaders and partners in the campaign to prevent the killing and maintain the peace.

I once had the opportunity to talk at length with a Navy Seal. The setting was casual. I asked him how he felt about the opportunity to develop his body and mind into peak form, to engage in activities requiring great skill and daring. He replied that it was terrific. And then, after a somber pause, he added, "But the price is too great." He did not elaborate and I didn't ask, but I suspected that he meant the killing and destruction to others involved, and perhaps even the emotional harm to himself, far outweighed the plusses. I also suspect that other men, like this elite warrior, would agree. We should learn from the experience of individuals who have seen the destruction and killing. Their stories about the evils of war should be so vividly and often told that they become stories that make kids around a campfire shudder at the horrors of an unfortunate human past.

Tony Perry wrote a column with the title "Marine Corps Adjusts its Recruiting Mission."[287] Arguably the efforts of the U.S. Marine Corps are felt around the globe, and its view of its mission is relevant to whether we can end war. Perry reports on a new 60-second television commercial, "Toward the Sounds of Chaos." It is intended for local theaters and social media sites. The commercial feeds the Marines' macho image as a supreme fighting force, but also suggests "that Marines are equally ready to help when disaster, natural or made-made, strikes."

What caused this shift in focus by the Marine Corps, however subtle? Perry writes that the Marines found that the patriotic lure of joining a military force that prides itself on being 'first to fight' remained strong among a segment of young Americans. But a second philosophy emerged as well. Many of the young audience for whom the commercials are directed—17-24 year-olds—were as attracted to humanitarian missions as they were to fighting terrorists. Sociologist Kathleen Barry describes how we can "remake men" by creating situations that foster their ability to get in touch with the empathy aspect of our nature. The Marines apparently intend to take advantage of the empathy we all have, and we can all benefit from encouraging that humanitarian impulse.[288]

The message of the new commercial, Perry explains, citing the commanding general for the Marine Corps Recruiting Command, Gen. Joseph L. Osterman, was, "It is going to be a chaotic future with a lot of unknowns," and the Marine Corps is still going to be an exciting place to be.

This shift in the views of the men (and women) about the mission of our military forces is a necessary component of our campaign, and another hopeful shift in the right direction. In the kind of future we seek, the orientation of military training would differ from that of an army being primed for conquest. The emphasis would be on putting down insurgencies, separating combatants, preventing violence, and enforcing good behavior. Simultaneously, the time young people spend in service could provide the valuable socialization benefits that a tour of duty in the military can: e.g., the values of discipline, duty, honor, and service.

9.2 Young men not subject to draft – In a distant future, mass killing conflicts would be a baffling memory from humanity's primitive past—much like head-hunting or cannibalism seem to us today. But if we stop waging wars now, what are we to do with massive numbers of young men not subject to a draft?

It would be high folly to simply ignore them and hope for the best. As they are the pool from which violent criminals and terrorists are created, doing something about all young men is a facet of everyone's defense. Moreover, young men become the fathers who teach what it means to be a man to the next generation.

The United States, which has embraced an all-volunteer military, already suffers a high crime rate. Too many of its male youths stumble from their teens into gangs and crime with no means of making a living and no vision for their future. We could expect crime to decrease dramatically if we required young men, without exception, to give four years, or even two, following high school to public service under the guidance of adults. During those years they could mature and emerge with useful skills, pride, and positive goals. We can task young minds to come up with new solutions to problems.

Even if compulsory public service is unacceptable to independence-loving citizens of some countries, there is an alternative. Make voluntary public service during those formative years extremely attractive, something to which young men and their parents will be powerfully drawn because of its obvious benefits (for example, scholarships or loans for school, or guaranteed work placement for a year or more).

Perhaps just as important, voluntary service could be something teens choose to do "because it's cool." Serving their country can be made into a matter of pride and honor, something "my father did, and his father before him." Many countries already require some form of compulsory public service (e.g., Austria, Greece,

Singapore, Brazil, Israel, Sweden, China, Switzerland, Norway, Finland, Germany, Russia).

It can be done. What we require is the decision to do it and the funding necessary to:

- set up programs and/or expand those already in place. In the United States these are numerous, from AmeriCorps to thousands of local programs sponsored by states and municipalities.
- recruit young men vigorously and creatively to "national service with honor." Enlist them in a "Be All That You Can Be" service program, and dedicate to that program something approaching the financial resources used today to promote military service.
- take note when the children of rock stars, movie stars, and sports heroes—the people our teens emulate—participate in voluntary national service, and make sure their service is given high profile as an example of humanity at its best.

9.3 Rites of passage - How do peaceful societies (without war and with low rates of interpersonal violence and crime) deal with their young men? Many cultures have created positive ways to tame and direct those restless urges while assuring their young men that they are an important and valued part of their community. Many put them through demanding initiations, rites of passage into manhood. Formal rites of passage were lost in many modern democracies as they experimented with freedom of choice where decisions for young people were made by families, not the state. Some families, communities, and faith groups do quite well at providing a transition to adulthood for their young men. Far too many do not.

The mythologist Joseph Campbell is often quoted as saying, "Boys everywhere have a need for rituals marking passage to manhood. If society doesn't provide them, they will inevitably invent their own."[289] As we see in many gangs and fraternities that rely on extreme hazing, young men don't always invent positive rites.

A year or two of service in their community, or perhaps elsewhere in the world, one that includes an official testing and reward for success, would help set young feet onto a positive path. Simply spending time, and especially doing something that feels like forced or unpaid labor, won't be sufficient. A hard test, one involving discipline, creativity, doing something constructive and which once accomplished brings a profound sense of pride, perhaps even that requires courage, is critical.

When a young man in a culture having rites of passage has completed his challenge or test, he knows he is a man. His community officially recognizes him as such, a part of fulfilling his legitimate, and according to scholars like Fukuyama, primal need for recognition which if not satisfied can lead to social instability. The community embraces him, meeting his most critical emotional need, for connectedness.

A word concerning young women and voluntary service. Many cultures also initiate girls. Empowered women are both catalyst and stabilizers for a future without war. Experience and education are critical to their empowerment. In preparation for careers, leadership roles, and roles as good mothers, young women should be given the same opportunity to mature and broaden their outlook under the guidance of caring and skilled adults. They also deserve to enjoy the benefits, honor, and satisfaction of contributing to the common good, an initiation rite of their own.

For society to ignore this particular "initiation" need of its young is astonishingly shortsighted. Since we know that developing positive connectedness to one's community is a critical component of wholesome development, failing to expend time, money, and creative resources to meet this youthful need is not only foolish but also morally bankrupt.

9.4 Work - Finally, meaningful work that brings meaningful reward is also critical to ward off disaffection. Young males who cannot find such work suffer lack of respect—from themselves and others. They become hostile. Discontent from many such young men leads to instability, often with tragic consequences in crime, suicide, or even eventually in revolt and war.

If a community finds that jobs for its youth are lacking, and the adults consider it their solemn responsibility to tackle this problem with urgency, serious problems would find solutions. Adults could call in experts. They could consult all available resources and learn from communities that have conquered this challenge. They should not rest until they have provided avenues to employment. If local governments attacked this problem with the focused passion—and money—that they would muster if they were at war and were devising means to halt a deadly enemy invasion or terrorist attack, we might all reap the benefits—because for a young person and his community, lack of meaningful work that promises a meaningful future *is* a deadly enemy.

9.5 *Summary to Enlist Young Men* - We certainly need to bring young men into a culture of nonviolence so they are part of the solution, not a cause of the problem. We can enlist them. In the past, organizations that worked to end young male violence have primarily thought of themselves as working to prevent crime, not wars. Yet there is an intimate connection. The solution to "the crime problem" is part of the campaign to end wars. Crime and terrorism share a common basis in young male social disaffection.

Nine Cornerstones and the Great Shift

These nine cornerstones highlight the wide variety of contributing factors that challenge any effort to end war and to prevent subsequent backsliding. The extraordinarily good news is that legions of efforts moving us in the right direction are already under way. Appendix I lists organizations roughly grouped according to the cornerstone that is their chief concern. As I write, these groups for the most part do not see themselves as working to end war. In the section below entitled "F.A.C.E.–Putting a Base on the Moon" I describe a mechanism to unite them for action. When these outstanding organizations and hundreds of others around the globe like them discover that

- ending war is possible,
- their work is critical to the campaign to end this abomination, and
- they unite to acknowledge a shared vision to make it happen and draw their combined memberships into a cooperative like F.A.C.E.,

we will have created a positive entity greater in number than all the military forces on the planet. We will have the people power for the next Great Shift in human history.

CHAPTER II – HOPE: WE CAN CHANGE AND CHANGE RAPIDLY

We have looked into the future and the future is ours....Once social change begins, it cannot be reversed. You cannot uneducate the person who has learned to read. You cannot humiliate the person who feels pride. You cannot oppress the people who are not afraid anymore.
Cesar Chavez
Commonwealth Club Address - 1984

Evidence increasingly suggests that war emerged when humans settled down around or gained access to reliable, rich and stable resources. This thrust people with an eons-long history of living in egalitarian groups pursuing a nomadic foraging and hunting way of life into a new environment. No one foresaw what unintended consequences might follow, but that new environment triggered the emergence of some "new" behaviors. Not biologically evolved adaptations, simply responses of complex nervous systems to a radically altered environment. These new responses included social stratification (with distinct roles such as chief or shaman), loss of status for women, and war.

Settling down on a grand scale happened a relatively short time ago, at the time of the Agricultural Revolution. The beginning of animal husbandry at around the same time would have brought a similarly dramatic change in resource availability, and the challenge of having to defend the resource from anyone willing to kill to control it.

Succeeding millennia have witnessed an elaboration of war beyond our ancient kin's wildest worst imaginings. It is legitimate to wonder if the change to agriculture and herding set us on an irreversible path to an inescapable future of war after war. Did that shift doom us to fight? For that matter, does high population density, a characteristic result of that shift, doom us to fight? Does living in hierarchical, sophisticated, technological nations doom us to fight? Should those of us who envision an evolution toward a more just and nurturing planet be seriously depressed?

The answer to all these questions of doom is *No*. What follows are a number of grounds for hope. First, we can consider sophisticated societies that resisted the lure of war (Minoans and Norwegians). Second, we consider how our time in history is poised to make another massive cultural shift, one that leaves war behind. A third source of encouragement comes from understanding that it would not take "forever" to make this shift; some historical and current examples of rapid social transformation make the case for the possibility of rapid change.

Internally Peaceful State-level Cultures, Ancient and Modern

Minoan, Caral, Harappa – One proposed hypothesis for the origins of state-level societies—civilizations as we think of it—is that leaders consolidated separate communities via violent conquest. This puts war at the heart of state-level civilization. Accepting that hypothesis as true has led a variety of thinkers to argue that, in spite of some admittedly unfortunate consequences, war was a good and necessary force in the development of civilization. Maybe all the killing was essential. Legitimate. Maybe even an inevitable part of any sophisticated, civilized future.

But was that violent path to civilization the only possible one? If a less brutal route to state-level status occurred, we would have encouragement that in order to build a highly sophisticated, creative, technologically advanced future, we also do not need war.

I was drawn into the study of war when promoting my novel, *Voice of the Goddess*.[290] I set the story on the island of Crete because I had read material that suggested that the Minoan culture had been nonviolent and nonwarring. I envisioned the heroine as a high priestess of a highly sophisticated, island-dwelling, woman-centered, goddess-worshipping, and nonviolent culture. In stark contrast, always important for good fiction, I created a hero who was a sea-faring warrior. He was from the mainland, warring Mycenaean culture—the people who hundreds of years later invaded Troy. I used what I knew of biology, anthropology, the known history of the Minoan culture and the Mediterranean world in general to create the heroine's society. What is true of them is that the Minoans invented indoor plumbing, massive architecture, distinctive nature-centered art, and paved roads, all at least one thousand four hundred years before the birth of Christ. At book signings I gave a talk, "If Women Ran the World, How Might Things Be Different," to explain why the Minoans of my story were nonviolent.

An editor friend, familiar with Konrad Lorenz's book, *On Aggression*, had never heard anyone stress that women in general might be biologically different from men when it came to using physical aggression, let alone how that might relate to war. After hearing the talk, she excitedly told me that this knowledge was so important that if I extended the material into book length, she would drop everything to edit it. I wrote *Women, Power, and the Biology of Peace*, and readers will recognize parts of it in *Shift*.

Creating the novel's Minoan world took me to libraries to read original work by the culture's discoverer, Sir Arthur Evans, to museums in Athens, Knossos, and Istanbul, and to ruins in Crete and Turkey.[291] The Minoans, as Sir Arthur named them, had a written language, but it is insufficiently deciphered. Even if we had good translations, we have so little material written by or about them that we are limited to art and artifacts for insight into their lives.

Experts hotly debate whether or not they made war; after all, the working assumption still is that "we have ALWAYS made war." I remain convinced that they likely were what anthropologist Chet Lancaster called a "woman-centered" culture, much like the contemporary Goba or Minangkabau. That they did not make war among themselves. And while they may well have maintained a navy capable of defending the island from invasion, they also did not engage in wars of aggression with outsiders.[292] For example, murals on Crete do not depict defeated warriors, or defeated rulers offering gifts to a Minoan king. They do not depict battle scenes. Burials may include hunting implements such as knives, but characteristically do not include major war weapons like axes, swords, or maces. No sites resembling workshops for making war weapons have been found. No Minoan period burials are found with skeletons having cuts suggesting death in battle, as opposed to being the result of a hunting accident or possible homicide. Minoan period burials do not include a warrior's armor. Structures that have been called fortifications because they have stone walls or a base for what appears to have been a stone wall can have served other functions.[293]

The general course of evolution of societies has progressed from an eons-long period as nomadic hunter-gatherers, to settled agriculture roughly 10,000 years ago (and an attendant increase in the practice of war), to living in towns, to formation of state-level, highly complex societies. To explain why the highly sophisticated people of Crete were able to retain their nonwarring condition while all mainland cultures around them were busily doing battle, I proposed six necessary conditions as these relate to what facts we do know about this culture.[294]

- Protection from aggressors.
- Resources that enabled self-sufficiency.
- A legitimate, strong, central authority.
- An ethos of nonviolence.
- Strong female influence.
- Population density did not exceed resource availability.

A consideration of each of these provides insight into causes of war, and suggests necessary conditions for social stability of any complex, highly sophisticated culture in any time period. For the sake of discussion, let's assume that the Minoans of Crete at roughly 1400 BCE did not make war among themselves nor did they launch wars with others.

1. Protection from aggressors. The Minoans lived on an island sufficiently far from the mainland (70 miles) that they would have been protected from invasion and conquest while they passed, over hundreds, or thousands, of years, from tribal to community to state level. At the height of the civilization, they likely had a navy for defending the island's shoreline, but we have no compelling evidence that they engaged in internal warfare or wars of aggression.

Clearly, without the protection of isolation, any unswerving inclination for peace would have doomed the culture in short order as soon as they came under attack by warring neighbors. One of the self-reinforcing properties of war is that even people who are peaceful are likely, when attacked, to fight back, especially if fleeing or moving away isn't an option. This introduces them to this horrible invention/cultural disease/meme that—once introduced—can take on a life of its own. Attack can initiate a vicious cycle.

The nonviolent cultures of our time usually share this same characteristic of isolation. Often it is physical: living on an island or high in a mountain valley or in a remote forest. They live in an unreachable place or one that has no resources that anyone wants to steal. Isolation can also be cultural, as when a people largely isolate themselves from the dominant culture around them and refuse to engage in wars launched by the dominant community (e.g., Hutterites and Amish).

If our full world is to have a peaceful future, ultimately all communities must renounce war because in a full world we no longer have the luxury the Minoans had of isolation as a defense from each other, nor can we escape by fleeing or moving on—as our nomadic forbearers could.

2. Resources that enable self-sufficiency and that meet the needs of all people. Crete is a large island, able to provide all, or nearly all, critical resources required to make the transition to state level (they did lack tin and copper necessary for making bronze, and we do find bronze artifacts). The Minoans could persist and do their own thing without being brought to their knees by outsiders upon whom they were critically dependent. They were apparently able to also avoid internal wars. If we want a future without war, our governments must have ways to ensure that all people have life's essential resources.

3. A legitimate, strong, central authority. Knossos was the center of the Minoan culture, a strong central authority that is one of the hallmarks of a state-level society. The reasons why Knossos rose to this status are not known, and may never be known.

As mentioned above, Crete was poor in the metals needed to make Bronze. At some point the Minoans must have made strategic alliances or trading contacts off-island because without such trading partners, they would have lacked these materials. In fact, it's possible that trade was the basis upon which the Minoans built their high civilization. Artifacts of Minoan origins are found as far away as Egypt and Asia Minor. The island is strategically positioned in the Mediterranean, off the southern coast of Europe, along navigable trade routes. One might suppose that the city/community (Knossos?) best able to make and keep such contacts might eventually have come to be the center of decision-making, maintenance of social order, and distribution of critical materials, and during difficult times, the distribution of life-sustaining essential resources.

Or perhaps negotiating skills of members of the religious community at Knossos were superior, and as religion became centered there, so did other functions. It is entirely likely that a combination of events elevated Knossos to central power and influence. Perhaps even the rise of a pivotal personality—perhaps a woman as High Priestess in Knossos who had the temperament and political skills of Elizabeth I, Queen of England.

If the Minoans were indeed free of war, their sophisticated society with a strong central authority suggests that we need not fear these attributes *per se*. What is essential is to ensure that the values guiding the centralized authority are ones that foster social stability and nonviolence.

4. An ethos of nonviolence. To avoid internal or external war as they made the transition to state-level would have required a longstanding, shared religious or ethical tradition, widespread on the island, that fostered a pacific lifestyle. An aversion to violence would have to have been deeply rooted in the culture to guide them through the stressful passage from local tribes, to larger communities, to state.

Short of on overarching military force, I can think of no influence sufficiently powerful to provide that kind of control and cohesion but religion. It seems likely that if we are to create a future without war, our religions will have to begin practicing what they preach, doing more than simply speaking out against aggression or enjoining us to love each other. In early September 2012, Pope Benedict XIV, spoke to an enthusiastic youth gathering in Lebanon as fighting was raging in next-door Syria. "It is time," said the Pope, "for Muslims and Christians to come together so as to put an end to violence and war."[295] The Pope is certainly speaking truth and wisdom. But words alone, of protest against war or calls to love others, are clearly not sufficient to end millennia-long behavior of armed aggression. Religions, if they choose, can bring strong measures to bear, urging their followers to risk prison rather than participate in something so morally repulsive, and forbidding their followers to make war upon pain of sanctioning such as expulsion/excommunication from the religious community.

5. Strong female influence. The Minoans maintained a tradition of goddess worship (indicated in their art and in some fragmentary texts), suggesting that women were not merely religious figureheads. For example, the central figure in a huge mural, The Procession, was a woman. The female inclination for social stability could have been exercised through religion. Their art indicates that women were also prominent and powerful in social life.[296] If so, the female tendency to anticipate and resolve problems before they produce serious unrest could have found effective expression.

A religion in which women were influential could have used the persuasive, even coercive, power of religion to foster peace and stability whenever more aggressive inclinations from any sources threatened to take the path to armed conflict. There are cultures that are peaceful where women are not important community decision-makers (e.g., the Hutterites). History suggests that over long periods of time, however, let's says hundreds of years, the absence of female input (in religion, in government) will allow male biology to run wholly unchecked, eventually allowing male urges for domination to eventually overwhelm and transform a society's cultural restraints on war.

6. Population density did not exceed resource availability. Finally, the Minoans must have made the transition to state level well before Crete's population density exceeded the island's capacity to provide any essential resource. Indeed, they must still have been quite resource rich. One function of central authority is to control, regulate, and distribute vital resources, perhaps especially in times of stress due to crop failure or other natural disasters. If done in a way that encouraged social stability over the long haul, extreme disparities that lead to social unrest would not have developed.

When any critical resource—water, food, fuel, or land—is insufficient to supply the basic needs of all, the inevitable result is either emigration or physical conflict over that resource or both. This is true regardless of who runs the state—men, women, powerful families, or the people in a democracy. It will be true of our future. Unless we find a way to match our rapidly growing population density with sufficient sustaining resources, we are likely to have war.

Two other sophisticated ancient cultures may have been similar to Minoans in avoiding war. These are the Caral of Peru and the Harappa of the Indus Valley. Initial excavations found no evidence of warfare and found extensive evidence of trading. As seems likely for the Minoans, it is possible that trade and business might have been the engine driving consolidation and state-building. Further excavations are under way. It will be interesting to see what will be found and to what extent the results will resemble what we know of Minoans.

If these people also created sophisticated, creative cultures without war, theories about the evolution of state-level societies that depend on consolidation by warfare as essential to the process will have to be changed. In a cultural context that perhaps rejected violence, cooperation and trade may have formed the basis for the formation of at least some early civilizations—and can be the basis for the warless future we envision.

Norwegians – The ongoing natural experiment in Norway provides a second, hopeful insight. Here is an example of how people accustomed to making war transitioned from war to peace. Fry includes Norwegians in a list of over 80 internally peaceful societies.[297]

From about 800 CE to roughly 1050 CE, the Norwegians were Vikings, war-making sea voyagers, traders, settlers, and notorious for invasion and raiding. The people then experienced an insurgence of Christian influence, and war continued. From the mid-fifteen hundreds to the mid-eighteen hundreds, Norway was essentially a tributary of Denmark, and in 1813, Norway-Denmark was defeated in the Napoleonic wars. In 1814, Norway was ceded to Sweden. The Swedes allowed the Norwegians to create their own constitution, and their union was severed in 1905.

It was during this period from roughly 1814 to 1905, called the time of Norwegian Romantic Nationalism, that Norwegians began to form their own unique way of living. They began creating a new environment, a new culture, for themselves. The people were no longer enamored with war. They forged a consensus that led

Norway to remain neutral in WWI and to also claim neutrality in WWII, although they were invaded by Germany and had to defend themselves as best they could.

In 2014, only a short two hundreds years later and accomplished without the speed afforded by modern modes of communication, their experiment with social democracy includes attending to many of the proximate causes of war. They are not living in Utopia, but they embrace a rejection of violence as a way to solve disputes. In a thought-provoking article entitled "How the Swedes and Norwegians broke the power of the 1%" George Lakey describes how, guided by their commitment to nonviolent struggle, the Norwegian society's "high level of freedom and broadly-shared prosperity began when workers and farmers, along with middle class allies, waged a nonviolent struggle that empowered the people to govern for the common good."[298]

Historians, ethologists, and sociologists could do us a service by careful study of how these people made the transition from Viking culture to an internally peaceful culture that rejects the call to wars. What aspects of their educational system, arts, economics, religion, social system, and so on now reflects and supports this shift? Focusing global attention on practices contributing to the Norwegian transition may enable us to speed up a global transition from war to peace.

Given the need to fight to defend themselves in WW II, Norwegians cannot yet be classified as a non-warring culture. I was pleased to give a speech to the International Humanist and Ethical Union in Oslo in 2011, and was seated at a dinner beside the noted Norwegian sociologist Johan Galtung, often called the father of peace studies. I mentioned my academic interest in watching this Norwegian experiment in transitioning to being a non-warring people. He quickly responded, with sharp disgust that shocked me. "We are not a non-warring people. We provide sharp-shooters to the Afghan war and make money off of munitions."

I think he, as an ardent pacifist, was excessively hard on his people. They do not live in total isolation from the rest of the world and are as filled with the same sense of threat many people have that powerful negative forces are at work, forces that threaten peace-loving people. It is understandable that some among them use this fear to argue for the use of weapons... as a response emerging from their personal fear or as a way to personally enrich themselves. The Norwegians are advocates for democracy, justice, and peace, but they live on a globe filled with a still extremely violent dominant culture. They will have to find a way to hold on to the progress they have made as increasing intrusion by the rest of the world presses them.

It won't be easy. As of now, they are a hopeful example of how a highly sophisticated culture can choose to create and walk a peaceful, nonviolent path. Their inspiring example would be magnified many times if they would stop providing sharp-shooters or creating munitions for the purpose of killing and make it clear that they do so because it is an historically proven fact that using violence only leads to cycles of violence. Make clear that they choose the path of nonviolence and dispute resolution by rule of law or negotiation because it is the only hope for bringing the violence of wars to an end.

Why Our Time in History Is Poised for a Great Change

Another reason to be hopeful, even confident, that we can achieve this tantalizing goal is because our time in history is crucially different from times preceding us when people who wanted to end war—maybe even tried—nevertheless failed.[299] Remarkable events have given us an open window of opportunity. It is most likely only a narrow opening—as already mentioned, we face many ominous threats that could derail our efforts at peace—but it is nonetheless an exciting opportunity.

I find six events, beginning roughly 700 years ago, particularly pivotal. Goldstein, Pinker and others describe these same or related trends.[300]

Why Our Time in History is Different:

- Renaissance and Reformation: Enlightenment
- Advent of Modern Scientific Method
- Return to Democratic/Republican Government
- Women Secure the Vote

- Women Gain Access to Reliable Family Planning
- Advent of the Internet

We entered a period of great opportunity for peace beginning in the Western world during the Renaissance (from the 14th to the 16th century) and the Reformation (beginning in the early 1500s), followed by the Enlightenment (1500s through 1700s). During this turbulent time, the individual view of the relationship between the individual and authority began to shift; worldly authorities such as kings and priests were no longer to be unwaveringly deferred to simply because they sat at the top of the grand dominance hierarchy. When Martin Luther nailed the Ninety-five Theses to the door of the Castle Church of Wittenberg, it spread throughout Europe in two months' time. Pinker stresses the importance during the Enlightenment of what he calls the "....Escalator of Reason..... the movement away from tribalism, authority and purity in moral systems and toward humanism, classical liberalism, autonomy, and human rights."[301]

A much later product of these changes is the phenomenon of conscientious objector. In some countries we have moved to the point where members of a community can decide that they will not answer a call to war, something that only a relatively short time ago might have shamed them within their entire community or even cost them their heads.

The second historical event opening the door of opportunity for global peace was introduction of the modern Scientific Method. Beginning roughly 350 years ago, this way to search out truth caused an extraordinary shift in how we acquire knowledge. Previously, philosophers and authorities proclaimed notions about the nature of men—and women—that fit preconceived religious, intellectual, or philosophical convictions. It used to be said for example:

- that black-skinned people are inferior, more animal-like than light-skinned people;
- that women are not quite fully developed humans, while men are the supreme creation;

- that men make war because they were born in "original sin," a tragedy that resulted from the trickery and defiance of the woman Eve as she was led astray by a devil.

The application of this new way of thought by anthropologists, primatologists, sociologists, psychologists, and evolutionary biologists has given us a fact-based understanding of human nature as it is, not as we imagine it might be. This carried us another step closer to abandoning war as the chosen means of resolving conflicts. Ideologies and philosophies that veer too far from scientifically proven facts provide increasingly weak justifications for armed aggression, particularly if they argue that the inclination for war is innate or that original sin or inherent human evil make it our inescapable fate.

Paradoxically, revolutions and wars for independence and democracy are a third major factor opening up the possibility of ending war, specifically the English (1688), American (1775), and French (1789) Revolutions. These resulted in a renewed attempt at republican/democratic governance that continues until today. As described earlier, this allows the people, not just kings or tyrants, to decide to make war or not.

A fourth historical event, the enfranchisement of women, began a little over a century ago. In the United States, Wyoming gave women the right to vote in 1869. New Zealand gave women the vote in 1893. Around the globe we now have women leading nongovernmental organizations, businesses, and even governments. In retrospect, it seems tragically shortsighted that the step of including women in governing was never taken by early democracies and republics like Athens and Rome. Perhaps one reason for ultimate failure of these impressive early attempts at government *by the people* was that they were immature: lacking among other things, any female governing input. Neither the democracy of Athens nor the laws of early Rome's republic could curb the natural inclination of dominant men to seek power by instigating wars to enlarge their wealth.

The most recent two events which give our generation a unique opportunity for establishing a world peace system began in the 1960s. The first was a quiet but profound revolution in family planning made possible by highly effective means of birth control. In the 1960's the global total fertility rate was nearly 5 children in a woman's lifetime. In 2012 this global rate had dropped to 2.45 children.[302] Women's ability to control the timing and numbers of their children is critical to their full empowerment in social and political affairs.[303] Women bearing and rearing large families of six or more children at 2-3 year intervals cannot participate in large numbers in higher levels of state. Because of its importance to controlling population growth and to enabling women to participate in large numbers in governance, women having access to reliable control over their reproduction is another essential step in the campaign to end war.

Finally, the 1960s saw initiation of what has become the Internet and World Wide Web. The explosive growth of this means of information and communication makes it possible for people across the globe to connect—to feel and act as one. Through associations maintained by instant global communication, organizations and individuals can coordinate powerful efforts to advance the cause to end war in ways and with a speed that was unthinkable only thirty years ago.

Literally hundreds of thousands before us have worked, and many have died, to bring us to this opportune moment. Our time is absolutely different. The challenge for us is to rise to the opportunity and seize the day.

Examples of Rapid Change

So we're poised to change. But what can encourage us that we can change rapidly? Or would putting an end to war have to take many generations and hundreds of years? Hardly worth any serious effort since we have so very many pressing problems. To answer these questions, consider examples of our capacity for rapid transformation.

First, an easy change. In the United States in the late 1800's and early 1900s, people, mostly men, chewed tobacco, and public places like bars, railroad cars, and offices provided spittoons. By 1915, concerns arose associated with tuberculosis. After the 1918 flu epidemic, the habit of public use of spittoons fell into strong disfavor. By 1939 they were still found in a few parts of the country, but most were donated to the war drive for metal in World War II. In less than 25 years, acceptance of the habit of spitting tobacco in public was over. The use of spittoons effectively lingers on only in the world of wine tasting, and the habit of spitting tobacco in public generally only on the baseball field.[304]

Next consider an example of a rapid change of a deeply embedded meme. For ten centuries in China, the definition of feminine beauty depended upon a woman's feet being extremely small. Ideally, no longer than 3 inches. For all practical purposes, such women could not walk. They hobbled. They suffered excruciating pain and infections. In 1911, the new Republic of China government banned foot binding. Although it was practiced in secret for years, the practice of binding the feet of young women is now defunct.[305] A deeply-held belief of a thousand years changed in less than one hundred.

A compelling example of the speed and profundity with which enormous cultural change on a huge scale can happen when sufficient financial and human resources are applied is the Christianization by Catholic, and other religious groups, of numerous native cultures in South America and elsewhere. This often took place within one generation. Major resources—human, financial and in some cases, military—were employed. This example is sad, even tragic, because of the frequent brutality of the military methods used and the savaging of indigenous cultures. But this effort is nevertheless an indisputable example of the *rapidity* of massive cultural shift of which we are capable. Although many Christian ideas were simply grafted onto the indigenous religions, many significant behaviors changed. For example, people adopted more modest clothing. The form of worship moved into churches. Sexual practices with respect to adultery or divorce often changed. Head hunting was abandoned. The ramifications were extremely widespread. What we can do is use the positive power of nonviolence—mentioned earlier and described in more detail in later chapters—to seek an equally or even faster transition to a warless future but do so with respect for human rights and dignity.

Current Examples of Rapid, Promising Change

Other recent examples of swift change that altered the course of human affairs are the fall of the Berlin Wall and the Arab spring in Tunisia, Egypt, and elsewhere. It is simply wrong to argue that we can't shape the future, or that making a big change would take many hundreds of years. It's a matter of deciding to do it and then doing the hard work to make it happen. Here are four out of hundreds of other events happening right now that give us additional confidence that we are primed for a rapid change.

An Increasing Global Sense that Change Is Needed and that War Is Maladaptive/Obsolete – It is arguably the case that we have reached a critical mass of individuals and organizations that see the path the global community currently treads to be dangerously reckless and war to be an expensive, destructive, maladaptive folly. This disquiet has been building for years. A famous quote from early in the last century is attributed to Einstein.[306] "I know not with what weapons World War III will be fought, but World War IV will be fought with sticks and stones." Many now agree that to preserve our civilization, we must change. Legions are doing hard labor to shift us from the old ways locally and nationally. Many are even uniting and thinking globally (see organizations listed under "Broad General Interest" in Appendix I).[307]

Most, however, are like the vast majority of people. They do not yet appreciate that we could stop making war. A principle goal of *Shift* is to bring that awareness to them, and to let them see how their work plays a role in such a campaign. Appendix I lists a tiny sampling of the legions of such organizations around the globe. If these thousands of groups representing many millions of global citizens can be united in common cause they will be an unstoppable force demanding a Great Shift—that possibility is grounds for hope.

Increasing Numbers of Men Who Recognize the Importance of Women - A second hopeful sign is increasing numbers of powerful men who have figured out that partnership with women is key to positive changes, men like United States President Barack Obama, Nobel Economics Prize Winner Muhammad Yunus,

United Nations Secretaries General Ban Ki Moon and Kofi Annan. Annan has said, "There is no development strategy more beneficial to society as a whole - women and men alike - than the one which involves women as central players."[308] These men may not know the biological reasons for why women make such an astonishing difference in governance, but experience has taught them that make a difference they do.

A significant contribution to this growing recognition of the value of women was the 2010 book *Half The Sky: Turning Oppression to Opportunity for Women Worldwide*, written by New York Times columnist Nicholas D. Kristoff and his wife Sheryl WuDunn.[309] This writing duo makes a powerful case for women's empowerment using vivid personal examples and evocative writing about women who achieved major changes in their families but also in their communities. With its focus on sex trafficking, maternal mortality, sexual violence, microfinance, and girls' education, the book immediately hit best-seller lists. Washington Post book critic Carolyn See said of *Half the Sky*, it is "a call to arms, a call for help, a call for contributions, but also a call for volunteers…I really do think this is one of the most important books I have ever reviewed."[310]

The progress these women create using microfinance for both family and community welfare even in grindingly difficult situations is entirely in harmony with innate female inclinations for creating stable places to raise children. A campaign to end war must ensure that people have essential resources and empowering women is now generally recognized by many influential men as an extraordinarily effective means through which this can be accomplished.

Increasing Status and Influence of Women Globally – Another hopeful sign of impending and positive rapid change is that we have *Newsweek* offering a report on women's progress around the globe.

They hold the highest political offices from Thailand to Brazil, Costa Rica to Australia. A woman holds the top spot at the International Monetary Fund; another won the Nobel Prize in economics. Self-made billionaires in Beijing, tech innovators in Silicon Valley, pioneering justices in Ghana—in these and countless other areas, women are leaving their mark.[311]

As of this writing, Angela Merkel, the Chancellor of Germany, is a pivotal player in holding the European Union together. Hillary Clinton was the Secretary of State of the world's richest and most powerful nation. The *Newsweek* article also highlights the very worst places for women to live. Globally things are far from good for women in many oppressive and regressive cultures, but the trend is moving in the direction of empowerment. By historical standards, the rate of change is rapid and accelerating. Even ten years ago a statement about having reached a critical mass of powerful women might not have rung true. It is arguably true now.

At the other end of the power spectrum, one of the greatest sources of confidence is legions of grassroots women's and peace movements around the globe. The conference held in San Diego by the Women PeaceMakers Program, cited earlier, featured examples of the work of a small sample of these women.[312] Globally, the number of such organizations instigated and led by women is easily in the tens of thousands.

One final inspiring example. There are ten living women Nobel Peace Laureates. If it is essential that women shake off helplessness and step up to the responsibility of governing and shaping the future, and it is, then the works of the Nobel Women's Initiative are another beacon of hope.[313]

Experts and lay people alike need to be aware that the impression gained from the all-pervasive media, which feeds on gloom and doom, is not the whole picture, maybe not even the main picture. The times are not hopelessly bad and spiraling ever downward. The main picture is CHANGE. Our survival instincts are in high gear. We, the people of this planet, want to rise to the greatest potential that our positive visionaries have imagined for us. We need to stoke those instincts with the financial and psychic energy that will rev them and propel a movement for positive change to maximum warp speed.

CHAPTER 12 – Pulling Elements of the Plan Together

What we are called to is, in fact, a kind of war. We will need 'armies,' or at least networks of committed activists willing to act in concert when necessary, to oppose force with numbers, and passion with forbearance and reason. We will need leaders—not a handful of generals but huge numbers of individuals able to take the initiative to educate, inspire, and rally others. We will need strategies and cunning ways of assessing the 'enemy's' strength and sketching out the way ahead. And even with all that, the struggle will be enormously costly. Those who fight war on this war-ridden planet must prepare themselves to lose battle after battle and still fight on, to lose security, comfort, position, even life.

Barbara Ehrenreich
Blood Rites, 240

First Step – It's Time to Bury the "Just War" Concept

Where do we begin this campaign? A first pivotal step is to bury what has been called the "just war" concept.

Are some wars justified while others, especially wars of aggression, are not? An encyclopedia or Internet search will reveal how the principle of a "just war" has varied considerably over time.[314] The concept has such a long and changing history that we can legitimately question whether, for our time, the entire idea that any war should any longer be considered "just."

The actual phrase "just war" is most commonly associated with Catholic theologian Thomas Aquinas, however in Howard Zinn's 1990 article, "A Warrior Turns Pacifist," the former bombardier and noted pacifist traces the notion even further back to artists, philosophers, and scholars as ancient as Euripides in the fifth century before Christ. In the 16th century after Christ, the monk Erasmus famously grappled with the brutality of indiscriminate, armed, mass killing.[315] In *Collapse of the War System*, J. J. English also reviews the evolution of the just war concept.[316]

So how does continued acceptance of it apply to our near and distant future? Why does it need to be buried? To put those questions into context, first consider the concept's origin and the way it shaped the past.

The term suggests that the idea was developed out of ignoble motives primarily, perhaps solely, to *justify* war. That assumption is wrong. Actually, to reduce war's brutality, people of good will who assumed (incorrectly) that war is inescapable sought to provide rules to limit the slaughter. They sought to outline conditions under which it would be okay to participate. Note that the view that a war could be "just" could also, perhaps inadvertently, allow participants to feel a bit better, if not actually righteous, about engaging in it.

Zinn quotes the Oxford scholar Michael Howard, who wrote that the sixteenth-century scholar Thomas More

> *... accepted, as thinkers for the next two hundred years were to accept, that European society was organized in a system of states in which war was an inescapable process for the settlement of differences in the absence of any higher common jurisdiction. That being the case, it was a requirement of humanity, of religion and of common sense alike that those wars should be fought in such a manner as to cause as little damage as possible....For better or worse, war was an institution which could not be eliminated from the international system. All that could be done about it was, so far as possible, to codify its rationale and to civilize its means.[317]*

In July 2009, Nicholas Goldberg, writing in the *Los Angeles Times*, took a long look back into the history of the idea.[318] In "Parsing the Rules of War" he pointed out that until the 17th century, armies were pretty much free legally and ethically to kill, wound, or enslave as many members of the enemy's civilian population as they wished. (Although Goldberg doesn't mention it, freedom to rape should probably have been included.) After the Thirty Years' War, which ended in 1648, European leaders began to question indiscriminate killing. Goldberg specifically mentions the Dutch jurist, Hugo Grotius, who was so shocked and repulsed that he developed rules of engagement as part of international law.[319] These rules included distinguishing between combatants and noncombatants. More recently, Geneva Conventions in 1864 and 1949 attempted to further "civilize" war.

In *Women, Power, and the Biology of Peace*, I accepted that some wars have been necessary. I cited WW II. Then, following seven years of writing and study, my mind was ready to receive a new idea. By the time I wrote the essay "To Abolish War" in 2010, I was already thinking that a campaign to end war would need to pressure the United Nations to declare that war is illegal. In April 2010, the noted pacifist and peace educator Colman McCarthy spoke about peace education to a rapt audience at the Joan B. Kroc Institute for Peace and Justice in San Diego, California.[320] He summarized in one line the situation for our period in history: "It's time to put the concept of a just war to rest."

McCarthy is on firm ground for at least two reasons. First, war is clearly not an inescapable expression of our biology. If we alter cultural conditions that foster war, replacing them with conditions that foster nonviolent forms of conflict resolution, we *could* abolish war.[321] Secondly, if culture is the main culprit, we have another reason to bury the idea that any war is "just." If we can avoid war, most people would concede that to continue to engage in it is profoundly immoral.[322]

How then, do we alter cultural conditions fostering war and replace them with conditions fostering peace? That's the focus of this chapter. A highly recommended resource for bringing about a desired social change nonviolently is *Waging Nonviolent Struggle: 20th Century Practice and 21st Century Potential*. It is written by Harvard Professor Gene Sharp and several co-authors.[323] To reach our full potential as rational, creative beings, we urgently need to start practicing alternatives we already know. We can begin to wage permanent peace by burying the outmoded, self-fulfilling, make-us-feel-better-as-we-kill-each-other concept that any war is just.

Major Barriers to Permanently Ending War

A second, equally important step to accomplish this Great Shift requires us to be realistic about barriers to success. The following five are, in my view, the most imposing ones. How we deal with them will shape all stages of planning a campaign to end war.

- The Widespread Belief that Ending War is Impossible
- The Money – The War Business, The War Machine
- The Glory of War – Its Glitzy Place in our Historical Narrative
- Failure to Acknowledge Innate Tendencies, the Biological Roots of War
- Underestimating (Dismissing) the Critical Importance of Women to Social Stability

The most formidable barrier—already highlighted as the first *Shift* cornerstone—is the widespread belief that ending war is impossible, that we are doomed by our biology, or by the strength of the war meme, or simply by the weight of thousands of years of wars, to always make war. Until we tear down that barrier, no campaign will have a prayer of a chance of succeeding.

Next we will quickly hit the money barrier. A well-known essay by Major General Smedley Butler is entitled "War is a Racket."[324] Butler was a Major General in the U.S. Marine Corps and an outspoken critic of U.S. military adventurism. At the time of his death he was the most decorated Marine in U.S. history, having received sixteen medals, five for heroism. He twice received the Medal of Honor. In his essay and 1935 book by the same title as his essay, he described the inner workings of the military-industrial complex, pointing out that war is essentially a business the overarching goal of which is to make money.

But it isn't just the war business or the war machine that makes money from war. Millions of just plain folks are employed by the war business. The immediate negative financial ramifications of ending war for some segments of the world's population are vast. A second great challenge will be to creatively address this financial reality, highlighted by the cornerstone Shift Our Economies.

Then there is the glory of war. We have imbued it with glitz and glamour in books and films, in our holidays, in our historical narratives of who we are as nations. Essayist Barbara Ehrenreich compellingly describes the glorious lineage of war as felt by warrior elites who see themselves as different from and far superior to the mere mortals who service their ability to make war.[325] A third major challenge will be to turn us to new narratives that celebrate the ways of peace.

Failure to understand our biological nature and how it makes us susceptible to war is a fourth major barrier to ending war, and a major theme of *Shift*. Culture is powerful, but if we attempt to live in any way that does not take human nature into account, whatever social or political arrangements we fashion—and historically we've tried quite a few—they will ultimately be unstable and will collapse. There is a genuine and legitimate fear of falling into the trap of genetic determinism. But that isn't what's involved when we consider our biology. We are not genetically fated to engage in war, but if out of a fear of genetic implications we cling to the idea that war is no more than an invention, that it is nothing more than a bad habit with no profoundly influential biological bases, we will utterly fail to understand how to create and then maintain an enduring peace. The challenge here will be finding ways to convey that understanding to leaders and activists.

A final barrier to keep in the forefront of our thinking is that much of the world remains ignorant of the critical stabilizing force of women. Rather steadily, women in developing nations are gaining power, but the pace of improvement in their status is dangerously, even pathetically, slow. Their influence needs to be felt in all aspects of their societies: law, education, health care, business, certainly politics. The entire world needs to be making the case everywhere and at every opportunity that women must be in vastly increased numbers in our governing bodies everywhere, including states where women are often of less value than men, sometimes of less value than cattle.[326] Our plan needs to figure out how best to leap that hurdle.

None of these barriers is insurmountable, and success most likely will be ours when all of them are realistically acknowledged so that we take them into account as we go forward.

Gandhi's Constructive and Obstructive Programs

Now let us assume that a group of leaders resolves to launch a directed campaign to end war. What would have to be the basic components of their effort? Fortunately, the principles of successful nonviolent social transformation have already been worked out. The example of the U.S. suffragists is admirable for its nonviolent tactics and tenacity, and like the Liberian Women's Peace Movement described shortly, it illustrates the way women who are engaged in social transformation organize themselves.[327] Their approach is structurally less hierarchical, more egalitarian than a male approach might be. We can learn much from their work.

Another early nonviolent social transformer, however, was Mohandas Gandhi and he wrote prolifically on the subject. Gandhi's efforts to pressure the British to grant India independence can be divided into what he called Constructive Program and what former Berkeley Professor Michael Nagler, by way of parallel construction, called Obstructive Program.[328] In "To Abolish War" I compare in some detail the roles of Constructive and Obstructive Programs.[329] What follows are some basics of these two mutually necessary and mutually reinforcing components of an ending war campaign, beginning with a consideration of Constructive Program.

Constructive Program - Good works people do to prepare the ground for the transformed future they are creating constitute Constructive Programs. These efforts tend to bring about change through a gradual evolution in social mores and norms. Gandhi's Constructive Programs were things like teaching Indian villagers how to be independent (spinning their own cloth, for example), and working to end the worst abuses of the caste system.

In the case of ending war, I grouped necessary good works into the nine cornerstones covered earlier. Spanning an enormous range of human endeavors, a few examples of the many hundreds of such good works would include running summer camps where Israeli and Palestinian teens get to know each other; running programs for reconciliation in villages after a war has ended; providing women with microloans; teaching women and girls how to run a business; providing negotiators to groups in conflict; setting up programs to eliminate diseases like malaria or polio; running a program that teaches teen males a useful job skill; running programs of peace education at high school, college, and graduate levels; writing a book about the dangers of nuclear proliferation or the counter-productive fallout of using drones; and the list goes on. These are the works of the cornerstones, our fronts in the struggle to bring an end to war.

So many challenges, contemplated all at once, are intimidating. They need not be. It's not as though we're starting from scratch. Legions of people from organizations such as those listed in Appendix I are already at work. Readers can find one or more of these organizations, contribute, join, and become part of the shared goal of ending war.

Unfortunately, few written resources systematically lay out all of these essential elements, and to date there is no sustained effort to coordinate them all so they work synergistically to abolish war. Each writer or expert tends to settle on one favored "solution," usually the focus of their particular expertise. While each of their insights for what we need to do to end war is necessary and true, stressing them more or less alone and then tossing in generalizations about other helpful changes to pursue grossly over simplifies the challenge.

In the section below called F.A.C.E., I describe how to coordinate and energize the legions of people and organizations of all nine cornerstones so that we create reinforcing efforts on all nine battlefronts. But first, a painful truth needs to be confronted and the implications internalized by all partners in the campaign: the issue of enablement.

Constructive Programs Can Enable War - An enabler is someone who helps another to persist in self-destructive behavior by helping that individual to avoid the consequences of his or her actions. An enabler can be kind and thoughtful, with no intention of fostering self-destructive behavior, nevertheless, they do. As wonderful as good works belonging to the Constructive Program aspect of the campaign are, they alone are not likely to be culturally transformative with respect to ending war. They can transform individuals, change communities, and shape history in powerful ways. These kinds of efforts, for example, gave us democracy, nurses, hospice care, food relief, health care, education, and improved human rights.

Good works alone, however, will not apply sufficient force to transform warrior cultures into nonwarring cultures. And what's worse—the painful part—is that they actually enable violent, dominator war cultures to persist. Constructive Programs alone have not, and will not, *dismantle* the war machine. When we bring education, economic progress, better health care, and even democracy to those in need, we give them hope...hope for a better life...someday. We do not thereby transform let alone dismantle the war system.

Giving help and hope to people has the effect of blunting peoples' wrath and thereby (inadvertently) allows the war machine to escape the consequences of its destruction and waste. This principle partially explains a puzzle. Why is it, with all the time, money and human resources poured into aid, our dominator cultures—whether communist, socialist, capitalist, or run by petty dictators—still have not changed with respect to many fundamentals? With rare exceptions—for example, increasingly the case in some of the Nordic countries—the elite at the top continue to live extravagantly well, the few in the middle class, where there is a middle class, are satisfied and pacified, the masses at the bottom suffer horribly, and we continue to make war.

No matter how many educated, healthy, and democratic countries we create, without pressure a dominator culture *will not* transform into a more egalitarian, nonwarring one. The old paradigm will persist with its control from the top down by deception, by "bread and circuses" where that works (as it often does), *and by force if necessary*. Even without achieving this most profound transformation of ceasing to make war, people may live much better in many ways. Consider, for example, what has evolved in the United States; historically, it's the good life. But significant inequality persists. So does violence in homes and communities. So does participation in war. All persist in spite of democracy, education, a relatively affluent lifestyle by historical standards, and remarkable, although not equally available, health care.

When viewed on a broad historical scale, Constructive Programs prevent the beneficiaries of aid from becoming so angry and desperate that they riot and pull down the elite and demand that not a penny, farthing, centime, or dinar be spent on war. Thus, despite abundant good intentions, Constructive Programs can inadvertently allow the war system to escape the consequences of its bad behavior, at least for a time. And when change does come, as it inevitably does, it is often by revolution. If by luck or visionary leadership a positive shift begins, it doesn't persist and flower into lasting peace because the necessary cultural factor—the absolute renunciation of using violence to dominate others—isn't in place.

Dominator systems of government, be they in small communities or nation-states, rely heavily on the use of force to regulate and maintain the social order. They perpetuate themselves by means of customs and cultural expectations built on a worldview that use of force is sometimes legitimate. Individuals, all of us, born into dominator systems are typically just swept along. Masses of good people get caught up in acceptance and support of the use of force and war. People sometimes even help to generate a war. The dominator system sets us all up.

The underlying worldview (working paradigm) of most of today's world is that domination of others using force and violence is inevitable and hence to be endured/accommodated/worked around. This is accepted as true by most of us without even having to think about it, and virtually every decision made, in homes, communities, nations, and internationally, is shaped by acceptance of it. Until we are believers in a different, nonviolent paradigm, violence in its many forms, not just war, will continue.[330] A paradigm that would underlie a warless future that persists and that provides for creating peace in our homes and communities can be stated to be *"Using force and violence against others is anathema, intolerable under any conditions."* That is the worldview (paradigm) that we must come to believe, and act upon without even thinking. It must be the paradigm undergirding laws, customs, and everyday life choices. To create a less violent future, it must be the paradigm we model and teach our children from their early childhood.

IMPORTANT NOTE: Even creating a peace system along the lines suggested by Fry (see Appendix III), perhaps under the auspices of the United Nations, would not automatically shift us away from the dominator paradigm that currently undergirds the global worldview. As Fry points out, although all the three models he used—the 10 Brazilian tribes, the Iroquois Confederacy, and the European Union—lived by nonwarring and peace-promoting values (e.g., in the Brazilian tribes, the role of warrior was shunned), they still made war with people outside their union. Close inspection would reveal instances of violence other than war in their daily lives. To make the final, permanent shift to a warless and less violent future that will last over time, we must undergo a global change of heart—if you will, embrace the shift in worldview described above.[331]

Ending War is the Foundation for Building a Future of Peace - Only time and history will tell if we make such a worldview shift. But as stated earlier, abolishing war is the foundation for making this great change. It's the horse we need to put before our cart, the horse that will pull the cart of change. How this works is similar to the process advocated by relationship counselors. For example, if someone must find a way to get along with someone in their family or at work that they can't simply ignore or avoid, one way to deal with the situation is to start to act toward that person "as if" you like them. Maybe even "as if" you love them. Go out of your way to respond with a smile rather than a frown. Make attempts to engage with them over some shared positive moment. Doing this changes you and it changes them, and somewhat to the surprise of a person who sincerely tries this approach, they eventually come to actually like the originally disliked person.

The process of ending war requires us to act "as if" we, the entire global community, have already emotionally absorbed and made ours an underlying worldview that use of force to control or dominate others is unacceptable under all conditions. The whole world need not, and likely will not, have come to so deeply believe this as truth that it unconsciously shapes every aspect of their daily lives before we end war. But that isn't necessary. The key is to act "as if." By our actions and laws in setting up a global peace system, we ultimately can end war. And by actually ending war—when we have achieved that goal—we will have simultaneously established conditions globally that allow us to build a culture of nonviolence. We can use time and resources now devoted to killing and recovering from killing to do the work of education and raising our children in new ways that over time will bring that massive worldview shift to reality. When that happens we will have created a peaceful worldview in the hearts of global citizens that will shape the human future in new and positive directions of our choosing.

Obstructive Program: The Driving Force for a Rapid Shift – Given that Constructive Programs alone cannot end war, we come to Obstructive Programs. To dismantle with any speed the war machine that underlies and is, in fact, enabled by Constructive Programs, we need something with teeth. Something with force. Obstructive Program is a strategy that has several names, among them nonviolent civil disobedience, nonviolent direct action, or nonviolent struggle. Gandhi created the term *satyagraha*. Successful nonviolent revolutions that we view as positive used Obstructive Program, from suffragists to Gandhi to Martin Luther King, Jr. to the first demonstrators in Egypt's Tahrir Square. Examples of actions that constitute nonviolent struggle are protest marches, flying forbidden flags, massive rallies, vigils, leaflets, picketing, social boycotts, economic boycotts, labor strikes, rejection of legitimacy, civil disobedience, boycott of government positions, boycott of rigged elections, strikes by civil servants, noncooperation by police, mutiny, sit-ins, hunger strikes, sit-down on streets, establishment of alternative institutions, occupation of offices, and creation of parallel governments.[332]

This strategy allows a social transformation movement to focus laser-like on the heart of the problem and challenge it directly. Such a movement can put fire into followers and galvanize a social upheaval and swift shift, even one as seemingly impossible to achieve as wiping out war.

Why nonviolent? Again I refer to Gandhi: "You must be the change you want to see in the world." What this means is that to end war, violent means can't be used. For example, the idea of WWI, the "war to end war," is contrary to this principle, and it clearly didn't work.

Many modern examples of major social transformations were achieved using nonviolent means. *Shift's* Introduction mentioned a number of them. We also have studies that show which strategies and tactics work and which don't, which movements created a lasting shift in the desired direction and which ones didn't.[333]

> *The practice of this type of struggle is not based on belief in "turning the other cheek" or loving one's enemies. Instead, the widespread practice of this technique is more often based on the undeniable capacity of human beings to be stubborn, and to do what they want to do or to refuse to do what they are ordered, whatever their beliefs about the use or nonuse of violence. Massive stubbornness can have powerful political consequences. In any case, the view that nonviolent struggle is impossible except under rare conditions is contrary to the facts. That which has happened in the past is possible in the future.*
>
> Gene Sharp[334]

Regrettably these options are rarely, if ever, taught systematically at any level of educational systems. For example, few schools K-12 in the United States offer classes in peace studies, let alone peace studies that promote use of nonviolent struggle for any cause. Our best minds are not challenged to perfect and use them. And since the present world system assumes that war is inevitable, relatively little time and resources are ever devoted to the art of using nonviolence to wage permanent peace.

Governing systems deeply entrenched in a war culture will let do-gooders do good until hell freezes over while their practice of domination by force remains unchanged and they remain fully in control. In the next section we now consider how to join all elements of Constructive and Obstructive Programs into a plan that has a genuine chance to engineer the demise of war.

F.A.C.E. – Like Putting a Permanent Base on the Moon[335]

> *No evil propensity of the human heart is so powerful that it may not be subdued by discipline.*
>
> Seneca
> Roman Senator, mid-1ˢᵗ century AD

Four key components constitute F.A.C.E., the instrument of directed change to be described:

- A shared goal,
- A clear, unifying strategy,
- A mechanism for leadership and coordination,
- A launch and follow-up plan.

A shared goal – do it for our children – why it's called F.A.C.E. – It's time to go beyond sharing generalizations about how to end war. What follows is a call to shared action. It is based on a mechanism of "massively distributed collaboration" used successfully by the International Committee to Ban Landmines (ICBL).[336] This concept is being adapted by other social transformation movements as well, described by John Kania and Mark Kramer in their article "Collective Impact."[337] They offer examples such as The Strive Partnership educational initiative in Cincinnati, Ohio, and the environmental clean up of the Elizabeth River in Virginia. Another effort using the ICBL/Collective Impact approach is GAIN, created in 2002 in a special session of the United Nations General Assembly and focused on improving health and nutrition globally.

Note that the first requirement for putting this kind of campaign, including an ending-war campaign, in gear is to embrace a shared goal. This enables stakeholder activists to overlook (less important) differences that might divide (and thus limit) them. Instead they focus effectively on shared actions that will move the campaign closer to the goal.

What could be powerful enough to unite an entire global movement behind one grand vision? What concept would transcend all barriers of nationality, religion, race, sex, and politics? What is something that all humans agree on that would allow them to set aside less important causes and differences they might have and that would also be a powerful motivator?

Virtually all humans are motivated by the powerful, driving passion of love for their children. We return to fundamental biology. This love is not something that is learned. Not something about which people have radically differing opinions. Love for children, even children that are not our own, is in our moral fabric, in our genes.

If we could shape a culture that allowed our children to grow up in safe, healthy, and nurturing communities, the vast majority of us would agree that we should use our collective powers to create that reality. By security and wellbeing we mean that we build and sustain communities where children have healthy food and clean water, access to education to the level they choose, medical care essential to a healthy body, freedom to think and speak freely, and they live without fear of outsiders or members of their own community. Whatever our differences may be, in religion, political views, or feelings about our nationality, we can find common grounds for action based on a shared vision to give our children that kind of security.

A good friend wrote to me, "Consider how acknowledgment of universality on this one issue could allow something splendid to evolve? Legions of individuals and organizations around the globe already work to create safe, healthy communities and preserve the environment that sustains them. Imagine the daring possibility that those legions become—within the space of a year or two—partnered in a powerful, united voice to create and ensure safe and nurturing communities for all children, now and into humanity's far distant future."[338]

In 1996, the United Nations commissioned Graça Machel—noted Mozambican politician, humanitarian educator, and children's champion—to study the effects of war on children.[339] Machel's report concluded with something we all know in our hearts:

> *The physical, sexual and emotional violence to which they [children] are exposed shatters their world. War undermines the very foundations of children's lives, destroying their homes, splintering their communities and breaking down their trust in adults.*

What moral ethos and worldview will be carried into the future by such children? War is a great destroyer in countless ways, not the least of which is this aspect of its self-perpetuating nature.

The plan to be described below is a directed movement. It would work by phased, integrated, achievable milestones. Partners in this campaign would be coordinated by an umbrella entity and for the reasons just stated, I've given it the tentative name F.A.C.E.—For All Children Everywhere.

The concept of F.A.C.E. is one of action. The goal is to purpose-fully hasten positive change to end war as a gift to our children. And of profound importance, it would be an awareness movement, to let the world know that massive change is possible, and that a massive shift to end war is being initiated *now*. We need to dream big. Who can accomplish anything grand based on a puny dream? So, let's imagine....

A clear, unifying strategy – After a shared goal, the second requirement of such a campaign is a unifying strategy. The over-arching strategy to be used by F.A.C.E. is nonviolent direct action/nonviolent direct struggle, the essence of Obstructive Program. As laid out above, we don't need to reinvent the wheel. How to use this powerful social transformation mechanism has already been worked out. The leaders of this ending-war movement, firmly com-mitted to unswerving use of nonviolent struggle, can draw upon hundreds of successful tactics, applying these as needed depending upon immediate goals.[340]

A mechanism for leadership and coordination – Thirdly, a directed movement, by definition, must have leadership and coor-dination. How are we to unite, coordinate, and move the world's masses to action? Can such a thing be done?

At this moment, the entire world, outside of the war industry (and terrorists), is hungry for an end to wars. Books like Pinker's, Horgan's, Fry's and Goldstein's are documenting this desire. Plenty of "people power" is available. But without focus, the world's people power is expended in thousands of different directions that have relatively little effect on war. Legions are putting out brushfires or even forest fires here and there (Appendix 1). Yet domination by force, the massive structure burning at the heart of the world, con-tinues to rage unabated and continues to be the source of thousands of fires of violence worldwide.

Fortunately there exists a successful model to which we can turn. In 1997, Jody Williams, as head of the International Committee to Ban Land Mines (ICBL), received the Nobel Peace Prize. Along with her allies, Williams devised a method for uniting hundreds of organizations that, before their encounter with the ICBL, thought they had no need to be involved with ending the use of land mines.

Williams called this coordination and leadership arrangement "massively distributed collaboration."[341]

Here are the basics:

- Joining requires no dues, just passion to participate.
- Members perform whatever aspect of the work best fits their mandate, political culture, and circumstances.
- There is no bureaucratic top-down structure. Agreements on projects the entire F.A.C.E. collaboration would take on are arrived at from the ground up, at regular local, regional, national, and global meetings [see the Moon project metaphor below].
- The central coordinating committee is relatively small: a few paid staff and volunteers [see Applying Pressure to Achieve a Shift below].

F.A.C.E. partners—organizations, groups, government agencies, and individuals—would join simply by signing up on the website and agreeing to a statement something like:

"I/we believe it is possible to shape a future for our children and theirs that is more egalitarian, just, ecologically sustainable, nonviolent, and without war. I/we will help shape this future for our children by coordinating my/our efforts with other F.A.C.E. partners."

In an essay elsewhere I describe this mechanism in detail, explaining how it can be applied to unite all elements working on the nine cornerstones.[342] The essay names names of current leaders and groups who could take up the cause, its necessary human elements (passionate luminaries, dedicated and skilled partner organizations, and determined grass roots groups and individuals) as well as issues of framing, naming, financing and promoting the movement globally.

First and foremost, for this movement to work fast and effectively, it must have leadership. Professor Gene Sharp's analyses show that a characteristic of the most successful, major social transformation movements is good leadership. F.A.C.E. needs a core group of men and women who find each other and resolve to devote their lives, and if they have it a good portion of their fortune, to making the Great Shift a reality.

A discovery in the world of science has resonance to the concept of initiating a F.A.C.E. campaign. In early July 2012, the scientific community, with great joy, announced the discovery of a particle, the long-sought elementary particle of the universe called a Higgs boson. Its existence—or lack of existence—is a profoundly important key to understanding the cosmos and the basis of all matter, including our own lives. The search for Higgs spanned decades. It represents an investment of tens of thousands of person years. In an article entitled "Science—It Takes a Global Village," Yale University Professor Paul Tipton wrote insightfully about the non-scientific significance of the search for the Higgs.[343] He noted that citizens from all corners of the globe made up the search team, based in Switzerland, and this created enormous communication challenges: cultural differences, language barriers, and 24 time zones. And physicists, he points out, are not noted as being skilled project managers. All of this was, says Tipton, "…a recipe for failure." But somehow, even without a profit motive or the need to survive—the things that usually motivate us—this team succeeded. The motivator, says Tipton, was "an overwhelming desire to comprehend the fascinating physical world we inhabit....The Higgs could well be the first science discovery brought about by all of us in the broadest sense, the planet-wide human community. It seems fitting that nature's secrets are unwrapped by all of us, that we own and enjoy the discovery corporately. Let us hope that this is the first of many such endeavors."

The Higgs searchers from across the globe put together a team and a plan and pursued it over decades out of pure passion to "know." I believe there are likewise individuals around the globe equally greatly motivated out of love for our children and the passion to create a new, less violent worldview for posterity who can come together to be the founders of a campaign to end war, For All Children Everywhere.

A permanent base on the Moon: a metaphor – In complexity and difficulty, F.A.C.E. would surely surpass the search for Higgs.

It would be much more like establishing a permanent base on the moon.[344]

Consider that a moon base project would have many divisions—areas of expertise focused on different challenges. Each division would be responsible for a part of the project, such as designing and building the rocket system to reach earth-orbit, designing a propulsion system for the moon ship, designing and building the ship, planning for the biological basic essentials such as oxygen, water, food, waste disposal both on the space journey and on the moon base, design of the space suit, finding the means to handle hazards like meteoroids, designing and building the physical moon habitat, and much more.

Using a moon project as a metaphor, the nine cornerstones of F.A.C.E. are analogous to these task divisions for a moon project. Rendering wars obsolete will require a concerted effort similar to the complexity of a moon base project—challenging—but not beyond the range of human endeavor or vision. And just as no moon base could be built without a coordinating body, F.A.C.E. will need one. Creating that body (a paid staff and volunteers) will be an early task of F.A.C.E.'s founding individuals and organizations.

Launch and follow-up plan - By signing a simple pledge to work for safe, healthy, nurturing communities for all children everywhere, and devoting some portion of their time and effort—large or small as they are able—to shared F.A.C.E. efforts to end war, hundreds of thousands of groups and individuals around the globe would stand united. Where there seemed to be a scatter-shot of charitable actions and sophisticated, dedicated volunteers and organizations achieving patchy effectiveness, the world could sense instead a mighty, united entity determined to end war, an entity determined to use our resources to shape a better destiny for us all, an entity whose members could quickly outnumber all the world's armed forces.

From this potentially huge collective commitment to a simple statement of intent, we have the engine of a paradigm shift, our stage-one rocket liftoff. With the beginnings of a paradigm shift occurring, a volunteer at an AIDS clinic in Africa, a school builder in Afghanistan, or a teacher of sustainable agriculture can begin to see herself or himself as a nonviolent soldier in a worldwide, ending-war campaign.

So the final piece of the movement's inception is to create the most amazing, heart-stopping and thrilling launch, along with a follow-up plan to ensure that the movement grows in numbers and influence. This movement must not be a stealth campaign. The entire world must know, using all available media, that something new and better is within our reach and there are people who have committed themselves to making it manifest. We are metaphorically going to build a colony on the Moon.

To date, other globally oriented movements and events with similar intentions tend to be one-time only or once-a-year efforts (e.g., Earth Hour, Billions Rising, Global Peace March, International Day of Peace). Ideally their experienced organizers or members would also be F.A.C.E. stakeholders. And from its inception, a F.A.C.E. launch would be followed up with monthly global events designed to capture media attention, annual meetings of stakeholders from the many cornerstones organizations to review successes and forge new shared plans of action, and five year grand assemblies of all partners.[345] The critical point is that media-catching and sustained follow up would be given great importance in the planning stages…before even one public step is taken. NASA will not launch the rocket to the moon that will create the actual moon base until, to the best of its ability, all elements for success are in place. A year, or more likely two or if necessary three years, of planning, networking, and coordinating by initial F.A.C.E. stakeholders would surely be required before launch.

Tentative success, defined as a future in which there are no ongoing wars, will not come in the lifetime of this writer. From the time the global community launches a movement to permanently end war, however, a world without wars could be achieved in two generations or less. As described earlier, when conditions favor it and we put our backs into it we are capable of enormous rapid change.

The ICBL continues adding signatories to the land mine treaty and tracking the removal of landmines in war-ravaged lands. The campaign to end war must likewise have a follow-up plan to carry the action forward for however many years it takes. Gandhi had to persist over 30 years to see his country gain its independence. From the time they resolved at a conference in Seneca Falls, New York, to win the vote for all women, it took women in the United States roughly 70 years to secure that right. There is every reason to believe our present generations and those that will directly follow us have that same capacity for perseverance.

The ICBL also discovered that success depends on putting in place mechanisms to gauge successes, to discover what is working and if something isn't working, the flexibility to change with circumstances. Reliable means for keeping score that are included in initial planning are also a key component of a successful strategy.

Lever and Fulcrums to Effect Change

Applying pressure to achieve a shift –The Obstructive Program of F.A.C.E. works by applying pressure to the war machine's weak points, to take the machine apart bit by fundamental bit until it collapses in defeat. These weak points can be thought of as fulcrums upon which to apply concerted lever of people-power force.[346] While each organization or project partner continues work on their cornerstone effort, the movement as a whole would launch shared direct actions and members would apportion some fraction of their resources, which could be large or small, to F.A.C.E. shared efforts.

Following the pattern worked out by the ICBL and also well described in the article by Kania and Kramer, F.A.C.E. would not be a bureaucracy, but a hub, an ongoing basis of cohesion and momentum. In this respect the analogy with something like the United States' space program, NASA, does not hold because F.A.C.E. would not be the location of actual work and planning, with a huge staff and many departments. It would not be dictated from the top down. The heavy lifting would be done by the partner organizations, with ideas for shared action being formulated at local levels, and then shared for consensus via regional, national, and finally international meetings where final choices for shared action would be agreed on. Through a process of discussion and elimination, all F.A.C.E. partners would settle on targets where all of them would direct action. The target goals picked would have three characteristics in particular:

- The goals would be achievable, not simply things wished for,
- Their accomplishment would move the campaign substantially forward, and,
- The goals would garner the most possible global attention and support and thereby provide opportunities to recruit more people and organizations to the campaign.

The assemblies where these targets would be chosen would have three additional important goals. To:

- assess the movement's progress,
- celebrate successes of cornerstone members, and
- allow cornerstone partners the opportunity to network so that efforts being pursued by all nine work synergistically.

The job of the F.A.C.E. staff would be to keep everyone aware of what everyone else is doing, to provide information to the media, to provide assistance and guidance to the organizers of national and/or international meetings, and to provide coordination when the entire F.A.C.E. body engages in shared, direct action.

The most popular variant of the idea of lever and fulcrum is a quote by Greek mathematician, scientist, and inventor Archimedes. "Give me a lever long enough and a fulcrum on which to place it, and I shall move the world." The world we intend to move, if you will, is the worldview that accepts the culture of war...of domination by force.

An example of lever and fulcrum - One instructive and triumphant example of using nonviolence to stop the war machine is the peace achieved in the west-African country of Liberia, in part by the united and unswerving nonviolent confrontation of their dictator, Charles Taylor, by Christian and Muslim women. This successful effort is documented in the film *Pray the Devil Back to Hell*.[347] The lever is the people-power of the women. The first fulcrum is the opportunity afforded to end the Liberian war because of a peace conference to be held in a neutral location in a nearby country. The women resolved to apply sufficient persuasion to force Charles Taylor to go to the conference. The second fulcrum, used at the conference, was Taylor's weakened position with respect to the world community. The women's visible pressure and determination at the peace conference to accept nothing less than peace drew strength from the attention and intentions of the world community.

Liberia was colonized in 1820 by freed American slaves. In 1847, it was officially founded as the Republic of Liberia by American slaves who had been repatriated to Africa. Through the years Liberia remained a republic until a military coup in 1980. By 1985, Liberia was again a republic, but in 1989 Charles Taylor, an Americo-Liberian (a descendant of American colonists), overturned the elected government. The country fell into civil war. By 2001, the brutality inflicted by various military forces included rape, murder, and the taking of children as soldiers.

The documentary film chronicles the actions of Liberian women who reached the end of tolerance for the brutality. What began as a Christian prayer meeting asking for divine help ended up uniting Christian and Muslim women in a joint effort to use sit-downs at the local market and along the road where Taylor's caravan passed each day to insist that Taylor grant them a hearing. Eventually, unable to avoid the women any longer, Taylor, who was being accused of war crimes by the international community, granted the women their request. In a dramatic confrontation, several hundred women came to support their representative as she respectfully asked Taylor to attend ceasefire talks in Ghana, and to make peace at those talks.

Under pressure from many sides, including these determined women, Taylor agreed. Later, when the men at the talks appeared to be more interested in enjoying the conference facilities while agreeing to nothing, the women who had come to observe organized a sit-in at the meeting site, refusing to leave until a peace agreement was signed. When threatened with arrest, the women responded that if they were arrested, they would recruit hundreds of other Liberian women residing in nearby refugee camps to come in their place. As described by the film's promotional material, "The women held the men hostage until there was a signed peace treaty."

After returning to Liberia, the women maintained their cohesion, with the result that Ellen Johnson Sirleaf was elected President in 2005, the first female elected head of state on the African continent. In 2011, Dr. Johnson-Sirleaf and one of the most prominent women leaders of the women's movement, Leymah Gbowee, were awarded the Nobel Peace Prize.

Possible Fulcrums - An ending-war campaign will have to be opportunistic, looking for appropriate fulcrums—causes and opportunities where the applied force of F.A.C.E. has a high likelihood of succeeding and where success forwards the movement's ultimate goal. One facet of the strategy of a directed campaign is to go from victory to victory. In every instance the approach is to use the full force of the F.A.C.E. people's power using tactics the partners determine are appropriate for each target/goal.

Some targets to focus on would be immoral practices, for example, an actual war somewhere that needs to come to an end. It's impossible to predict which opportunistic subjects might present themselves in the near future as fulcrums, but here are examples of some possible starting points, ongoing efforts, possible future issues, and longer-term objectives:

1. Use the full force of the F.A.C.E. partners to pressure the United Nations to set up an ending-war think tank along the lines envisioned by F.A.C.E., a place within the UN where all elements of Constructive Program and Obstructive Program are coordinated for maximum effect. Goldstein presents a compelling case for the United Nations as an already extraordinarily successful, if still flawed, location for the home of a global peace movement.[348]

2. Block any attempt to put offensive weapons in space.

3. Demand until it is achieved, the dismantling of all nuclear arsenals.

4. Encourage the spread of unilateral demilitarization (a la Costa Rica, Panama, and as of 2009, 27 other nations) and support countries wanting to demilitarize by giving them UN guarantees of peacekeeping protection.

5. Put an end to use of robots (drones) as offensive, killing weapons as they frequently kill innocents while presenting no risk whatsoever to those using them (emphasize that they are in fact cowardly).

6. Put selling small arms across borders out of business.

7. Pressure the United Nations to declare that war for any reason is illegal, and that leaders and heads of governments or factions responsible for launching a war will be punished by the international community. In spite of a treaty signed by many nations, the Kellogg-Briand Pact, and similar resolutions, at this time, 2012, war is not treated or considered illegal under threat of punishment by the United Nations if it is undertaken as "self-defense." It may take years from the time a serious use of Obstructive program is begun to give the movement the strength to accomplish this goal, but the time MUST come. Law is our guidepost and social regulator. We make illegal what we want to prevent: murder, rape, torture, slavery, genocide – it's time to add war. As long as war's instigators face no penalties by claiming self defense as they begin the bloodshed we signal that we are not resolved to end it.

At this time, any of these efforts already being pursued, eliminating nuclear weapons for example, tend to be stymied because there isn't sufficient people-power mobilized behind them. When this movement is fully global and composed of hundreds of millions of people and they are given focus, not even the war machine can stand for long against that power.

A Radical Change in Tactics – Women on the Front Lines

A great battle plan employs new and surprising tactics. Albert Einstein famously said, "Insanity is doing the same thing over and over and expecting different results." It is pretty certain that if we want to abolish war, the last 10,000 or so years of history indicate that we're going to have to do something radically different—maybe even shockingly different.

Here is a radical proposition. Rather than mobilize men as the majority front line participants of marches, sit-ins, demonstrations, work-stoppages and so on, movements committed to pressuring for social transformation using nonviolence should, whenever feasible, deploy women as the primary protestors.[349] Together men and women plan, but tactically let the men be the supporters, providing backup from transport to arrest monitors, to legal support, etc.

Why? Because this immediately alters the conflict chemistry. Biology is involved here. The context on the front line becomes no longer a male contest of wills, which provokes emotions that easily escalate into violence. Instead, men who are the enforcers of the system are facing, and threatening, determined women: their mothers, grandmothers, sisters, and daughters.

This single change maximally reduces the likelihood that the situation will turn violent. Male enforcers facing women are far less inclined to turn water hoses, dogs, or weapons fire on women. The change does not guarantee a peaceful protest. As with all nonviolent direct actions, there will be risks for the activists, perhaps even arrest or beatings. If their opposition is led by a brutal dictator—a Hitler, Kadafi, or Assad—the risk may be to life itself.

But women are not fragile flowers, by nature fearful and retiring, unable to bear any enormous strain. In battle they can be as fearless or heroic as men. They endure the trauma of birthing babies almost too large to exit their bodies. Women are the primary hard laborers in the field in much of the world. When we grasp this truth, provocative possibilities are presented, and this one is among them. "Grannies of the world unite!"

As an added plus, this tactic does not require laborious training of men in how to respond nonviolently when attacked, something that is essential to well-planned nonviolent protests where men are going to be the chief protestors; women are already strongly inclined to avoid turning physically violent. Consider that the successful U.S. women's movement to secure the vote was nonviolent. As a recent, real-world example, we have the peace campaign of the Liberian Women's Peace Movement described above.[350] Recall that estimates are that 25% of the original protestors in Egypt's Tahrir Square yelling "Peaceful...Peaceful" were women.[351]

Many if not most men and women will initially respond negatively to this reversal of traditional roles. We are used to men being out front and women lagging behind as helpers. But nonviolence movements should not automatically dismiss the potential for tactical advantage of putting women on the front lines whenever conditions reasonably allow.

Gradualism vs. Obstructive Program

In *The Better Angels of our Nature*, Stephen Pinker's thesis is that historically there has been a massive downward trend in violence from the times of hunter-gatherers until the present. Aside from the fact that I strongly disagree with that assessment and agree instead with Goldstein's finding that violence goes in grand cycles, I have another major problem. The dominant implication one is left with from *The Better Angels* is that we may expect this downward trend to continue with the result of less and less violence, fewer and fewer wars. In my view, it would be a serious mistake to come away from *The Better Angels of our Nature* with the notion that this trend is inexorable or irreversible, that forces will gradually move us in the direction we want to go. Pinker himself says at one point, "Declines of violence are a product of social, cultural, and material conditions. If the conditions persist, violence will remain low or decline even further; if they don't, it won't."[352]

The opportunity to build the kind of positive future our finest visionaries imagine is right at our fingertips. But if we are to do it quickly enough to avoid a potential descent into chaos and war, wisdom and foresight suggest that we ought not rely on a hopeful trend or even the slow work of Constructive Programs. We must adopt a directed plan and get busy.

The gradualist approach—which would rely on Constructive Programs alone—faces at least two serious problems. First, there is the time factor; it's not possible to know how long a gradual shift away from war might take—negative ecological, social, or political events may overwhelm us before any positive shift that ends war can reach completion. Additionally, the gradualist approach depends on a key assumption: that the war machine will not find some way or have the time to co-opt future culture in a way to let us keep making war. The war machine is actually very likely to find a way to keep sucking up resources. Drone wars. Robot wars. Space-based wars. Whatever it can invent. All through history this machine has managed to outflank any efforts to stop war.

Second, if we don't consciously learn and *internalize* our understanding of the causes of war and most especially, what it takes to avoid war, at some future point we can end up like an alcoholic falling off the wagon. We have invented and become addicted to war—like alcohol—and we can successfully stop ourselves from being ruined by it as a recovering alcoholic would conquer his or her addiction. Just as an alcoholic must, however, resist the pull of bad friends, bad environments, bad attitudes, and available alcohol, we need to counter the biological and other causes of war that will always be there to pull us back into the insanity of self-destruction. It is critical to realize that we will always need to be on guard; we will never be cured. Short of genetic engineering, we will always be recovering addicts.

Twelve-step programs have saved alcoholics. A nine cornerstone program, vigorously pursued and internalized, has the power to save us from war. And we can speed up movement in the direction we intend to go using directed, Obstructive Program.

Biological Factors Working Against and For Us

A facet of our biology that works against us is xenophobia—the fear of strangers, fear of foreign customs, fear of things that are different from the familiar. Earlier I listed xenophobia as a built-in tendency warmongers can exploit to rile people up for war. In our deep, evolutionary past xenophobic tendencies had strong survival benefits. The strange and unfamiliar might have been dangerous. Better to have been wary.

In the twenty-first century global community, however, lives all over the planet have become ever more intertwined. Unexamined xenophobic responses hinder more than help us. Fortunately, if such tendencies, say relating to cultural and racial differences, are countered early in life, by education and by example, they can be controlled/suppressed/reduced. Children taught that our cultural differences are a rich heritage and a tribute to the unique character of our species enthusiastically embrace diversity. One of the most successful advertising jingles ever produced was made for Coca-Cola: "I'd like to teach the world to sing in perfect harmony." Its success is not explained simply because the tune is catchy, but because the message taps into an innate human proclivity, a profound longing for community. We can build on this.[353] In *War No More*, Hinde and Rotblat describe this challenge to cultivate a sense of connectedness that goes beyond family or even nation as the need to develop a "loyalty to humanity."[354]

Another way our full world environment presents another challenge related to xenophobia is the issue of multiculturalism. It used to be that people were born into and lived their entire lives within a single culture. This was the case with nomadic hunter-gatherers or even villagers in nation states in times when communication and transport were extremely limited. Now we often find ourselves living beside or with people of different ethnicities, values, and customs. Scholars are exploring what it takes to move people from us-versus-them categorizing in a way that divides us to more sophisticated thinking that facilitates making allies and building coalitions.[355] These insights can be tools for us to use.

A powerful biological factor working for us is that killing another human is not natural.[356] A broad survey by Fry and Szala of fighting by many mammal species, including primates, reveals behaviors and signals used to avoid actually killing an opponent. As Lorenz also described in *On Aggression*, among mammals, fighting to the death, which involves risk of getting killed to both opponents, is actually rare. Instead, species-typical signals and behaviors establish who is the "winner" of the conflict or competition. Losers typically submit and offer a signal of submission (in group-living species) or they depart the scene when it is clear to them that they can't win.

With humans, as in other mammalian species, we see that striking or fighting can come relatively easily, but this typically stops before actual killing. Fry and Szala conclude that, as in other mammalian species, a key principle in the evolution of human aggression is *restraint*. A nonsociopathic, normal man who is to be a soldier must be trained to kill.[357] In today's armies, an enemy must be dehumanized and demonized to make killing possible, and the psychological brutality this inflicts on the soldiers is vividly explored by sociologist Kathleen Barry in *Unmaking War. Remaking Men.*[358]

This revulsion to killing, however, exerts its strongest effect close-up. One challenge to preventing the use of weapons of mass destruction (bombs, chemicals, biotoxins) or killing robots (aerial drones) is that individuals who unleash them do not look another human being in the eye when they act, nor do they see, smell, hear, or feel the results.[360] One reason why media coverage of the action in wars is censored is that if people supporting a war see what is happening and who it is happening to, they are deeply repulsed and the required support declines precipitously.

Policy makers, and especially voters, should understand the danger of making the killing entirely impersonal. Even as we on one hand have progressed to value each human life highly, we have on the other hand adopted the practice of killing other people by delivering death from the air with drones. It's as if we've taken a big ethical step forward, but two big violence steps back. One way the war machine can keep the killing (and money-making) going is to make the killing entirely impersonal and disassociated from moral repugnance...and they are fully aware of that fact and are shifting their recruiting and warfare tactics accordingly.

Four Keys to Avoid Backsliding into War

The people have always some champion whom they set over them and nurse into greatness ... This and no other is the root from which a tyrant springs; when he first appears, he is a protector.

Plato - The Republic, Bk. VIII

Pick Leaders Wisely (Watch out for Warmongers) – As part of the campaign's end game, the world community needs to have stamped onto its global forehead the following keys to prevent backsliding into war once we've achieved the goal of no ongoing wars anywhere.

First, in our current stage of social evolution, we're still beset with a dangerous number of warmongers: we have created warrior, dominator cultures that generate these men (and an occasional woman) so our responsibility is to recognize them and refuse to give them decision-making positions in matters of war.

Most citizens don't yet clearly see the danger warmongers pose. A recent egregious example in the United States was former Pennsylvania Senator, Rick Santorum.[361] On 1 January 2012 on "Meet the Press" he addressed the issue of Iranian nuclear facilities and said that if he were to become President, "We will degrade those facilities through airstrikes, and make it very public that we are doing that." He clearly outed himself as willing to launch a war, and yet, as his wins in Republican primary contests showed, a great many citizens were willing to elect him President of the United States, leader of the free world, with the power to wage war in his hands.

We can account for what John Horgan called the mystery of war: why analyses have shown its causes to be hit and miss. As he put it, "Many conditions appear to be sufficient for war to occur, but none are necessary. Some societies remain peaceful even when significant risk factors are present, such as high population density, resource scarcity, and economic and ethnic divisions between people. Conversely, others societies fight in the absence of these conditions."[362]

The presence of at least one warmonger (a person willing to kill others who have not wronged them) in a position of final decision-making or leadership may be the critical, explosive detonator. Where such an individual is lacking—either as chief, dictator, or as a member of the inner circle of final decision-makers—war is not begun no matter what the conditions may be. Some other solution will be sought. Consider: if the United States President had been the leftist Al Gore and his inner circle rather than the hawkish George W. Bush and his inner circle, would history have seen the 2003 Iraq War?

In the book *Opting out of War,* Mary B. Anderson and Marshall Wallace detail how thirteen communities that found themselves in danger of being drawn into a brutal war instead found creative ways to escape participation. Common to their success was the central importance of accessible, accountable leadership determined to avoid being drawn in and systems within the community of consultations that gave voice to all citizens. If instead a charismatic warmonger had been in a key leadership position, arguably the community would have opted in, not out.[363]

How common are warmongers in our societies? Individuals so driven by the need for power/domination/control that they are willing to indiscriminately kill many other people—men, women, and children? No studies have quantified their numbers. Given that most people, even very powerful people, draw a moral line at killing other people to accomplish their personal desires, the number of warmongers in any society is likely small. Maybe at the very most 10%. Most men and women hate war and would happily be free of it. Warmongers are a dominance-fueled tail that has been wagging the dog of civilization for far too long.

Pick Your Society's Philosophy or Religion Wisely – Here is a second key to preventing backsliding. Religions serve many positive functions. They affect decisions most people make. And they are not the cause of wars. To end war we do not need to eliminate religions as many have argued. As already discussed, wars are virtually always fought over control of resources that give some individuals power. Beliefs, when they are involved, tend to be marshaled by a warmonger and espoused by followers to justify the killing. In their books, Ehrenreich and Goldstein[364] make compelling arguments that *war can almost be defined by the fact that the community decision* *to kill members of some other group is given the blessing of religious leaders.* The leaders of the Crusades found texts in the Bible to justify conquest, just as many texts in the Koran can be used by modern Islamic terrorists.

But of course, the reverse is equally true. The Bible and Koran stress love, mercy, forgiveness, and other peace-promoting concepts. The reality is that all of our faiths could be the most potent possible allies in this campaign. Many "spiritual movements" already are deeply involved. Some faiths oppose war totally and consistently (e.g., Anabaptists, Quakers, Bahai).

Sadly, however, the world's most dominant religious establishments talk a good show of peace, but still rationalize, justify, and in some instances, facilitate or foment the killing. An article by Brian Bennett on the rising use of drone warfare—the war machine's latest ploy to keep the money flowing into its coffers—cites Air Force Lt. Col. Douglas Cunningham, a Roman Catholic priest. He has clearance to work in control rooms where drone pilots wage war on people thousands of miles away. The job is seriously stressful. Bennett says that Cunningham works to gain the pilot's trust so that he can see if the stress of dropping bombs for a few hours to provide support for fighting ground troops and then going home to kiss and hug one's family is creating debilitating wear on those he is observing. Cunningham is quoted as saying to the drone warriors, in order to provide comfort, "I let them know, 'If it wasn't for you, they wouldn't be as safe as they are over there, because we bring them a lot of security just watching over them.'" Cunningham's rationale is "They are protecting life."[365] But whose life, and at what costs, and does this not serve to facilitate making war? Perhaps religious authorities who enable war can be somewhat forgiven: perhaps they don't yet realize that ending war is possible and (incorrectly) see war, as many people do, as the only option to protect a community. But as covered earlier, it's time to bury the "just war" concept.

Unfortunately, religious belief and practice is one of the last cultural aspects of a society to shift, so it is not likely that the major religions, in an official capacity, will lead the way in a campaign to end war. Once a movement is begun, however, virtually all religions may soon come on board since virtually all tend to view killing as a sin.

While few of us pick a religion of choice (the vast majority of people practice the religion of their parents), to prevent backsliding into war we can all be sensitive to whether our religious leaders oppose war, and if so, by what means and with what vigor.

Parity Government - A third necessity to prevent backsliding addresses the suggestion by Margaret Mead that war is an invention, the result of culture not genes. Once invented, she explains in her essay "War is Only an Invention – Not a Biological Necessity," they do not just disappear by themselves.[366] Rather, they are only replaced when a better invention to do the same service comes along. A central argument of *Shift* is that the old invention of all-male governments that we've been laboring under for at least 10,000 years needs to be replaced with a new invention of gender parity in governing. Or perhaps more accurately, we need to return to gender parity governing.[367]

Furthermore, in order to create a peace system globally, this change cannot be unilateral, characteristic of only the Western democracies, for example. We need empowerment of women on all sides of conflicts.

Parity does not require a pure 50-50 sex ratio in leadership: but there must be enough independent-thinking women to change the "chemistry" of a decision-making body to substantially reflect female priorities. An earlier section, Empowering Women, cites the few studies done so far to investigate the relationship between women's empowerment and the effects this has on issues like government corruption, or the success of reconciliation after a war. Many more studies are needed to enable us to know just what percentage of women in a decision-making body causes a "tipping point" at which feminine values begin to have substantial weight.

This change, if extended to all levels of societies, will foster future cultures steeped in values that promote social stability in all aspects of people's lives. But certainly with respect to maintaining a permanent peace, parity government must be in place in perpetuity at the highest levels of decision-making.

Attend to All Cornerstones – Finally, to avoid backsliding we need to recognize that ending war is not going to be something we do once and never need concern ourselves about it again. Abolishing war also does not translate into immediate disarmament. Because of our biology, eternal vigilance will be required to create and maintain a future without war just as vigilance is required to maintain a democracy. Because of our biology, we may always need peacekeeping forces to immediately counter the next dominating warmonger who appears on the stage and is eager to raise an army to kill other humans standing in the way. We can hope that over time the size of such forces will diminish, their task becoming one primarily of policing an ever more peaceful world community. We can even enjoy imagining the possibility that in some far future, humans will have so completely absorbed a new paradigm of nonviolence that the very idea of making war is ridiculous, nor do we practice violence in our homes or communities. But for now, and into that future, we will be obliged to always attend to all nine cornerstones that are foundations of enduring security and order.

CHAPTER 13 – SUMMING IT ALL UP

You have brain in her head.
You have feet in your shoes.
You can steer yourself any direction you choose.

Dr. Seuss, *Oh, the Places You'll Go*

Choice

The scientific method has changed our moral landscape. Before we knew how to find out why we behave the way we do, we lived in a state of ignorance. Evolution, a blind and amoral process, shaped us to want and need certain things in order to reproduce. We reacted to those wants and needs and justified them with laws and religions and customs. Our wants and needs as codified in our adapted nature came first. Laws, religions, and customs to regulate or rationalize our behavior came second.

In every society, individuals who survived the struggle to live and to reproduce were moved by their biological priorities. Matters such as the fair distribution (or hoarding) of resources, and the challenges posed by young males (to create warriors or fashion men of peace) were decided by expedience rather than sure and certain knowledge of consequences. Since the time of the great settling down during the Agricultural Revolution the interplay between male and female priorities grew dangerously out of balance. Humans have followed the dictates of biology and did what worked best in a given time and place with particular sets of resources, and essentially heedless of future consequences.

In the past, people of good will came to different conclusions about the best way to organize society. Those who felt that subordinating women was best could marshal their arguments. Those who felt the sexes should be treated equally could marshal contrary arguments. Everyone could and did build religions and customs to support one view or the other and often defied anyone to question their "clearly evident truths."

We know now the root causes of wars. Moreover, we have changed our environment: we no longer occupy a world with available habitat to be filled with our kind. We occupy a full world, and this profound change challenges us. To survive and thrive, we need to create a cultural "new normal."

We can and will debate how best to make necessary changes—how best to bring hope to young men, equality to women, and a fair distribution of the earth's bounty to all her people. But we can no longer hide behind ignorance. A truly informed and hence deeply moral choice is ours to make: we can continue doing those things that foster war, or we can create laws, customs, a mindset (worldview), and institutions that foster peace.

Balance and the End Game

Man may be excused for feeling some pride at having risen, though not through his own exertions, to the very summit of the organic scale; and the fact of his having thus risen, instead of having been aboriginally placed there, may give him hope for a still higher destiny in the distant future.

Charles Darwin
The Descent of Man and Selection in Relation to Sex - 1883

The long history of wars of so many kinds fought for so many different reasons led by men from social structures of every imaginable kind demonstrates that it is impossible for men to help themselves. They cannot free themselves from the call to war. Most men do not love war. War games, perhaps. Planning war (or how to win), yes. But not actual war. This is especially true for men who have been in battle where they could feel the fear, engage the enemy, and smell and see the results. Men who have been in battle, without exception, have told me they *hate* war.

Most men, given a choice, would rather make love, not war.

The problem is that some men, the warmongers, thrive on war. Regrettably, other men—strongly predisposed to exciting group action, male bonding, and willingness to protect their group—too easily find themselves unable to resist the call to battle, honor, bonding, sacrifice and glory—the buzzwords used to summon the necessary followers.

There is a rapidly growing appreciation for the importance to our survival and success as a species of our abilities for cooperation. Equally expanding is our appreciation for our enormous capacity for empathy. These are the traits that will enable us to successfully adapt to our new, full world with all of its ecological, technological, and social challenges. We have every reason to believe in ourselves, in our capacity to create a positive future.

Consider the many organizations listed in the appendix below, knowing that each represents thousands of good-hearted people. Combined, their memberships represent millions of people, and these organizations are only a tiny sample of similar endeavors across the globe.

The section entitled Empower Women, introduced the Joan B. Kroc Institute for Peace and Justice's Women PeaceMakers Program, located in San Diego. It honors and promotes women who work directly in peacemaking and/or human rights efforts at a grassroots, national, or international level. Women like Nora Chengeto Tapiwa who was employed in a bank in what has become Zimbabwe under the tyrant Robert Mugabe. Violently persecuted for protesting, she and 700,000 refugees fled the country. Nora realized their collective power and has helped to organize some forty groups to stand for the humane treatment of refugees and keep pressure on the Mugabe government.

PeaceMaker honoree and Nobel Prize nominee Rubina Feroze Bhatti of Pakistan wanted to be a chemistry professor, but when her uncle was sentenced to death for insulting Islam, she began a crusade that saved not only him, but women being brutalized as well—all in a way that effectively calls her fellow Pakistanis to remember the Fullness of Humanity—the name of her organization.

Juliano Mer-Khamis was born the son of an Israeli Jewish mother and an Arab Christian father. Handsome and charismatic, he was an actor, director, and filmmaker of recognized talent who could have pursued a life of wealth and fame. Instead he chose to work in the huge Jenin refugee camp in the dangerous West Bank. He founded The Freedom Theater—a place of security for Jenin's children, where they could learn what Juliano believed…that it was not with violence or guns, but through culture—art, poems, songs and books—that Palestinians could find the freedom they long for. In 2011, he was brutally assassinated by a masked gunman outside his theater, thought by most people to be because Juliano was unwilling to submit to anyone else's orthodoxy. He touched hundreds of lives and inspired others with his vision of nonviolence.

Many concerted efforts by legions of heroic people have resolved, mitigated, and even prevented certain conflicts, but an important component necessary to effect binding, long-range changes vital to the survival of our species has been missing. To counter the inherited male inclination for dominance that can lead to group aggression, an equally unstoppable female participation—equally deeply rooted in its inclination for social stability—must share the levers of power. When "masculine" and "feminine" inclinations are encouraged simultaneously, male tendencies that can be manipulated to form armies will be bound by limits that foster social stability. Mature liberal democracies are the forums through which this pivotal, peace-affirming partnership of men and women can be expressed.

Think of the legions of individuals—the unsung heroes—who have been the engines behind wonderfully positive changes. Imagine hundreds of millions who are already engaged becoming united by a shared vision to create a better, less violent world for children now and the generations to come. We have nobility within us. Our time in history is uniquely poised to make manifest this Great Shift to a future without war—and make it last.

There are thousands to tell you it cannot be done,
  There are thousands to prophesy failure;
There are thousands to point out to you, one by one,
  The dangers that wait to assail you.
But just buckle in with a bit of a grin,
  Just take off your coat and go to it;
Just start to sing as you tackle the thing
  That "cannot be done," and you'll do it.
                    Edgar A. Guest

Appendix I

Organizations and the Cornerstones

Listed here is a small sampling of organizations or projects. URL links to them can be found at www.AFutureWithoutWar. org/links_overview.html.

They are arranged for convenience under their primary focus cornerstone. For some, their interest overlaps two or more cornerstones; this may not be indicated. Almost all provide links to many other organizations. The list is not complete and is provided for information only; no endorsement or responsibility for the work of any organization is intended.

Broad General Interest/Miscellaneous

4 Years Go	Jazz for Peace
Alliance for Peace Building	KOSMOS
Better World Links	New Tactics for Human Rights
FastCompany.com – Social	Peace Dot Directory
Entrepreneurs Awards Program	Peace Parks Foundation
Citizens for Global Solutions	Positive Futures Network (PFN) –
Culture of Peace News Network	Yes! Magazine
Global Directory of Peace Studies and	Pro-Peace - Imagine
Conflict Resolution Programs	Psychologists for Social Responsibility
Global Giving	Survivors of Torture International
Global Shapers	The Earth Charter Initiative
Great Transition Initiative	The Widening Circle
InterAction	Time Out for Peace Project
International Committee to Stop	Veterans for Peace
Rape and Gender Violence in	Vision of Humanity–Global Peace
Conflict	Index
	WiserEarth
	Z Magazine, Z Net, Z Media, Z
	Video

Embrace the Goal

This list is unfortunately short, awaiting lengthening. It includes only organizations or groups that, as of 2012, explicitly express as some part of their mission statement that *they work to abolish (end) war*. Organizations that work to promote peace, teach peace or nonviolence, or do peace research are not included as those goals entail a significantly different challenge.

A Future Without War
Center for Global Nonkilling
Citizens for Global Solutions
FCNL – Friends Committee on
    National Legislation
FOR – The Fellowship of
    Reconciliation

Nuclear Age Peace Foundation
Global Strategy of Nonviolence
Going For A Global Truce, Inc
Veterans for Peace

Empower Women

About.com: Womens Issues: Third
    World
Afghan Women's Education Center
Amnesty Int. USA
The Center for Development and
    Population Activities
Center for Womens Global
    Leadership-Rutgers
Central Asia Institute
Code Pink
Council of Women World Leaders
Feminst Peace Network
FINCA - Village Banking: Credit for
    Change
Foundation for Women
Freedom from Hunger
Global Fund for Women
Global Goods Partners
Heifer Project: Women in
    Development
IFOR Women Peacemakers Program
iKnowPolitics - International
    Knowledge Network of Women in
    Politics
Initiative for Inclusive Security
International Committee to Stop Rape
    and Gender Violence in Conflict
International Womens Health
    Coalition
JASS
MADRE
Mothers Acting Up
Network of East-West Women
NGO Working Group on Women,
    Peace, Security
Nobel Womens Initiative
NOW Foundation
PeaceXPeace

Soroptimist International of the
    Americas
UNIFEM - United Nations
    Development Fund for Women
Voices of Women
New Moon Magazine
The Malala Fund
The Whitehouse Project
Win with Women Global Initiative
The WIP
UN Women
Women and Public Policy Program -
    Kennedy School of Government
Women for Women
Women Leaders Intercultural Forum
Women Peace and Security Network
    Africa
Women Peacemakers Program – Joan
    B. Kroc Institute for Peace and
    Justice
Women Thrive Worldwide
Women Waging Peace Network-Hunt
    Alternatives Fund
Women's Action for New Directions
    (WAND)
Women's Environment and
    Development Organization
    (WEDO)
Women's Human Rights Net
Women's Human Rights Resources-
    University of Toronto
Women's International League for
    Peace and Freedom – (WILPF)
Women's Learning Partnership
World Pulse – a Social Media
    Enterprise

Enlist Young Men

The Desmond Tutu Peace Foundation	Peace It Together
Dream Project	PeaceJam
Global Youth Action Network (GYAN)	PeacePlayers International
Global Youth Connect	Students Against Violence Everywhere
Mentoring Male Teens	Seeds of Peace
Metta Center for Nonviolence	Student Peace Alliance
National Center for the Preservation of Democracy	Tariq Khamisa Foundation (TKF)
National Organization of Men Against Sexism	United Network of Young Peacebuilders
	Yes!

Foster Connectedness

ADay.org	Green Net
Alliance for a New Humanity	Lifebridge Foundation
American Youth Soccer Organization	National Peace Academy - USA
Caretakers/USA	Network For Good
Center for Partnership Studies	Organization Development Network
Challenge Day	Pachamama Alliance
Common Ground News	PeaceXPeace
The Clinton Global Initiative	People to People International
The Dalai Lama Center for Peace and Education	Teaching Tolerance
	Tikkun - A Jewish Magazine, An Interfaith Movement
Esperanto - USA	Wiser Earth
The Gandhi Institute	World Pulse – a Social Media Enterprise
Global Citizens Initiative	

Ensure Essential Resources

Best Futures	Heifer International
Bill and Melinda Gates Foundation	Initiative for Global Development
Buy Different	InterAction
The Carter Center - Health Program	Mothers Acting Up
The Clinton Global Initiative	National Resource Defense Council
Creating Hope International	One!
Center for Global Development	Peace Parks Foundation
Dream Project	Physicians for Peace
Earth Force	Project Concern
Environmental Defense	Sierra Club
Global Campaign for Education	Tamera: Healing Biotope
Global Goods Partners	Women for Women
Global Warming Central	World Water Council
	4YearsGo

Promote Nonviolent Conflict Resolution

Abolition 2000
The Albert Einstein Institution
Alliance for Peace Building
Americans for a Department of Peace
American Friends Service Committee
Center for Global Nonkilling
Code Pink
Center for Partnership Studies
Citizens for Global Solutions
Center for Peace and Conflict Studies –
    Univ. Sydney
FOR - The Fellowship of Reconciliation
Friends Committee on National
    Legislation - FCNL
Global Action to Prevent War
Global Alliance for Ministries and
    Departments of Peace
Global Nonviolent Action Base
Global Strategy of Nonviolence
Mediators Beyond Borders
Mediators Without Borders
M.K. Gandhi Institute for Nonviolence
Mothers Against Killing
Joan Kroc Institute for Peace and Justice
School for Conflict Analysis and
    Resolution
Institute on Violence, Abuse and
    Trauma (IVAT)
Interactions for Peace
International Center for Conciliation
International Center for Nonviolent
    Conflict
International Committee to Stop Rape
    and Gender Violence in Conflict
International Women's Commission
Iraqi Nonviolence Group

Mahatma Gandhi Center for Global
    Nonviolence
National Conflict Resolution Center
National Peace Academy - USA
Nonviolence.org
Nonviolent Peaceforce
The Metta Center
Nuclear Age Peace Foundation
Peace Brigades
Peace Conferencing
Peace Party
Peacepeople
Peaceful Tomorrows
Ploughshares Fund
SAVE
Seeds of Peace
Search for Common Ground
Solidarity and Sustainability Research
    Newsletter
Tariq Khamisa Foundation (TKF)
Toda Institute for Global Peace and
    Policy Research Institute
The Center for Nonviolent
    Communication
The King Center
The Peace Alliance
Traprock Foundation
The University for Peace
Transnational Foundation for Peace and
    Future Research
Veterans for Peace
Voices for Creative Nonviolence
Waging Nonviolence
Women's International League for Peace
    and Freedom - WILPF
Women, War, Peace

Provide Security and Order

Arms Control Association
The Boston Consortium on Gender,
    Security, and Human Rights
Business Leaders for Sensible Priorities
Center for Advanced Defense Studies
Center for Global Security and
    Democracy - Rutgers University
Center for Security Studies -
    Georgetown University
The Century Foundation
Liveable World
Federation of American Scientists
Geneva Center for the Democratic
    Control of Armed Forces (DCAF)
Global Security
Global Zero

Henry L. Stimson Center
Institute for Global Security Law and
    Policy-Case School of Law
Institute on Global Conflict and
    Cooperation – University of
    California
Institute for Inclusive Security
International Action Network on Small
    Arms
Nuclear Age Peace Foundation
Nuclear Weapons Free World
SIPRI – Stockholm International Peace
    Research Institute
Social Science Research Council –
    Program on Global Security and
    Cooperation
Women in International Security –
    WIIS – Georgetown University

Shift Our Economies

Alliance for a Caring Economy
Archie's Acres - Veterans Sustainable
    Agricultural Training
Bioneers - Collective Heritage Institute
Business Leaders for Sensible Priorities
Center for Global Development
Climate Crisis
Earth Institute - Columbia University
Environmental Defense Fund
Gaia Foundation

Global Giving
Global Marshall Plan–Project of Tikkun
Grandmothers for Peace
Great Transition Initiative
Interface
National Priorities Project
Organization for Economic Co-
    operation and Development
Peace Action
Rocky Mountain Institute
Women's Action for New Directions

Spread Liberal Democracy

Annenberg Foundation Trust at
    Sunnylands
The Carter Center
The Center for the Study of Democracy
    - UC Irvine
Citizens for Global Solutions
Freedom House
International Humanist and Ethical
    Union (IHEU)
International Institute for Democracy
    And Electoral Assistance (IDEA)

League of Women Voters
National Center for the Preservation of
    Democracy
National Democratic Institute
Peace Action
Students for Global Democracy -
    Uganda
The Open Society Institute (OSI)

Appendix II

Stephen Pinker's *Better Angels of Our Nature* and F.A.C.E.

In *The Better Angels of Our Nature: Why Violence is Declining*, Steven Pinker's analysis of the most consistent reducers of violence throughout history focuses on five major forces.[368] Here we consider how these forces relate to F.A.C.E. and to the nine *Shift* cornerstones. The objective of this comparison is to indicate commonalities between different, broad approaches to ending war. Instances of overlapping or common features deemed to be important or critical, derived independently by different experts, cast a spotlight on elements of a campaign to end war that are the most obvious requirements. Appendix III adds to this search for commonalities by presenting a similar comparison with a paper by Douglas Fry, "Life Without War."

Pinker named these five forces as most consistently related to reduction in violence:

- Leviathan (named after the book by Thomas Hobbs on the nature of the state and government, and Pinker includes Leviathan's female counterpart Justitia, the goddess of Justice)
- Gentle Commerce
- Feminization
- Expanding Circle, and
- The Escalator of Reason[369]

In separate chapters he explores, in detail, how each of these forces reduced violence. All do so by changing the cost/benefit ratio of parties involved in a way that fosters peaceful cooperation and conflict resolution rather than fighting.[370]

Leviathan – Leviathan, as used by Pinker, is the condition in which a state with a monopoly on force uses force to protect its citizens from other groups. Pinker says this is the most consistent violence-reducer encountered in his review of the history of violence. Justitia, Leviathan's counterpart, represents a condition in which a third, neutral party, namely the law, mediates disputes.

The former situation happens when potential warring parties come under the control of a power with overwhelming military force that imposes penalties for violence and can enforce those penalties using physical punishment. All parties under sway of such an overarching power are inclined to keep the peace. Among a number of examples, he writes, "When bands, tribes, and chiefdoms came under the control of the first states, the suppression of raiding and feuding reduced their rates of violent death fivefold."[371] It also includes situations where the rule of law for settling disputes is enforced.

The commonality here is that for *Shift* and F.A.C.E., this represents the cornerstone Provide Security and Order. We find reinforcement for the point that giving some entity or entities—such as the United Nations and the International Court of Justice—the ability to make war a crime and the power to enforce any violation is essential to a campaign to end war.

Gentle Commerce - The reality here is that by exchanging mutual benefits, the cost/benefit ratio of a war is altered so each adversary's incentive to attack is significantly reduced. Each party benefits much more by avoiding war damage plus gaining more benefit from exchange than they might have benefitted from attacking and winning. This assumes that each party produces something the other wants or needs. This gets reflected in a tilting of the culture's values away from national glory toward making money instead. The ability of Gentle Commerce to reduce violence is qualified: "governments that base their nation's wealth on digging oil, minerals, and diamonds out of the ground rather than adding value to it via commerce and trade are more likely to fall into civil wars."[372] To the extent that making money swamps all other values, particularly those reflected in the nine *Shift* cornerstones, commerce can become a destructive and destabilizing force. To the extent that it enables purchases of needed goods and services and provides employment, it can be a positive force.

Gentle Commerce is "….consistent with a phenomenon long known to anthropologists: that many cultures maintain active networks of exchange, even when the goods exchanged are useless gifts, because they know it help keep the peace among them."[373]

The *Shift* cornerstone Foster Connectedness covers all efforts we make to create a sense of global oneness, to promote empathy and understanding of our fellow humans whatever their culture. To the extent that "gentle commerce" (as opposed to exploitative commerce) facilitates this goal of fostering connectedness, it appears to be another common element in a campaign to avoid or end war. It is generally recognized that "countries that trade with each other are less likely to cross swords."[374]

Feminization - Pinker defines Feminization as "the process in which cultures have increasingly respected the interests and values of women. Since violence is largely a male pastime, cultures that empower women tend to move away from the glorification of violence and are less likely to breed dangerous subcultures of rootless young men."[375] Pinker discusses five varieties of feminization—direct political empowerment, the deflation of manly honor, the promotion of marriage on women's terms, the rights of girls to be born, and women's control over their own reproduction. Each has the effect of "draining the swamps" that promote violence, including war.

He is aware of what he calls the psychological legacy of basic biological (innate) differences between the sexes, "namely that males have more of an incentive to compete for sexual access to females, while females have more of an incentive to stay away from risks that would make their children orphans."[376] Nevertheless, his discussion omits any sense that empowering women as equal partners in governing is in any way critical to ending violence, or war. Nor does he convey any sense that empowering women as equal partners in governing would be key to preventing backsliding into a new dark age of violence should there be a change in conditions, environmental or ones we cannot anticipate.

In fact he writes: "Feminization need not consist of women literally wielding more power in decisions of whether to go to war. It can also consist in a society moving away from a culture of manly honor, with its approval of violent retaliation for insults, toughening of boys through physical punishment, and veneration of martial glory."[377] Having men who are governing get more in touch with their "feminine side," which seems to be the process Pinker is describing, suggests that perhaps women are not really necessary to good governing or to negotiating war and peace or to fixing anything; in the face of extensive data showing how the presence of women is correlated with a decline in violence, in summing up Pinker still projects the sense that if men embrace a more feminine, less martial, culture—stress more "feminine" and less "masculine" values—they might achieve the Great Shift from violence and war all on their own.

Although it is laudable progress to acknowledge the power of feminine input, the *Shift* cornerstone Empower Women would require that we do more than have men adopt more feminine values; we must empower women themselves. Failing to do so, over time male biology will erode any progress made as the urge to dominate once again takes center stage. For example, in an essay, "Locked in the embrace of male biology," I remind readers how this process ultimately undermined the original egalitarian and nonviolent character of early Christianity and replaced it with a male-dominated and militant religion.[378]

Consider a contemporary example of the way power drifts from a place where it is dispersed and shared to a place where only a few or even one holds it. This was the shift from the United States' founders' vision that only the people's representatives, those that form the Congress, were to have the power to declare war (in the Constitution of 1787), to the current situation where a few in the inner circles of the Executive Branch now launch even preemptive war (2003). This trend—driven by the male urge to accumulate power at the very top of a dominance hierarchy—is another example of the geological-like power of biology over time.

Like geological forces, biology is an unrelenting force. We can adopt laws and customs to channel and contain male urges for domination. We can encourage men, as Pinker does, to stress more feminine values as a way to reduce violence. I think, however, that this approach is like putting inadequate dams and levees in place that will only weaken over time. If actual women aren't empowered, over time we will find ourselves back in the same condition we've experienced during the last ten millennia.

Note, however, that we do have yet another commonality, this one between Pinker's force of "feminization" and the *Shift* cornerstone Empower Women.

Expanding Circle - The Expanding Circle is the idea that when humans have opportunities to see into the lives of others, to read about the feelings of others when they are abused or treated unjustly, to have social contact in a cosmopolitan world with people from other places, they become less likely to want to harm those others. This phenomenon relies on our innate sense of empathy; basically, the idea that humans are essentially good and prefer to act justly and fairly in accordance with what their culture, and their "common sense" tells them is just and fair.[379]

In several chapters, Pinker gives examples of a link between getting to know other people better and major positive changes. For example, beginning in the 17th century, technological advances in publishing and transportation created what he calls a "Republic of Letters" and a "Reading Revolution." These allowed people to read and learn about other people and places and ways of being. In these, he argues, the seeds of the "Humanitarian Revolution" took root. He then traces how that revolution led to a decline in violence.

Here again we have a commonality with a *Shift* cornerstone. All organizations and individuals working to enhance our sense of oneness and lift up our sense of what is just and fair are part of the cornerstone Foster Connectedness. We will, indeed, have to rely on an Expanding Circle of empathy for others that can manifest in an unwillingness to kill them.

Escalator of Reason - The Escalator of Reason is the last of the forces Pinker found to be the most consistent reducers of violence. It is an argument in favor of a humanistic value system. He writes:

> "Throughout the book we have seen the beneficial consequences of an application of reason to human affairs. At various time in history superstitious killings, such as in human sacrifice, witch hunts, blood libels, inquisitions, and ethnic scapegoating, fell away as the factual assumptions on which they rested crumbled under the scrutiny of a more intellectually sophisticated populace."[380] (p. 690)
> And ….

"A broader effect of the escalator of reason....is the movement away from tribalism, authority and purity in moral systems and toward humanism, classical liberalism, autonomy, and human rights."[381]

Reason, in this view, is given very high regard as a force that moves us away from violence. It is supposedly "....an Olympian, superrational vantage point...."[382]

Pinker writes that "A humanistic value system, which privileges human flourishing as the ultimate good, is a product of reason because it can be justified: it can be mutually agreed upon by any community of thinkers who values their own interests and are engaged in reasoned negotiation...."[383]

But that is not quite the entire story. A phrase that paraphrases one by Emily Dickenson comes to mind: The human heart wants what the human heart wants. The reason negotiators can come to agreements to get rid of the evils Pinker has named is because the human heart indeed wants to flourish, and the values we call humanist are values that most allow us as humans to flourish. It is not just that reason produces a humanistic value system, although reason (practical good sense) plays an important part. But it's also that a built-in human sense of what kind of world works best to raise children and for a community and the individuals within it to flourish tends to respond positively when it finds itself living in a community that embraces cooperation, democracy, classical liberalism, and nonviolence. In short, although reason and logic are essential and necessary to figure out how to proceed, ultimately reason is the servant of what the human heart wants.

A campaign to end war will likewise be given force because it is also in tune with what the human heart wants. F.A.C.E., a campaign designed around creating safe, nurturing communities in which to raise our children is in tune with one of the human heart's most profound desires. And this is true of the people in the most backward and repressive countries we have on the globe. It is the leadership, not the people, of those countries that is out of touch with those values, drunk instead on power.

There is a commonality here between what Pinker is describing and a *Shift* cornerstone, Spread (Mature) Liberal Democracy, although the commonality is not based on "reason" *per se*. The key here is humanistic value systems, and liberal democracy is based on a humanistic value system as it honors, among other things, religious and personal freedoms, individual dignity, and rule of law. The recognition of and spread of humanistic values thus appears to be another key commonality.

In summary, we find five stressed commonalities for a campaign to end war that emerge from my analysis and Pinker's:

- We must provide security and order.
- We must foster connectedness.
- We must shift economies to foster shared commerce.
- We must bring feminine values into governing arenas.
- We must promote humanist values (by whatever means, but most readily by putting liberal democracies in place).

Appendix III

Douglas Fry's "Life Without War" and F.A.C.E.

In "Life Without War," Douglas Fry continues his explorations of how to move our global community beyond war by comparing characteristics of three peace systems.[384] Here we consider how these characteristics relate to F.A.C.E. and the nine *Shift* cornerstones. The objective of this comparison is to indicate commonalities between different, broad approaches to ending war. Instances of overlapping or common features, derived independently by different investigators, cast a spotlight on the most obvious key elements of a campaign to end war. Appendix II added to this search for commonalities by presenting a similar comparison with the book by Stephen Pinker, *The Better Angels of our Nature: Why Violence is Declining*.

Fry proposes the establishment of a global peace system. This was also the proposal of Robert Irwin in his 1988 book, *Building a Peace System*.[385] But while Irwin focused the elements of his book essentially around issues that are similar to the *Shift* cornerstones, in his "Life Without War" article in *Science*, Fry compares characteristics of three actual peace systems on different continents:

- ten tribes of the Upper Xingu River basin of Brazil,
- the Iroquois Confederacy of upper New York State, and
- the European Union.[386]

Fry points out that some people with peace systems renounce all war, but these particular people did engage in armed conflicts with people outside of their union. Within their union, however, they developed attitudes and institutions that allowed them to live in peace. His comparison leads him to suggest six essentials of a successful peace system:

- An overarching social identity.
- Interconnections among subgroups.
- Interdependence.
- Nonwarring values.

- Symbolism and ceremonies that reinforce peace.
- Superordinate institutions for conflict management.

All six of these overlap with or are embraced by *Shift* cornerstones. In his discussion of "overarching social identity" he takes on the question of "us-versus-them" mentality that can foster conflicts and willingness to use violence against the "other." He describes the methods used by his three peace systems to "expand the us" to encompass a sense of common identity, and the methods are unique to each setting. This corresponds to the work done and institutions embraced by the *Shift* cornerstone Foster Connectedness.

Addressing "intergroup ties," he points out that intergroup bonds of friendship and kinship discourage violence. He describes how peace systems use ceremonial unions, fictive and genuine intermarriage that establishes a sense of kinship, economic partnerships, and personal friendships to create such ties. These practices are, again, ones being advanced by F.A.C.E.'s Foster Connectedness cornerstone partners.

"Interdependence" in Fry's paper refers primarily to economic interdependence and its power to promote cooperation. It includes, however, engaging in cooperation for any kinds of beneficial reasons. For example, in the dry desert of Australia's west, local groups reciprocally allow other groups access to water and food in lean times, because a time will come when they may be the needy ones. Peace systems also tend to specialize in production of particular trade goods that they exchange, again creating interdependence. Potential F.A.C.E. partners of the cornerstone Shift Our Economies would also be stressing the importance and potential power of creating this kind of interdependence.

Fry begins his discussion of "nonwarring values" by pointing out the obvious fact that some value orientations are more conducive to peace than others, and that peace systems live by "nonwarring values." In the Upper Xingu tribes, for example, the warrior role is shunned. Peace is considered moral; war is not. Fry describes the means by which peace-promoting values were enshrined by the Iroquois Confederation. He points out that an explicit goal for the European Union was to bring peace and prosperity to the region. In the case of the EU, he describes how actualization of the values of democracy, social equality, human rights and respect for the law serve as the EU's moral compass. The *Shift* cornerstone Spread Liberal Democracy also places emphasis on the pacifying effect of these facets of liberal democracies when you have large, modern societies. The cornerstone Promote Nonviolent Conflict Resolution embraces the need to teach the philosophy and skills of peace. So here we have commonality between Fry's assessment of what it will take to move us beyond war and two *Shift* cornerstones.

Fry illustrates a need for "symbolism and ceremonies that reinforce peace" citing participation of all the Upper Xingu tribes in ceremonies to mourn the deaths of deceased chiefs and inaugurate new ones. Joint ceremonies help unify the tribes, again helping to foster connectedness and create a sense of common identity. The Iroquois League was symbolized by a powerful symbol of unity and peace, the Tree of Peace. The tree's white roots represented the desire for peace to spread beyond the confederacy. Clearly the Iroquois understood that peace requires work to maintain it; an eagle perched on top of the tree was a reminder that the tribes must remain vigilant to the threats to peace. A F.A.C.E. campaign, built around the shared goal of creating safe, secure, and healthy places for all children will likewise need to create an appropriate, unifying symbol to represent the desire to bring and maintain such a peace. The campaign should also invent ceremonies to celebrate its creation.

If a life without war is to be won and maintained, there must be "superordinate institutions for conflict management." Fry points out that there are many different ways to address conflicts between groups, and that one key to managing them is to create higher levels of governance to facilitate these processes by creating a new common identity and a new unity of purpose. He describes the Council of Chiefs of the Iroquois Confederacy. He describes higher levels of governance created by the EU, such as the European Court of Justice. The formation of the United States from thirteen separate colonies created that kind of higher level of governance in which people with differences do not take up weapons and battle it out; they take their case to the Supreme Court. The commonality here is that F.A.C.E. partners working in the *Shift* cornerstones Provide

Security and Order and Promote Nonviolent Conflict Resolution are concerned with these issues of how to nonviolently manage conflicts. The United Nations, as discussed earlier, is perhaps the best candidates for creating a key superordinate institution for a global peace system. The International Court of Justice is another step we have already taken in the right direction.

Fry concludes that creating a peace system for the entire planet would involve many synergistic elements "including the transformative vision that a new peace-based global system is in fact possible…." Here the commonality with getting the very concept that it is possible to create such a peace system and end war widely understood is with *Shift* cornerstone Embrace the Goal.

Two notable cornerstones that Fry's analysis does not directly, or even very indirectly, touch are Empower Women and Enlist Young Men. First, the challenge of making young, restless males part of the solution—making them supporters of building this peace system—is arguably the least appreciated element of creating a future without war. It is seldom mentioned by anyone writing on this subject since the general assumption is that we will never end war so thinking about the specific problem of what to do with young men as part of the process of ending or what to do with them when war is absent has no relevance.

Fry also doesn't acknowledge the importance of empowering women, although women were powerful in the Iroquois Federation and women certainly have influence and the vote in the members of the European Union. The biological facets of our problem are not generally stressed, however, by most scholars, the emphasis being placed on culture. Furthermore, it is virtually universally recognized that war is a male behavior, not a controversial idea and not requiring discussion. The issue of how women relate to peace and social stability, however, is only now coming into the discussion. Many scholars are cautious, like Yale University professor Nicholas Sambanis. Mara Hvistendahl quotes him in her *Science* article "Gender and War" as thinking that perhaps what I would call a "female effect" on peace and stability is perhaps "a proxy for other, more fundamental things, like cultural differences, rule of law, [and] institutional development."[387] In other words, Sambanis is expressing the view that perhaps the fact that empowerment of women in a society is strongly related to its level of peace is simply a correlation, not part of causation. One goal of *Shift* is to make the importance of biological traits of men and women as these relate to war explicit, and to stress that women's influence is, in fact, a critical, causative factor.

Summing up, if we decide to pursue the goal of a warless future with sufficient will, we have actual examples and models to learn from and they encourage us to know that we can succeed. The following are the commonalities between *Shift* cornerstones and elements that Fry puts forth:

- We must foster personal and cultural connectedness.
- We must foster economic interconnectedness (as part of fostering connectedness in general and related to shifting our economies appropriately)
- We must foster human rights (by whatever means, but most readily by spreading mature liberal democracy)
- We must foster behaviors and institutions that promote non-violent conflict resolution.
- We must foster the rule of law (part of providing security and order and promoting nonviolent conflict resolution)
- We must embrace the goal.

BIBLIOGRAPHY

'Abdu'l-Bahá. 1982. *The Promulgation of Universal Peace*. US Bahá'í Publishing Trust. 2nd Ed. p. 135.

Aker, Dee (ed.) and Emiko Noma, Laura Taylor and Susan Van Schoonhoven. 2007. *Is Peace Possible? Women PeaceMakers in Action*. San Diego, CA: Joan B. Kroc Institute for Peace and Justice. http://tinyurl.com/7cvmkzj (accessed 8 July 2012.)

Anderlini, Sanam Naraghi. 2007. *Women building peace: what they do, why it matters*. Boulder, CO: Lynne Rienner Publishers.

Andersen, Steffen, Erwin Bulte, Uri Gneezy, and John A. List. 2008. "Do Women Supply More Public Goods than Men? Preliminary Experimental Evidence from Matrilineal and Patriarchal Societies." American Economic Review: Papers & Proceedings 2008, 98:2, 376–381. http://www.aeaweb.org/articles.php?doi=10.1257/aer.98.2.376 (accessed 5 April 2010).

Anderson, Mary B. and Marshall Wallace. 2012. *Opting Out of War: Strategies to Prevent Violent Conflict*. Boulder, Co: Lynne Rienner Publishers.

Archie, Elizabeth A., Jeanne Altmann, and Susan C. Alberts. 2012. *Social status predicts wound healing in wild baboons*. Proceedings of the National Academy of Sciences. http://www.pnas.org/content/early/2012/05/14/1206391109. abstract (accessed 30 May 2012).

Ardrey, Robert. 1966. *The territorial imperative*. New York: Delta.
     1976. *The hunting hypothesis: a personal conclusion concerning the evolutionary nature of man*. New York: Macmillan Publishing Co.

Atran, Scott and Ara Norenzayan. 2004. "Religion's evolutionary landscape: counterintuition, commitment, compassion, communion." Behavior and Brain Sciences 27: 713-770.

Barry, Kathleen. 2011. *Unmaking war. Remaking men*. Santa Rosa, CA: Phoenix Rising Press.

Benjamin, Medea. 2012. *Drone warfare: killing by remote control*. NY: OR Books.

Benjamin, Medea and Jodie Evans. 2005. *Stop the next war now*. Makawao, HI: Inner Ocean Publishing.

Bennett, Brian. 2012. "More pilots wage war from home." Los Angeles Times. July 29.

Blum, Deborah. 1997. *Sex on the brain. The biological differences between men and women*. NY: Viking Penguin.

Boehm, Christopher. 1999. *Hierarchy in the forest. The evolution of egalitarian behavior*. Cambridge, Mass.: Harvard Univ. Press.

2012. "Ancestral hierarchy and conflict." Science 336: 844-847.

Brizendine, Louann. 2006. *The female brain*. NY: Broadway Books.

2010. *The male brain*. NY: Broadway Books.

Brock. Peter. 1992. *A brief history of pacifism from Jesus to Tolstoy*. Toronto: Syracuse University Press.

Butler, Smedley. *War is a racket*. http://www.veteransforpeace.org/war_is_a_racket_033103.htmXX (accessed 10 April 2012).

Campbell, Anne. 1999. "Staying Alive: Evolution, culture and women's intra-sexual aggression." Behavioral and Brain Sciences 22: 203-252

Caprioli, Mary. 2003. "Gender equality and state aggression: the Impact of domestic gender inequality on state first use of force." International Interactions 29: 195–214;

2005. "Primed for violence: the role of gender inequality in predicting internal conflict." International Studies Quarterly 49:161–178.

Caprioli, Mary and Mark A. Boyer. 2001. "Gender, Violence, and International Crisis." Journal of Conflict Resolution 45:503–518.

Chagnon, Napoleon A. 1977. *Yanomamö: The fierce people*. NY: Holt, Rinehart and Winston.

Chopra, Deepak. 2005. *Peace is the way*. New York: Three Rivers Press.

Cohen, D. (Ed.). 1991. *The circle of life—rituals from the human family*. London: The Aquarian Press.

Collins, Suzanne. 2008. *The hunger games*. New York: Scholastic.

Crisp, Richard J. and Rose Meleady. 2012. "Adapting to a multicultural future." Science 336: 853-855.

Cunningham, Karla. 2012. "Terror's 'Invisible Women.'" Los Angeles Times, April 4.

Daly, Hermann. 2005. "Economics in a full world." Scientific American 293: 100-107

Daly, Martin, and Margo Wilson. 1985. "Competitiveness, risk-taking, and violence: The young male syndrome." Ethology and Sociobiology 6: 59-73.

1988. *Homicide*. Hawthorne, NY: Aldine de Gruyter.

Davis-Kimball, Jeannine. 1997. "Warrior women of the Eurasian steppes." Archaeology 50: 44-48.

Davis-Kimball, Jeannine and Mona Behan. 2002. *Warrior women: An archaeologist's search for history's hidden heroines*. NY: Warner Books

Dawkins, Richard. 1986. *The blind watchmaker*. New York: Norton.

Diamond, Jared. 1992. *The third Chimpanzee. The evolution and future of the human animal*. NY: HarperCollins.

1999, 1997. *Guns, germs, and steel. The fates of human societies.* NY: W. W. Norton.

2005. *Collapse. How Societies Choose to Fail or Succeed.* NY: Viking.

Disney, Abigail and Gini Ritiker. 2009. *Pray the devil back to hell.* A film.

Dollar, David, Raymond Fisman, and Roberta Gatti. 1999. "Are women really the "fairer" sex?" women and corruption in government." World Bank. Development Research Group. Poverty Reduction and Economic Management Network. Journal of Economic Behavior & Organization, Volume 46, Issue 4, December 2001, Pages 423-429.

Dye, David H. 2013. "Trends in Cooperation and Conflict in Native Eastern North America." In *War, peace, and human nature: the convergence of evolutionary and cultural views.* Douglas P. Fry (ed.). New York: Oxford University Press.

Eagly, A. H. and V. Steffen. 1986. "Gender and aggressive behavior: a meta-analytic review of the social psychological literature." Psychological Bulletin 100: 309-330.

The Economist. 2012. "The Anthropocene. A man-made world." The Economist. http://www.economist.com/node/18741749 (accessed 10 April 2012).

Ehrenreich, Barbara. 1997. *Blood rites: Origins and history of the passions of war.* New York: Henry Holt Publishing Company.

2012. "The End of War by John Horgan review." Special to the SF Chronicle. http://tinyurl.com/7xspvn8 (accessed 20 April 2012).

Ehrlich, Paul R. 1968. *Population Bomb.* New York: Ballantine.

Ellemers, Naomi. 2012. "The group self." Science 336: 848-852.

Ember, Carol R. and Melvin Ember. 1993. *Cultural anthropology. 7th Ed.* Englewood Cliffs, New Jersey: Prentice-Hall, Inc.

Ember, Melvin and Carol R. Ember. 1994. "Cross-cultural studies of war and peace: recent achievements and future possibilities." In Reyna and Downs eds. *Studying War: anthropological perspectives.* Langhorne, PA: Gordon & Breach. pp. 185-208.

English, J.J. 2007. *Collapse of the War System. Developments in the Philosophy of Peace in the Twentieth Century.* Ireland: Saor-Ollscoil Press in association with Choice Publishing.

Eisler, Riane. 2007. *The Real Wealth of Nations. Creating a Caring Economics.* San Francisco, CA: Barrett-Koehler Publishers, Inc.

Evans, Sir Arthur. 1921-35. *The palace of Minos: An account of the early Cretan civilization as illustrated by the discoveries at Knossos.* London: Macmillan.

Ferguson, R. Brian. 2003. "The birth of war." Natural History 112: July/Aug. http://iweb.tntech.edu/kosburn/history-444/birth_of_war.htm. (accessed 15 June 2012).

2013. "The Prehistory of War and Peace in Europe and the Near East. In War, peace, and human nature: the convergence of evolutionary and cultural views." Douglas P. Fry (ed.). New York: Oxford University Press.

Fisher, Helen. 1999. *The first sex. The natural talents of women and how they are changing the world.* NY: Random House.

Fox, Robin. 1967. *Kinship and marriage. An anthropological perspective.* NY: Penguin.

Frank, Adam. 2008. "Is war inevitable? A view from the stars." NPR Radio blog. http://tinyurl.com/9cbdtdz (accessed 30 August 2012)

Fry, Douglas P. 2006. *The human potential for peace: an anthropological challenge to assumptions about war and violence.* New York: Oxford University Press.

2007. *Beyond war: the human potential for peace.* New York: Oxford University Press.

2011/2012. *Peace in our time.* Book Forum. http://www.bookforum.com/inprint/018_04/8575 (accessed 5 April 2012).

2012." Life without war." Science 336: 879-884.

Fry, Douglas P. and Anna Szala. 2013. "The evolution of agonism: the triumph of restraint in nonhuman and human primates." In *War, peace, and human nature: the convergence of evolutionary and cultural views.* Douglas P. Fry (ed.). New York: Oxford University Press.

Fry, Douglas P. and Patrik Söderberg. 2013. "Lethal aggression in mobile forager bands and implications for the origins of war." Science 341: 270-273.

Fukuyama, Francis. 1992. *The end of history and the last man.* New York: Free Press.

1999. *The Great Disruption: Human Nature and the Reconstitution of Social Order.* NY: Simon & Schuster.

Gat, Azar. 2006. *War and human civilization.* New York: Oxford University Press.

Gilbert, Susan. 2000. *A field guide to boys and girls.* NY: HarperCollins.

Gibbs, W. Wayt. 2005. "How should we set priorities?" Sci. Am. 293: 108-115.

Gizelis, Theodora-Ismene. 2009. "Gender empowerment and United Nations peacebuilding." International Peace Research. 46 (4): 505 –523. http://tinyurl.com/6vvqpxv. (accessed 31 May 2012).

Goldberg, Nicholas. 2009. "Parsing the rules of war." Los Angeles Times. July 26.

Goldstein, Joshua. 2001. *War and gender.* Cambridge, UK: Cambridge University Press.

2011. *Winning the war on war: the decline of armed conflict worldwide.* New York: Dutton.

Goodall, Jane. 1990. *Through a window: My thirty years with the Chimpanzees of Gombe.* Boston: Houghton Mifflin.

Goodenough, Ursula. 1998. *The sacred depths of nature.* NY: Oxford University Press.

Gray, John. 1992. *Men are from Mars, women are from Venus: a practical guide for improving communication and getting what you want in your relationships.* New York: HarperCollins.

Grobman, K. H. 2003-2008. Sex/gender differences. http://www.devpsy.org/teaching/gender/sex_differences.html (accessed 10 March 2012).

Grossman, Lt. Col. Dave. 2000. "Teaching kids to kill." Phi Kappa Phi National Forum. Fall issue. http://www.killology.org/print/print_teachkid.htm. (accessed 2 May 2012).

2009. *On Killing: the psychological cost of learning to kill in war and society.* Boston, MA: Back Bay Books.

Gőetner-Abendroth, Heidi. 1991 and 1999. *Das Matriarchat, vol II I. contemporary matriarchal societies in East Asia, Indonesia, Oceania.* Stuttgart: Verlag Kohlhammer.

2000. *Contemporary matriarchal societies in America, India, Africa.* Stuttgart: Verlag Kohlhammer.

Grotius, Hugo. 1623. *The rights of war and peace.* Translated by A.G. Campbell. London: Universal Classics Library. 1901.

Haidt, Johnathan. (accessed 17 June 2012). http://people.virginia.edu/~jdh6n/home.html.

Hand, J. L. 1981. "Sociobiological implications of unusual sexual behaviors of gulls: the genotype/behavioral phenotype problem." Ethology and Sociobiology 2: 135-145. 1981.

1985. "Egalitarian resolution of social conflicts: a study of pair-bonded gulls in nest duty and feeding contexts." Z. Tierpsychol. 70: 123-147.

1986. "Resolution of social conflicts: Dominance, egalitarianism, spheres of dominance and game theory." Quart. Rev. Biol. 61: 201-220.

2001. *Voice of the Goddess.* Cardiff, CA: Pacific Rim Press.

2006. "What makes people happy." http://www.afww.org/WhatMakesPeopleHappy.html. (accessed 5 April 2012).

2006. "How far we have already come." http://www.afww.org/HowFar.html. (accessed 8 Sept 2011).

2009. "Changing the biological chemistry of nonviolence movements: women on the front lines." http://wp.me/p45hl-8F (accessed 1 April 2012).

2009. "How long will it take to reach the goal?" http://afww.org/HowLong.html (accessed 20 June 2012).

2009. "Liberian women demand and get peace." http://tinyurl.com/2aq2xe6 (accessed 1 April 2012).

2009. "Locked in the embrace of male biology: a barrier to positive paradigm shift." http://afww.org/EmbraceOfMaleBiology.html. (accessed 1 April 2012).

2009. Book Review: Mothers and others – on the origins of mutual understanding. ISHE Bulletin 24 (3): 3. http://afww.org/MothersAndOthers.html (accessed 2 April 2012).

2009. Gort, Climate Change, Abolishing War. http://tinyurl.com/yl9syow. (accessed 15 April 2012).

2010. "To Abolish War." Journal of Aggression, Conflict, and Peace Research 2 (4): 44-56.

2010. "The origin of war and human destiny." http://wp.me/p45hl-8b (accessed 4 April 2012).

2010. "Sarah Palin and why all women are not progressive." http://tinyurl.com/2c2o2tl (accessed 5 April 2012).

2011. "Shaping the Future: A Proposal to Hasten a Global Paradigm Shift for the Security and Well-being of All Children Everywhere." www.afww.org/ShapingTheFuture.html. (accessed 28 March 2012).

2011. "No more war: the human potential for peace." A filmed lecture (58 minutes). San Diego, CA: Questpath Publishing. Available at: http://afww.org/NoMoreWar_TheHumanPotentialForPeace.html.(accessed 25 May 2012).

2012 "Rick Santorum is a U.S. Presidential Candidate – and a Warmonger" – http://wp.me/p45hl-el (accessed 1 April 2012).

2012. "The moral molecule: the source of love and prosperity." Book Review. http://www.afww.org/TheMoralMolecule.html. (accessed 10 October 2012).

Hand, J. L., Sigrid Hopf, and Detlev Ploog. 1967 "Observations on mating behavior and sexual play in the Squirrel Monkey *(Saimiri sciureus)*." Primates 8: 229-246.

Hart, Gary. 2004. *The Fourth Power. A Grand Strategy for the United States in the Twenty-First Century.* NY: Oxford University Press.

Hart, Michael H. 1978. *The 100. A ranking of the most influential persons in history.* NY: A & W Publishers, Inc.

Haviland, William A. 1999. *Cultural anthropology. 9th Ed.* Orlando, Florida: Harcourt Brace & Company.

Hawkin, Paul. 2007. *Blessed Unrest: How the Largest Movement in the World Came into Being and Why No One Saw It Coming.* NY: Viking.

Hawkes, Kristen, J.F. O'Connell, N.G. Blurton Jones, H. Alvarez, and E.L. Charnov. 1998. "Grandmothering, menopause and the evolution of human life histories." Proceedings of the National Academy of Sciences 95: 1336-1339.

Hedges, Chris. 2002. *War is a force that gives us meaning.* NY: Public Affairs.

Hewlett, Barry S. 2005. "The cross-cultural nexus of Aka father-infant bonding." In: Brettell, Caroline B. and Carolyn F. Sargent (eds). 2005. *Gender in cross-cultural perspective.* New Jersey: Prentice Hall.

Hinde, Robert. 1970. *Animal behaviour: A synthesis of ethology and comparative psychology.* McGraw-Hill.

Hinde, Robert & Rotblat, J. 2003. *War No More. Eliminating Conflict in the Nuclear Age.* Stirling, VA: Pluto Books.

Hiraiwa-Hasegawa, Mariko. 2005. "Homicide by men in Japan, and its relationship to age, resources and risk taking." Evolution and Human Behavior 26: 332-343.

Hoffman, Martin. 1978. "Sex differences in empathy and related behaviors." Psychology Bulletin 84: 712-722.

Holman, Jeanine. 2010. "Bound feet." http://www.josephrupp.com/history.html (accessed 17 June 2012).

Horgan, John. 2012. *The end of war.* San Francisco: McSweeney's Books

Hrdy, Sarah Blaffer. 1981. *The women who never evolved.* Cambridge, MA: Harvard University Press.

1999. *Mother Nature: a history of mothers, infants, and natural selection.* New York: Pantheon Books.

2009. *Mothers and others: on the origins of mutual understanding.* Cambridge, MA: Harvard University Press.

Hua, Cai. 2001. *A society without fathers or husbands: the Na of China.* Translated by Asti Hustvedt. NY: Zone Books.

Hudson, Rex A. 1999. "The sociology and psychology of terrorism: who becomes a terrorist and why?" Prepared by Library of Congress, Federal Research Division. See: www.loc.gov/rr/frd/pdf-files/Soc_Psych_of_Terrorism.pdf. p.50 "Terrorists are generally people who feel alienated from society and have a grievance or regard themselves as victims of an injustice." (accessed 10 April 2012).

Hudson, Valerie M., Bonnie Ballif-Spanvill, Mary Caprioli, and Chad F. Emmett. 2012. *Sex and world peace.* NY: Columbia University Press.

Hvistendahl, Mara. 2012. *Gender and violence.* Science 336: 839-840.

Internet Encyclopedia of Philosophy (IEP). http://www.iep.utm.edu/justwar/#H2 (accessed 1 April 2012).

Interparliamentary Union. http://www.ipu.org/english/home.htm (accessed 4 April 2012).

Irwin, Robert A. 1988. *Building a peace system: exploratory project on the conditions of peace.* Washington, D.C.: Expo Press.

Jandt, Fred E. 1985. *Win-win negotiating: turning conflict into agreement.* NY: Wiley.

Kania, John, and Mark Kramer. 2011. "Collective Impact." Stanford Social Innovation Review. Winter. http://www.ssireview.org/articles/entry/collective_impact. (accessed 8 August 2012.)

Kano, Takayoshi. 1992. *The last ape: pygmy Chimpanzee behavior and ecology.* Translated by Evelyn Ono Vineberg. Stanford, CA: Stanford University Press.

Keeley, Lawrence. 1996. *War before civilization: the myth of the peaceful savage.* NY: Oxford Univ. Press.

Kelly, Raymond C. 2000. *Warless societies and the origin of war.* Ann Arbor, MI: University of Michigan Press.

Korten, David. C. 2006. *The Great Turning: from Empire to Earth Community.* San Francisco, CA: Berrett-Koehler.

2009. *Agenda for a new economy. From phantom wealth to real wealth.* San Francisco, CA: Barrett-Koehler Publishers.

Krause, Kenneth W. 2012. "Gender Personality Differences: Planets or P.O. Boxes, Evidence or Ideology?" Skeptical Inquiror, May/June.

Krober, Clifton B., and Bernard L. Fontana. 1986. *Massacre on the Gila: An account of the last major battle between American Indians, with reflections on the origin of war.* Tucson: University of Arizona Press.

Kristof, Nicholas D. and Sheryl WeDunn. 2009. *Half the Sky: Turning Oppression Into Opportunity For Women Worldwide.* New York: Alfred A. Knopf

Kunzig, Robert. 2011. "Population 7 Billion." National Geographic 219(1): 32-69.

Lakey, George. 2012. "How Swedes and Norwegian broke the power of the '1 %." Nation of Change. http://www.nationofchange.org/how-swedes-and-norwegians-broke-power-1-percent-1327762223 (accessed 28 April 2012).

Lancaster, Chet S. 1981. *The Goba of the Zambezi: sex roles, economics and change.* Norman: University of Oklahoma Press.

Layard, Richard G. 2005. *Happiness:Lessons from a New Science.* New York:Penguin

Le Blanc, Stephen A. and Katerine B. Register. 2003. *Constant Battles*. New York: St. Martin's Press.

Lippa, Richard. A. 2010. "Gender differences in personality and interests: When, where, and why?" Pers. and Soc. Psych. Compass 4/11: 1098-1110.

Lorenz, Konrad. 1974, c1966. *On aggression*. Translated by Marjorie Kerr Wilson. New York: Harcourt Brace Jovanovich.

Lovins, Amory B. 2005. "More profit with less carbon." Sci. Am. 293:74-83.

Machel, G. 1996. *Impact of armed conflict on children*. NY: United Nations Department of Policy Coordination and Sustainable Development (DPCSD).

Malthus, Thomas. 1798. *An essay on the principle of population*. London: J. Johnson.

Marshall, Andrew Garvin. 2011. "Lies, war, and empire: NATO's "Humanitarian Imperialism" in Libya." http://www.andrewgarvinmarshall. com. (accessed 5 July 2012).

McCarthy, Coleman, Ed. Undated. *Strength through Peace: The ideas and people of Nonviolence*. Washington, D.C.: Center for Teaching Peace.

McDermott, R., and J. Cowden. 2001. "The Effects of Uncertainty and Sex in a Simulated Crisis Game." International Interactions 27: 353-380.

McElvaine, Robert S. 2002. *Eve's seed: biology, the sexes, and the course of history*. New York: McGraw Hill Companies.

Mead, Margaret. 1940. "War is Only an Invention − Not a Biological Necessity." ASIA, XL (accessed at http://www.andrew.cmu.edu/user/jdegolia/Interpretation%20and%20Argument/Suggested%20Readings/Mead. pdf_- 20 March 2012.

Mealey, Linda. 1995. "The sociobiology of sociopathy." Behavior and Brain Sciences 18:523-541.

    2000. *Sex differences: Developmental and evolutionary strategies*. San Diego: Academic Press.

Melander, Erik. 2005. "Gender equality and intrastate armed conflict." International Studies Quarterly 49: 695-714. http://www.iepcd.org/files/ Download/genderequality.pdf (accessed 31 May 2012.)

Moir, Anne and David Jessel. 1991. *Brain Sex. The real difference between men and women*. NY: Carol Publishing Group.

Mowrey, William R. and Douglas S. Portman. 2012. "Sex differences in behavioral decision-making and the modulation of shared neural circuits." Biol. Sex Differences: March, 3(1): 8.

Mueller, John. 1989. *Retreat from Doomsday: the obsolescence of major war*. New York: Basic.

2006. "Accounting for the waning of major war." In Raimo Väyrynen, ed. *The Waning of Major War: theories and debates*. London: Routledge. pp. 64-79.

Muir, Kate. 1992. *Arms and the woman. Female soldiers at war*. London: Sinclair-Stevenson Ltd.

Mustafa, Nadia. 2005. "What about gross national happiness?" Time/Health http://tinyurl.com/4krm4 (accessed 12 April 2012).

Myers, Winslow. 2009. *Living beyond war: a citizen's guide*. MaryKnoll, NY: Orbis Books.

Nagler, Michael N. *Hope or Terror? Gandhi and the Other 9/11*. Minneapolis, MN: Nonviolent Peaceforce and Tomales, CA: Metta Center. To obtain copies go to: http://www.mettacenter.org/?page_id=18.

Nathan, Otto and Heinz Norden. 1963. *Einstein on peace*. London: Methuen.

Nowak, Martin and Roger Highfield. 2011. *Supercooperators: Altruism, evolution, and why we need each other to succeed*. New York: Simon and Schuster.

Nyborg, H. 1994. *Hormones, sex and society*. Westport, Conn.: Praeger.

Panksepp, Jaak. 1998. *Affective neuroscience: the foundations of human and animal emotions*. New York: Oxford University Press.

Peach, Lucinda J. 2005. "Gender and war: are women tough enough for military combat?" In: Brettell, Caroline B. and Carolyn F. Sargent (eds). *Gender in cross-cultural perspective*. New Jersey: Prentice Hall.

Perry, Tony. 2012. "Marine Corps adjusts its recruiting mission". Los Angeles Times, 11 March.

Pinker, Steven. 1997. *How the mind works*. New York: W.W. Norton & Company.

2011. *The better angels of our nature: why violence has declined*. New York: Viking.

Polaskovic, Gary. 2012. "Are women greener than men?" Los Angeles Times. June 13. http://tinyurl.com/6p3k7c5 (accessed 13 June 2012).

Potts, Malcolm and Thomas Hayden. 2008. *Sex and war*. Dallas, TX: Benbella Books.

Radcliff, Benjamin. 2013. *The political economy of human happiness: How voters' choices determine the quality of life*. Cambridge, MA: Cambridge University Press.

Richardson, Lewis Fry, Quincy Wright, and Carl C. Lienau. 1960. *Statistics of Deadly Quarrels*. New York: Boxwood Press.

Rotblat, Joseph. 2006. "A world without war. Is it desirable? Is it feasible?" ISYP Journal on Science and World Affairs, Vol. 2, No. 1. http://www.pugwash.org/publication/tran/Rotblat-En.pdf (accessed 3 May 2012).

Sachs, Jeffrey D. 2005. "Can extreme poverty be eliminated?" Sci. Am. 293: 56-65.

2008. *Common Wealth*. New York: Penguin.

Salmonson, Jessica Amanda. 1991. *The encyclopedia of Amazons. Women warriors from antiquity to the modern era*. NY: Paragon House.

Sánchez, Oscar. A. 1995. "Understanding, tolerance, freedom and democracy." In: *Peace!* (Thee, M., ed.). UNESCO, Paris, p. 50.

Sanday, Peggy Reeves. 2002. *Women at the center: Life in a modern matriarchy*. Ithaca, NY: Cornell University Press.

Sandels, Alexandra. 2012. "A rebirth in Syria's peace movement." Los Angeles Times. 6 May

Scheper-Hughes, Nancy. 2005. "Lifeboat ethics: mother love and child death in northeast Brazil." In: Brettell, Caroline B. and Carolyn F. Sargent (eds) *Gender in cross-cultural perspective*. New Jersey: Prentice Hall.

Schlegel, Alice, and Herbert Barry III. 1991. *Adolescence: An anthropological inquiry*. NY: Free Press.

See, Carolyn. 2009. "Carolyn See reviews Kristoff and WuDunn's 'Half the Sky.'" Sept. 11. http://tinyurl.com/6uayu3u. (accessed 17 June 2012).

Sharp, Gene. 2005. *Waging Nonviolent Struggle. 20th Century Practice and 21st Century Potential*. Boston: Porter Sargent Publishers.

Shaywitz, B. A., S. E. Shaywitz, et. al. 1995. "Sex differences in the functional organization of the brain for learning." Nature 373: 607-608.

Shermer, Michael. 2001. "Spin-doctoring the Yanomamö." In *Skeptic* 9: 36-47.

Shostak, Marjorie. 1983. *Nisa. The life and words of a !Kung woman*. NY: Random House.

Silk, Joan B. 2002. "The form and function of reconciliation in primates." *Annual Reviews of Anthropology*, 31: 21-44. doi:10.1146/annurev.anthro.31.032902.101743.

Solomon, Norman. 2005. *War made easy: how presidents and pundits keep spinning us to death*. Hoboken, NJ: John Wiley & Sons, Inc.

Stephan, Maria J. and Erica Chenoweth. 2008. "Why civil resistance works. The strategic logic of nonviolent conflict." International Security 33 (1): 7-44. http://tinyurl.com/5ko7s9. (accessed 17 June 2012).

Swanson, David. 2013. *War no more. The case for abolition*. Charlottesville, VA: David Swanson.

Tannen, Debra. 1998. *The argument culture: stopping America's war of words*. NY: Ballantine.

Thottam/Thimphu, Jyoti. 2012. "The pursuit of happiness." Time Magazine-Business Section, October, pp. 1-5.

Tierney, Patrick. 2000. *Darkness in El Dorado*. NY: Norton.

Tiger, Lionel. 2001. "Osama Bin Ladin's Man Trouble." http://tinyurl. com/7wccyxq (accessed 10 April 2012.

Tipton, Paul. 2012. "Science—it takes a global village." Los Angeles Times. July 9.

Toffler, Alvin. 1970. *Future Shock*. NY: Random House.
    1980. *The Third Wave*. NY: Bantam Books.

Ury, William. 1999. *Getting to peace: transforming conflict at home, at work, and in the world*. NY: Viking.

Verbeek, Peter. 2008. "Peace ethology." Behaviour 145: 1497-1524.
    2013. "An ethological perspective on peace." In *War, peace, and human nature: the convergence of evolutionary and cultural views*. Douglas P. Fry (ed.). New York: Oxford University Press.

Waal, Frans B. M. de. 1989. *Primate Reconciliation. A review of Peacemaking Among Primates*. Cambridge, MA: Harvard University Press.
    1997. *Bonobo: the forgotten ape*. Berkeley: University of California Press.
    2009. *Primates and Philosophers: How Morality Evolved*. Stephen Macedo & Josiah Ober (eds.). New York: Princeton University Press.
    2012. "The antiquity of empathy. Science 336: 874-875.

Walton, Mary. 2010. *A Woman's crusade: Alice Paul and the battle for the ballot*. New York: Palgrave Macmillan.

Waters, Frank. 1963. *Book of the Hopi*. New York: Penguin.

Weiner, Eric J. 2012. "Not their fathers' economics." Los Angeles Times, April 11.

Weintraub, Pamela. 2012. "Jaak Panksepp. The man who makes rats laugh." Discover, May: 58-66. p. 60.

White, Tim D. 2009. "*Ardipithecus ramidus* and the paleobiology of early hominids." Science 326: 64. This issue presents many articles on the analysis of this fossil.

Wiessner, Polly and Nitze Pupu. 2012. "Toward peace: foreign arms and indigenous institutions in a Papua New Guinea society." Science 337: 1651-1654.

Williams, J., S. Goose, and M. Wareham. 2008. *Banning Landmines: Disarmament, Citizen Diplomacy, and Human Security*. Lanham, Md.: Bowman & Littlefield Publishers, Inc.

Williams J, and S. D. Goose. 2008. "Citizen diplomacy and the Ottawa Process: a lasting model?" In *Banning Landmines: Disarmament, Citizen Diplomacy, and Human Security*. Lanham, Md.: Bowman & Littlefield Publishers, Inc.

Wilson, Edward O. 1975. *Sociobiology*. Cambridge: Harvard University Press.
    2012. *The social conquest of earth*. New York: W.W. Norton Company.

Wilson, Marie C. 2004. *Closing the leadership gap: why women can and must help run the world.* New York: Penguin.

Wing, Walter with Richard Deats. 2000. *Peace is the Way: Writings on Nonviolence from the Fellowship of Reconciliation.* NY: Orbis Books.

Winter, Peter, Detlev Ploog and Judith Hand. 1966. "Vocal repertoire of the Squirrel Monkey *(Saimiri sciureus),* its analysis and significance." Experimental Brain Research 1: 359-384.

Wrangham, Richard and Dale Peterson. 1996. *Demonic males. Apes and the origins of human violence.* NY: Houghton Mifflin.

Zak, Paul J. 2012. *The moral molecule: the source of love and prosperity.* New York: Dutton/Penguin.

Zakaria, Fareed. 2001. "Why do they hate us? Newsweek: Oct. 15[th.]

Zinn, Howard. 1990. "A Warrior Turns Pacifist." In: *Strength Through Peace: The Ideas and People of Nonviolence.* McCarthy, C. Ed. Washington, D.C.: Center for Teach Peace.

Endnotes

1   Hand, Judith. 2011. "Shaping the Future: a proposal to hasten a global paradigm shift for the security and well-being of all children everywhere." www.afww.org/ShapingTheFuture.html. (accessed 27 March 2012).

2   Zimmer, Carl. 2012. "What Does E. O. Wilson Mean By a "Social Conquest of the Earth?" Smithsonian.com. (accessed at http://www.smithsonianmag.com/science-nature/What-Does-EO-Wilson-Mean-By-a-Social-Conquest-of-the-Earth.html#ixzz1qWEW22B1 1 April 2012).

3   Lewis, Susan K. (editor) 2005. "The man who predicted Katrina." http://www.pbs.org/wgbh/nova/earth/predicting-katrina.html. (accessed 9 June 2012).

4   Zeller, Tom Jr. 2012. "Nuclear security advocates accuse industry and regulators of foot-dragging on basic safety measures." Huff Post Green. http://tinyurl.com/ch7scqx. (accessed 9 June 2012).

5   Ardrey, Robert. 1966. *The territorial imperative*. New York: Delta; Ardrey, Robert. 1976. *The hunting hypothesis: a personal conclusion concerning the evolutionary nature of man*. New York: Macmillan Publishing Co

6   Pinker, Steven. 2011. *The better angels of our nature: why violence has declined*. New York: Viking.

7   Goldstein, Joshua. 2011. *Winning the war on war: the decline of armed conflict worldwide*. New York: Dutton; Mueller, John. 1989. *Retreat from Doomsday: the obsolescence of major war*. New York: Basic; Mueller, John. 2006. "Accounting for the waning of major war." In Raimo Väyrynen, ed. *The Waning of Major War: theories and debates*. London: Routledge. pp.. 64-79.

8   Horgan, John. 2012. *The end of war*. San Francisco, CA: McSweeney's Books.

9   Boehm, Christopher. 2012. *Ancestral hierarchy and conflict*. Science 336: 844-847; Dye, David H. 2013. "Trends in Cooperation and Conflict in Native Eastern North America." In *War, peace, and human nature: the convergence of evolutionary and cultural views*. Douglas P. Fry (ed.). New York: Oxford University Press; Fry, Douglas C. 2012. "Life without war." Science 336: 879-884; Kelly, Raymond C. 2000. *Warless societies and the origin of war*. Ann Arbor, MI: University of Michigan Press. Chapters 3 & 4.

10   Chopra, Deepak. 2005. *Peace is the way*. New York: Three Rivers Press.

11   Walton, Mary. 2010. *A Woman's crusade: Alice Paul and the battle for the ballot*. New York: Palgrave Macmillan.

12   Nagler, Michael N. *Hope or Terror? Gandhi and the Other 9/11*. Minneapolis, MN: Nonviolent Peaceforce and Tomales, CA: Metta Center. To obtain copies go to: http://www.mettacenter.org/?page_id=18. Includes brief relevant biographical material, history of his movement, and the philosophy and tactics of successful nonviolent struggle.

13   Wing, Walter with Richard Deats. 2000. *Peace is the Way: Writings on Nonviolence from the Fellowship of Reconciliation*. NY: Orbis Books.

14 Hand, J. L., Sigrid Hopf, and Detlev Ploog. 1967. "Observations on mating behavior and sexual play in the Squirrel Monkey (Saimiri sciureus)." Primates 8: 229-246; Winter, Peter, Detlev Ploog, and Judith Hand. 1966. "Vocal repertoire of the Squirrel Monkey (Saimiri sciureus), its analysis and significance." Experimental Brain Research 1: 359-384.

15 Hand, J. L. 1985. "Egalitarian resolution of social conflicts: a study of pair-bonded gulls in nest duty and feeding contexts." Z. Tierpsychol. 70: 123-147; Hand, J. L. 1986. "Resolution of Social Conflicts: Dominance, Egalitarianism, Spheres of Dominance and Game Theory." Quart. Rev. Biol. 61:201-220.

16 Hand, J. L. 1981. "Sociobiological implications of unusual sexual behaviors of gulls: the genotype/behavioral phenotype problem." Ethology and Sociobiology 2:135-145.

17 Daly, Hermann. 2005. *Economics in a full world*. Scientific American 293:100-107.

18 Fukuyama, F. 1999. *The Great Disruption: Human Nature and the Reconstitution of Social Order*. NY: Simon & Schuster; Hawken, Paul. 2007. *Blessed Unrest: How the Largest Movement in the World Came into Being and Why No One Saw It Coming*. NY: Viking; Korten, D. C. 2006. *The Great Turning: from Empire to Earth Community*. San Francisco, CA: Berrett-Koehler; Toffler Alvin. 1970. *Future Shock*. NY: Random House; Toffler, Alvin. 1980. *The Third Wave*. NY: Bantam Books.

19 In situations where dispersal was not possible because of physical barriers (see for example the discussion of Andaman Islanders) or because of dependency on a fixed food resource that favored settled living, what emerged was the development of peacemaking and peacekeeping rituals and behavior. War appears to be a late development in human evolutionary history, also associated with settled living.

20 Ehrlich, Paul R. 1968. *Population Bomb*. New York: Ballantine; Malthus. Thomas. 1798. *An essay on the principle of population*. London: J. Johnson.

21 Kunzig, Robert. 2011. "Population 7 Billion." National Geographic 219(1): 32-69.

22 Russell-Einstein Manifesto. 1955. Pugwash Conferences on Science and World Affairs.

23 Rotblat, Joseph. 2006. "A world without war. Is it desirable? Is it feasible?" ISYP Journal on Science and World Affairs, Vol. 2, No. 1. http://www.pugwash.org/publication/tran/Rotblat-En.pdf (accessed 3 May 2012).

24 Hinde, Robert and Joseph Rotblatt. 2003. *War no more. Eliminating conflict in the nuclear age*. Stirling, VA: Pluto Press.

25 Swanson, David. 2013. *War no more. The case for abolition*. Charlottesville, VA: David Swanson.

26 Frank, Adam. 2008. "Is war inevitable? A view from the stars." NPR Radio blog. http://tinyurl.com/9cbdtdz (accessed 30 August 2012).

27 Fry, Douglas P. 2007. *Beyond War: the human potential for peace*. New York: Oxford University Press. p. 13-17.

28 Kroeber, Clifton B., and Bernard L. Fontana. 1986. *Massacre on the Gila. An Account of the Last Major Battle Between American Indians, with Reflections on the Origin of War*. Tucson: Arizona University Press.

29 Fry, Douglas P. and Anna Szala. 2013. "The evolution of agonism: the triumph of restraint in nonhuman and human primates." In *War, peace, and human nature: the convergence of evolutionary and cultural views.* Douglas P. Fry (ed.). New York: Oxford University Press.

30 Fry, Douglas P. 2007. *Beyond War: the human potential for peace.* New York: Oxford University Press. p. 16.

31 Hand, Judith L. 2012. "Rick Santorum is a U.S. Presidential Candidate – and a Warmonger." http://wp.me/p45hl-el (accessed 1 April 2012).

32 Hand, Judith L. 2010. "To Abolish War." Journal of Aggression, Conflict, and Peace Research 2 (4): 44-56.

33 Ehrenreich, Barbara. 1997. *Blood Rites: origins and history of the passions of war.* New York: Henry Holt. pp. 122-123.

34 Mealey, Linda. 1995. "The sociobiology of sociopathy." Behavior and Brain Sciences 18:523-541.

35 Horgan, John. 2012. *The end of war.* San Francisco, CA: McSweeney's Books. pp. 62-64.

36 Ehrenreich, Barbara. 1997. *Blood Rites: origins and history of the passions of war.* New York: Henry Holt. pp.13–22.

37 Atran, Scott and Ara Norenzayan. 2004. "Religion's evolutionary landscape: counterintuition, commitment, compassion, communion." Behavior and Brain Sciences 27: 713-770.

38 Ehrenreich, Barbara. 1997. *Blood Rites: origins and history of the passions of war.* New York: Henry Holt. pp.81–82.

39 Barry, Kathleen. 2011. *Unmaking war. Remaking men.* Santa Rosa, CA: Phoenix Rising Press; Grossman, Lt. Col. Dave. 2000. *Teaching kids to kill.* Phi Kappa Phi National Forum. Fall issue. http://www.killology.org/print/print_teachkid.htm. (accessed 2 May 2012); Grossman, David A. 2009. *On Killing: the psychological cost of learning to kill in war and society.* Boston, MA: Back Bay Books.

40 Benjamin, Medea. 2012. *Drone warfare: killing by remote control.* OR Books.

41 Ellemers, Naomi. 2012. "The group self." Science 336: 848-852.

42 Solomon, Norman. 2005. *War made easy: how presidents and pundits keep spinning us to death.* Hoboken, NJ: John Wiley & Sons.

43 Barry, Kathleen. 2011. *Unmaking war. Remaking men.* Santa Rosa, CA: Phoenix Rising Press.

44 McElvaine, Robert S. 2002. *Eve's seed: biology, the sexes, and the course of history.* New York: McGraw Hill Companies.

45 Kroeber, Clifton B., and Bernard L. Fontana. 1986. *Massacre on the Gila. An Account of the Last Major Battle Between American Indians, with Reflections on the Origin of War.* Tucson: Arizona University Press. pp. 165-174.

46 Ehrenreich, Barbara. 1997. *Blood Rites: origins and history of the passions of war.* New York: Henry Holt. p. 127.

47 Kroeber, Clifton B., and Bernard L. Fontana. 1986. *Massacre on the Gila. An Account of the Last Major Battle Between American Indians, with Reflections on the Origin of War*. Tucson: Arizona University Press. p. 163.

48 Ember, Melvin and Carol R. Ember. 1994. "Cross-cultural studies of war and peace: recent achievements and future possibilities." In Reyna and Downs eds. *Studying War: anthropological perspectives*. Langhorne, PA: Gordon & Breach. pp. 185-208; Gat, Azar. 2006. *War and human civilization*. New York: Oxford University Press; LeBlanc, Steven A. 2003. *The myth of the peaceful, noble savage*. New York: St. Martin's Press; Marx, Karl; Richardson, Lewis F. 1960. *Statistics of deadly quarrels*. Quincy Wright and Carl C. Lienau, Eds.; Boxwood Press; Sachs, Jeffrey D. 2008. *Common wealth*. New York: Penguin.

49 Horgan, John. 2012. *The end of war*. San Francisco, CA: McSweeney's Books. p. 87.

50 English, John Jacob. 2007, *The Collapse of the War System. Developments in the Philosophy of Peace in the Twentieth Century*. Ireland: Saor-Ollscoil Press in Cooperation with Choice Publishing. Chapter 1.

51 Verbeek, Peter. 2008. "Peace ethology." Behaviour 145, 1497-1524.

52 Ibid.

53 Sánchez, O.A. 1995. "Understanding, tolerance, freedom and democracy." In: *Peace!* (Thee, M., ed.). UNESCO, Paris, p. 50.

54 Verbeek, Peter. 2013. "An ethological perspective on peace." In *War, peace, and human nature: the convergence of evolutionary and cultural views*. Douglas P. Fry (ed.). New York: Oxford University Press.

55 Waal, Frans B. M. de. 1989. *Primate Reconciliation. A Review of Peacemaking Among Primates*. Cambridge, MA: Harvard University Press.

56 English, John Jacob. 2007, *The Collapse of the War System*. Developments in the Philosophy of Peace in the Twentieth Century. Ireland: Saor-Ollscoil Press in Cooperation with Choice Publishing.

57 Hinde, Robert. 1970. *Animal behaviour: A synthesis of ethology and comparative psychology*. McGraw-Hill; Wilson, E. O.1975. *Sociobiology*. Cambridge: Harvard University Press.

58 Gray, John. 1992. *Men are from Mars, women are from Venus: a practical guide for improving communication and getting what you want in your relationships*. New York: Harper Collins.

59 Wilson, Edward O. 2012. *The social conquest of earth*. New York: W.W. Norton Company.

60 Zak, Paul J. 2012. *The Moral Molecule: The Source of Love and Prosperity*. New York: Dutton/Penguin.

61 Joshua Goldstein's *War and Gender* (2001) and Potts and Hayden's (2008) *Sex and War* are notable exceptions. These scholars do not, however, contribute the perspective of an evolutionary biologist.

62 Hand, Judith. 2003. *Women, Power, and the Biology of Peace*. San Diego, CA: Questpath Publishing. pp. 114-121, 124-125.

63 Hrdy, Sarah Blaffer. 1999. *Mother nature; a history of mothers, infants, and natural selection*. New York: Pantheon Books.

64 Scheper-Hughes, Nancy. 2005. "Lifeboat ethics: mother love and child death in northeast Brazil." In: Brettell, Caroline B. and Carolyn F. Sargent (eds). 2005. *Gender in cross-cultural perspective*. New Jersey: Prentice Hall.

65 Hewlett, Barry S. 2005. "The cross-cultural nexus of Aka father-infant bonding". In: Brettell, Caroline B. and Carolyn F. Sargent (eds). 2005. *Gender in cross-cultural perspective*. New Jersey: Prentice Hall.

66 Blum, Deborah. 1997. *Sex on the brain. The biological differences between men and women*. NY: Viking Penguin.

67 Hua, Cai. 2001. *A society without fathers or husbands: the Na of China*. Translated by Asti Hustvedt. New York: Zone Books.

68 In egalitarian cultures this urge to rise in dominance is socially suppressed. Boehm, Christopher. 1999. *Hierarchy in the forest. The evolution of egalitarian behavior*. Cambridge, Mass.: Harvard Univ. Press.

69 Goldstein, Joshua S. 2001. *War and gender*. Cambridge, UK: Cambridge University Press. pp. 204-208.

70 Hrdy, Sarah Blaffer. 1981. *The women that never evolved*. Cambridge: Harvard University Press.

71 See for example Potts, Malcolm and Thomas Hayden. 2008. *Sex and war*. Dallas, TX: Benbella Books.

72 Goldstein, Joshua S. 2001. *War and gender*. Cambridge, UK: Cambridge University Press.

73 Archie, Elizabeth A., Jeanne Altmann, and Susan C. Alberts. 2012. "Social status predicts wound healing in wild baboons." Proceedings of the National Academy of Sciences. http://www.pnas.org/content/early/2012/05/14/1206391109.abstract (accessed 30 May 2012).

74 Goldstein, Joshua S. 2001. *War and gender*. Cambridge, UK: Cambridge University Press. pp. 206-207.

75 Hand, J. L. 1986. "Resolution of social conflicts: Dominance, egalitarianism, spheres of dominance and game theory." Quart. Rev. Biol. 61:201-220.

76 Goldstein, Joshua S. 2001. *War and gender*. Cambridge, UK: Cambridge University Press. pp. 194-199.

77 ibid. pp. 203-210.

78 Horgan, John. 2012. *The end of war*. San Francisco, CA: McSweeney's Books. pp. 109-112.

79 English, John Jacob. 2007, *The Collapse of the War System. Developments in the Philosophy of Peace in the Twentieth Century*. Ireland: Saor-Ollscoil Press in Cooperation with Choice Publishing.

80 Fry, Douglas P. 2006. *The Human Potential for Peace. An Anthropological Challenge to Assumptions about War and Violence*. NY: Oxford University Press. p. 92.

81 Fry, Douglas P. and Patrik Soderberg. 2013. Lethal aggression in mobile forager bands and implications for the origins of war. Science 341: 270-273.

82 http://www.peacefulsocieties.org

83 http://afww.org/map.html (accessed 15 April 2012).

84 Kelly, Raymond C. 2000. *Warless societies and the origin of war.* Ann Arbor, MI: University of Michigan Press.

85 ibid p. 32.

86 Mead, Margaret. 1940. "War is Only an Invention – Not a Biological Necessity." ASIA, XL http://www.andrew.cmu.edu/user/jdegolia/Interpretation%20and%20 Argument/Suggested%20Readings/Mead.pdf_ (accessed 20 March 2012.

87 Ehrenreich, Barbara. 1997. *Blood Rites: origins and history of the passions of war.* New York: Henry Holt. pp. 232-234.

88 For an extended exploration of how genes relate to behavior see Dawkins, Richard. 1986. *The blind watchmaker.* New York: Norton; also see Goodenough, Ursula. 1998. *The sacred depths of nature.* New York: Oxford University Press; Pinker, Steven. 1997. *How the mind works.* New York: W.W. Norton & Company.

89 Panksepp, Jaak. 1998. *Affective neuroscience: the foundations of human and animal emotions.* New York: Oxford University Press; Weintraub, Pamela. 2012. Jaak Panksepp. The man who makes rats laugh. Discover, May: 58-66. p. 60.

90 Zak, Paul J. 2012. *The moral molecule: the source of love and prosperity.* New York: Dutton/Penguin.

91 Ibid p. xviii.

92 Hand, Judith. 2012. "The moral molecule: the source of love and prosperity." Book Review. http://www.afww.org/TheMoralMolecule.html. (accessed 10 October 2012).

93 Mowrey, William R. and Douglas S. Portman. 2012. "Sex differences in behavioral decision-making and the modulation of shared neural circuits." Biol. Sex Differences: Mar 21, 3(1): 8.

94 Grobman, K. H. 2003-2008 *Sex/Gender Differences.* http://www.devpsy.org/teaching/gender/sex_differences.html (accessed 1 April 2012).

95 Krause, Kenneth W. 2012. "Gender Personality Differences: Planets or P.O. Boxes, Evidence or Ideology?" Skeptical Inquirer, May/June; Lippa, Richard. A. 2010. "Gender differences in personality and interests: When, where, and why?" Pers. and Soc. Psych. Compass 4/11: 1098-1110.

96 Eagly, Alice and Valerie Steffen.1986. "Gender and aggressive behavior: a meta-analytic review of the social psychological literature." 1986. Psychological Bulletin 100 (3): 309-330.

97 Ember, Carol R. and Melvin Ember. 1993. *Cultural anthropology. 7ᵗʰ Ed.* Englewood Cliffs, New Jersey: Prentice-Hall, Inc.; Haviland, William A. 1999. *Cultural anthropology. 9ᵗʰ Ed.* Orlando, Florida: Harcourt Brace & Company.

98 Gilbert, Susan. 2000. *A field guide to boys and girls.* New York: HarperCollins. pp. 16, 24-25, 44.

99 Blum, Deborah. 1997. *Sex on the brain. The biological differences between men and women.* NY: Viking Penguin; Fisher, Helen. 1999. *The first sex. The natural talents of*

women and how they are changing the world. NY: Random House; Mealey, Linda. 2000. *Sex differences: Developmental and evolutionary strategies*. San Diego: Academic Press; Moir, Anne and David Jessel. 1991. *Brain Sex. The real difference between men and women*. NY: Carol Publishing Group; Brizendine, Louann. 2006. *The female brain*. NY: Broadway Books; Brizendine, Louann. 2010. *The male brain*. NY: Broadway Books.

100   Fisher, Helen. 1999. *The first sex. The natural talents of women and how they are changing the world*. NY: Random House. p.9.

101   Blum, Deborah. 1997. *Sex on the brain. The biological differences between men and women*. NY: Viking Penguin. p. 60.

102   Blum, Deborah. 1997. *Sex on the brain. The biological differences between men and women*. NY: Viking Penguin. p. 46-48; Fisher, Helen. 1999. *The first sex. The natural talents of women and how they are changing the world*. NY: Random House. p.11.

103   ibid. Blum p. 46-48; ibid. Fisher p.11.

104   Fisher, Helen. 1999. *The first sex. The natural talents of women and how they are changing the world*. NY: Random House.

105   Shaywitz, B. A., S. E. Shaywitz, et. al. 1995. "Sex differences in the functional organization of the brain for learning." Nature 373: 607-608.

106   Gilbert, Susan. 2000. *A field guide to boys and girls*. New York: HarperCollins.

107   Tannen, Debra. 1998. *The argument culture: stopping America's war of words*. NY: Ballantine. p. 169

108   Blum, Deborah. 1997. *Sex on the brain. The biological differences between men and women*. NY: Viking Penguin.

109   Gilbert, Susan. 2000. *A field guide to boys and girls*. New York: HarperCollins.

110   Hand, Judith. 2003. *Women, Power, and the Biology of Peace*. San Diego, CA: Questpath Publishing.

111   Daly, Martin, and Margo Wilson. 1988. *Homicide*. Hawthorne, NY: Aldine de Gruyter.

112   Campbell, Anne. 1999. "Staying Alive: Evolution, culture and women's intra-sexual aggression." Behavioral and Brain Sciences 22:203-252.

113   Hand, Judith. 2010. "Sarah Palin and why all women are not progressive." http://tinyurl.com/2c2o2tl
         (accessed 5 April 2012).

114   In chimpanzees and children, females provide comfort more often than males – Waal, Frans B. M. de. 2012. "The antiquity of empathy." Science 336: 874-875.

115   Polaskovic, Gary. 2012. "Are women greener than men?" Los Angeles Times. June 13. http://tinyurl.com/6p3k7c5   (accessed 13 June 2012).

116   Fisher, Helen. 1999. *The first sex. The natural talents of women and how they are changing the world*. NY: Random House.

117   Lorenz, Konrad. 1974, c1966. *On aggression*. Translated by Marjorie Kerr Wilson. New York: Harcourt Brace Jovanovich.

118   Radcliff, Benjamin. 2013. *The political economy of human happiness: How voters' choices determine the quality of life*. Cambridge, MA: Cambridge University Press.

119　Hedges, Chris. 2002. *War is a Force that Gives Us Meaning*. NY: Public Affairs.

120　Goodall, Jane. 1990. *Through a window: My thirty years with the chimpanzees of Gombe*. Boston: Houghton Mifflin.

121　Kano, Takayoshi. 1992. *The last ape: pygmy chimpanzee behavior and ecology*. Translated by Evelyn Ono Vineberg. Stanford, CA: Stanford University Press; Waal, Frans B. M. de. 1997. *Bonobo: the forgotten ape*. Berkeley: University of California Press.

122　Wrangham, Richard and Dale Peterson.1996. *Demonic males. Apes and the origins of human violence*. NY: Houghton Mifflin.

123　Boehm, Christopher. 1999. *Hierarchy in the forest. The evolution of egalitarian behavior*. Cambridge, Mass.: Harvard Univ. Press.

124　Hand, Judith. 2003. *Women, Power, and the Biology of Peace*. San Diego, CA: Questpath Publishing. p. 82.

125　White, Tim D. 2009. "*Ardipithecus ramidus* and the paleobiology of early hominids." Science 326: 64. This issue presents many articles on the analysis of this fossil.

126　Hrdy, Sarah. Blaffer. 2009. *Mothers and others: on the evolutionary origins of mutual understanding*. Cambridge, MA: Harvard University Press; Hand, Judith L. 2009. "Book Review: Mothers and others – on the origins of mutual understanding." ISHE Bulletin 24 (3): 3. http://afww.org/MothersAndOthers.html (accessed 2 April 2012).

127　Hrdy, Sarah. Blaffer. 2009. *Mothers and others: on the evolutionary origins of mutual understanding*. Cambridge, MA: Harvard University Press. p. 65.

128　Ehrenreich, Barbara. 1997. *Blood Rites: origins and history of the passions of war*. New York: Henry Holt.

129　Fry, Douglas P. 2006. *The Human Potential for Peace. An Anthropological Challenge to Assumptions about War and Violence*. NY: Oxford University Press; Fry, Douglas P. 2007. *Beyond War: the human potential for peace*. New York: Oxford University Press.

130　Hrdy, Sarah. Blaffer. 2009. *Mothers and others: on the evolutionary origins of mutual understanding*. Cambridge, MA: Harvard University Press. pp. 30-31.

131　ibid p. 194.

132　ibid. p.92.

133　ibid. p.73.

134　ibid. p.80.

135　Hrdy, Sarah Blaffer. 1999. *Mother Nature: a history of mothers, infants, and natural selection*. New York: Pantheon Books.

136　Hrdy, Sarah. Blaffer. 2009. *Mothers and others: on the evolutionary origins of mutual understanding*. Cambridge, MA: Harvard University Press. pp. 99-100.

137　ibid pp. 101-102, 177-178.

138　ibid. pp.101-102.

139　ibid pp. 177-178.

140　ibid. pp.47-62.

141　ibid. p. 19.

142   Fry, Douglas P. 2006. *The Human Potential for Peace. An Anthropological Challenge to Assumptions about War and Violence.* NY: Oxford University Press; Fry, Douglas P. 2007. *Beyond War: the human potential for peace.* New York: Oxford University Press; Fry, Douglas P. and Anna Szala. 2013. "The evolution of agonism: the triumph of restraint in nonhuman and human primates". In *War, peace, and human nature: the convergence of evolutionary and cultural views.* Douglas P. Fry (ed.). New York: Oxford University Press.

143   Kelly, Raymond C. 2000. *Warless societies and the origin of war.* Ann Arbor, MI: University of Michigan Press.

144   See Kelly, Raymond C. (2000) pp. 152-158 for a review of data suggesting that the social structure of human societies before roughly 15,000 years ago was that of simple, nomadic hunter-gatherers.

145   Fry, Douglas P. and Patrik Söderberg. 2013. "Lethal aggression in mobile forager bands and implications for the origins of war." Science 341: 270-273.

146   Kelly, Raymond C. 2000. *Warless societies and the origin of war.* Ann Arbor, MI: University of Michigan Press. Chapter 3.

147   ibid. p. 147.

148   Wiessner, Polly and Nitze Pupu. 2012. "Toward peace: foreign arms and indigenous institutions in a Papua New Guinea society." Science 337: 1651-1654.

149   Fry, Douglas P. 2007. *Beyond War: The Human Potential for Peace.* New York: Oxford University Press. pp. 129, 151, 155.

150   ibid. p. 163.

151   ibid. p. 109.

152   ibid. p. 203.

153   Since this table was created other data indicates that the "primary food" of nomadic African hunter-gatherers like the Hadza comes from roughly 60% plant food although meat is prized and important. Band level hunter-gatherers in other habitats (e.g., in the sub-Arctic) do depend heavily on local animal protein. The common feature is that the resource is not sufficiently rich and reliably available over long periods so that settled living is possible.

154   Fry, Douglas P. and Patrik Söderberg. 2013. "Lethal aggression in mobile forager bands and implications for the origins of war." Science 341: 270-273.

155   Kelly, Raymond C. 2000. *Warless societies and the origin of war.* Ann Arbor, MI: University of Michigan Press. Chapter 2 and .pp. 47 & 62.

156   Dye, David H. 2013. "Trends in Cooperation and Conflict in Native Eastern North America." In *War, peace, and human nature: the convergence of evolutionary and cultural views.* Douglas P. Fry (ed.). New York: Oxford University Press.

157   Boehm, Christopher. 1999. *Hierarchy in the forest. The evolution of egalitarian behavior.* Cambridge, Mass.: Harvard Univ. Press.

158   Ehrenreich, Barbara. 1997. *Blood Rites: origins and history of the passions of war.* New York: Henry Holt. p. 120.

159   ibid. p. 118.

160   ibid. p. 120.

161   Kroeber, Clifton B., and Bernard L. Fontana. 1986. *Massacre on the Gila. An Account of the Last Major Battle Between American Indians, with Reflections on the Origin of War.* Tucson: Arizona University Press. p. 169-170.

162   ibid. p. 173.

163   McElvaine, Robert S. 2002. *Eve's seed: biology, the sexes, and the course of history.* New York: McGraw Hill Companies.

164   ibid. p. 174.

165   Keeley, Lawrence. 1996. *War before civilization: the myth of the peaceful savage.* NY: Oxford Univ. Press.

166   Pinker, Steven. 2011. *The better angels of our nature: why violence has declined.* New York: Viking. pp. 47-50.

167   Fry, Douglas P. 2007. *Beyond War: the human potential for peace.* New York: Oxford University Press. p. 54

168   Ferguson, R. Brian. 2003. "The birth of war." Natural History 112: July/Aug. http://iweb.tntech.edu/kosburn/history-444/birth_of_war.htm. (accessed 15 June 2012); Ferguson, R. Brian. 2013. "The Prehistory of War and Peace in Europe and the Near East." In *War, peace, and human nature: the convergence of evolutionary and cultural views.* Douglas P. Fry (ed.). New York: Oxford University Press.

169   Ferguson, R. Brian. 2003. "The birth of war." Natural History 112: July/Aug. http://iweb.tntech.edu/kosburn/history-444/birth_of_war.htm. (accessed 15 June 2012).

170   Kelly, Raymond C. 2000. *Warless societies and the origin of war.* Ann Arbor, MI: University of Michigan Press. pp. 152-158.

171   Diamond, Jared. 1997. *Guns, Germs, and Steel: The Fates of Human Societies.* NY: W.W. Norton.

172   See for example Ember and Ember, 1993, *Cultural Anthropology.* pp 154-156.

173   Shostak, Marjorie. 1983. *Nisa. The life and words of a !Kung woman.* NY: Random House.

174   ibid. pp. 237-238.

175   ibid. p. 240.

176   Goldstein, Joshua S. 2001. *War and gender.* Cambridge, UK: Cambridge University Press; McElvaine, Robert S. 2002. *Eve's seed: biology, the sexes, and the course of history.* New York: McGraw Hill Companies.

177   Fox, Robin. 1967. *Kinship and Marriage: an anthropological perspective.* New York: Penguin.

178   Ember, Carol R. and Melvin Ember. 1993. *Cultural anthropology. 7th Ed.* Englewood Cliffs, New Jersey: Prentice-Hall, Inc. p. 191.

179   ibid. p. 191.

180   Hrdy, S. B. 2009. *Mothers and Others: the Evolutionary Origins of Mutual Understanding.* Cambridge, MA: Harvard University Press. pp. 240-250.

181   Hawkes, Kristen, J.F. O'Connell, N.G. Blurton Jones, H. Alvarez, and E.L. Charnov. 1998. "Grandmothering, menopause and the evolution of human life histories." Proceedings of the National Academy of Sciences 95: 1336-1339.

182   Hrdy, S. B. 2009. *Mothers and Others: the Evolutionary Origins of Mutual Understanding.* Cambridge, MA: Harvard University Press. p. 245.

183   Lancaster, Chet S. 1981. *The Goba of the Zambezi: sex roles, economics and change.* Norman: University of Oklahoma Press.

184   Boehm, Christopher. 1999. *Hierarchy in the forest. The evolution of egalitarian behavior.* Cambridge, Mass.: Harvard Univ. Press.

185   Ember, Carol R. and Melvin Ember. 1993. *Cultural anthropology. 7th Ed.* Englewood Cliffs, New Jersey: Prentice-Hall, Inc. p. 152.

186   Fisher, Helen. 1999. *The first sex. The natural talents of women and how they are changing the world.* NY: Random House.

187   Jandt, Fred E. 1985. *Win-win Negotiating: Turning Conflict Into Agreement.* New York: Wiley; Ury, William. 1999. *Getting to Peace: Transforming Conflict at Home, at Work, and in the World.* New York: Viking. pp. 104-105.

188   Tannen, Debra. 1998. *The argument culture: stopping America's war of words.* NY: Ballantine. p. 174.

189   Pinker, Steven. 2011. *The better angels of our nature: why violence has declined.* New York: Viking.

190   Goldstein, Joshua. 2011. *Winning the war on war: the decline of armed conflict worldwide.* New York: Dutton.

191   Hand, Judith. "How far we have already come." http://www.afww.org/HowFar/html. (accessed 8 Sept. 2012).

192   Cunningham, Karla. 2012. "Terror's 'Invisible Women.'" Los Angeles Times, April 4.

193   Muir, Kate. 1992. *Arms and the woman. Female soldiers at war.* London: Sinclair-Stevenson Ltd.

194   Peach, Lucinda J. 2005. "Gender and war: are women tough enough for military combat?" In: Brettell, Caroline B. and Carolyn F. Sargent (eds). 2005. *Gender in cross-cultural perspective.* New Jersey: Prentice Hall.

195   Salmonson, Jessica Amanda. 1991. *The encyclopedia of Amazons. Women warriors from antiquity to the modern era.* NY: Paragon House.

196   Davis-Kimball, Jeannine. 1997. "Warrior women of the Eurasian steppes." *Archaeology* 50: 44-48; Davis-Kimball, Jeannine and Mona Behan. 2002. *Warrior women: An archaeologist's search for history's hidden heroines.* NY: Warner Books.

197   Hvistendahl, Mara. 2012. "Gender and violence." *Science* 336: 839-840.

198   Hart, Michael H. 1978. *The 100. A ranking of the most influential persons in history.* NY: A & W Publishers, Inc.

199   Chagnon, Napoleon A. 1983. *Yanomamö: the fierce people.* New York: Holt, Rinehart, Winston.

200   Shermer, Michael. 2001. "Spin-doctoring the Yanomamö." In *Skeptic* 9: 36-47; Tierney, Patrick. 2000. *Darkness in El Dorado.* NY: Norton.

201   Fry, Douglas P. 2007. *Beyond War: the human potential for peace.* New York: Oxford University Press. pp. 135-13954

202 Ury, William. 1999. *Getting to peace: transforming conflict at home, at work, and in the world.* NY: Viking.

203 Goldstein, Joshua. 2011. *Winning the war on war: the decline of armed conflict worldwide.* New York: Dutton. p.224.

204 Goldstein, Joshua S. 2001. *War and gender.* Cambridge, UK: Cambridge University Press. p. 412.

205 Horgan, John. 2012. *The end of war.* San Francisco, CA: McSweeney's Books. p. 124.

206 Ehrenreich, Barbara. 2012 "The End of War by John Horgan review." Special to the SF Chronicle. http://tinyurl.com/7xspvn8 (accessed 20 April 2012).

207 AFWW.org. Cornerstones. http://afww.org/logo.html. (accessed 3 May 2012).

208 Hinde, Robert and Joseph Rotblat. 2003. *War no more.* Stirling, VA: Pluto Press.

209 Irwin, Robert A. 1988. *Building a peace system: exploratory project on the conditions of peace.* Washington, D.C.: Expo Press; Myers, Winslow. 2009. *Living beyond war: a citizen's guide.* MaryKnoll, NY: Orbis Books.

210 Anderson, Mary B. and Marshall Wallace. 2012. *Opting Out of War: Strategies to Prevent Violent Conflict.* Boulder, Co: Lynne Rienner Publishers.

211 Rotblat, Joseph. 2006. "A world without war. Is it desirable? Is it feasible?" ISYP Journal on Science and World Affairs, Vol. 2, No. 1. http://www.pugwash.org/publication/tran/Rotblat-En.pdf (accessed 3 May 2012).

212 Pinker, Steven. 2011. *The better angels of our nature: why violence has declined.* New York: Viking.

213 Fry, Douglas C. 2012. "Life without war." Science 336: 879-884.

214 Goldstein, Joshua. 2011. *Winning the war on war: the decline of armed conflict worldwide.* New York: Dutton. Chapt. 12.

215 Hinde, Robert & Rotblat, J. 2003. *War No More. Eliminating Conflict in the Nuclear Age.* Stirling, VA: Pluto Books. p. 210.

216 English, J.J. 2007. *Collapse of the War System.* Ireland: Saor-Ollscoil Press in association with Choice Publishing. p. 231.

217 Hart, Gary. 2004. *The Fourth Power. A Grand Strategy for the United States in the Twenty-First Century.* NY: Oxford University Press.

218 Marshall, Andrew Garvin. 2011. "Lies, war, and empire: NATO's "Humanitarian Imperialism" in Libya." http://www.andrewgarvinmarshall.com. (accessed 5 July 2012).

219 Dupont, Daniel G. 2004. "Test Drive. Will a planned defense shield defeat real missiles?" Sci. Am. - Sept.; Garwin, Richard L. 2004. "Holes in the Missile Shield." Sci. Am. – Nov.

220 Goldstein, Joshua. 2011. *Winning the war on war: the decline of armed conflict worldwide.* New York: Dutton. Chapt. 12

221 Butler, Smedley. "War is a racket." http://www.veteransforpeace.org/war_is_a_racket_033103.htmXX

222 Daly, Hermann E. 2005. "Economics in a full world." Scientific American 293:100-107.

223   Daly, Herman E., 2005. "Economics in a full world." Scientific American. http://tinyurl.com/76yg46 (accessed 4 April 2012.)

224   see for example Tamera: Healing Biotope 1. http://www.tamera.org/index.html. (accessed 15 April 2012); Transition Network. http://www.transitionnetwork.org/. (accessed 15 April 2012).

225   Intergovernmental Panel on Climate Change. http://tinyurl.com/7tlupax (accessed on 4 April 2012).

226   Hand, Judith L. 2010. "The origin of war and human destiny." http://wp.me/p45hl-8b (accessed 4 April 2012); Nowak, Martin and Roger Highfield. 2011. *Supercooperators.: Altruism, evolution, and why we need each other to succeed.* New York: Simon and Schuster.

227   Hand, Judith L. 2009. "Gort, Climate Change, Abolishing War." http://tinyurl.com/yl9syow. (accessed 15 April 2012).

228   Hand, Judith L. 2009. "How long will it take to reach the goal?" http://afww.org/HowLong.html (accessed 20 June 2012). This essay describes the biological basis for female reproductive choices of the Demographic Transition.

229   Wilson, Edward O. 2002. *The Future of Life.* Excerpted from Scientific American, Feb. pp. 84-91.

230   Potts, Malcolm and Thomas Hayden. 2008. *Sex and war.* Dallas, TX: Benbella Books.

231   Layard, Richard G. 2005. *Happiness:Lessons from a New Science.* NY:Penguin.

232   Hand, J.L. 2006. "What makes people happy." http://www.afww.org/WhatMakesPeopleHappy.html. (accessed 5 April 2012).

233   Layard, Richard G. 2005. *Happiness:Lessons from a New Science.* NY:Penguin; Hand, J.L. 2006. "What makes people happy." http://www.afww.org/WhatMakesPeopleHappy.html. (accessed 5 April 2012).

234   Layard, Richard G. 2005. *Happiness:Lessons from a New Science.* NY:Penguin.

235   Hedges, Chris. 2002. *War is a Force that Gives Us Meaning.* NY: Public Affairs.

236   Lorenz, Konrad. 1974, c1966. *On Aggression.* Translated by Marjorie Kerr Wilson. NY: Harcourt Brace Jovanovich.

237   Ury, William. 1999. *Getting to peace: transforming conflict at home, at work, and in the world.* NY: Viking.

238   Benjamin, Medea. 2012. *Drone warfare: killing by remote control.* OR Books.

239   Kelly, Raymond C. 2000. *Warless societies and the origin of war.* Ann Arbor, MI: University of Michigan Press. Chapter 1 & Table 2.

240   Collins, Suzanne. 2008. *The hunger games.* New York: Scholastic.

241   Fukuyama, Francis. 1992. *The end of history and the last man.* New York: Free Press.

242   Zakaria, Fareed. 2003. *The Future of Freedom: Illiberal Democracy at Home and Abroad.* NY: Norton.

243 Interparliamentary Union. http://www.ipu.org/english/home.htm(accessed 4 April 2012).

244 Hand, Judith. 2003. *Women, Power, and the Biology of Peace*. San Diego, CA: Questpath Publishing. p. 124.

245 Fukuyama, Francis. 1992. *The end of history and the last man*. New York: Free Press.

246 Fry, Douglas P. 2006. *The Human Potential for Peace. An Anthropological Challenge to Assumptions about War and Violence*. NY: Oxford University Press; Hand, Judith L. 2003. *Women, Power, and the Biology of Peace*. San Diego, CA: Questpath Publishing: Goldstein, Joshua S. 2001. *War and gender*. Cambridge, UK: Cambridge University Press.

247 Benjamin, Medea and Jodie Evans. 2005. *Stop the next war now*. Makawao, HI: Inner Ocean Publishing.

248 Aker, Dee (ed.) and Emiko Noma, Laura Taylor and Susan Van Schoonhoven. 2007. "Is Peace Possible? Women PeaceMakers in Action." San Diego, CA: Joan B. Kroc Institute for Peace and Justice. http://tinyurl.com/7cvmkzj (accessed 12 July 2012).

249 Ibid p.38.

250 Anderlini, Sanam Naraghi. 2007. *Women building peace: what they do, why it matters*. Boulder, CO: Lynne Rienner Publishers.

251 Dollar, David, Raymond Fisman, and Roberta Gatti. 1999. "Are women really the "fairer" sex?" women and corruption in government." World Bank. Development Research Group. Poverty Reduction and Economic Management Network. Journal of Economic Behavior & Organization, Volume 46, Issue 4, December 2001, Pages 423-429.

252 Andersen, Steffen, Erwin Bulte, Uri Gneezy, and John A. List. 2008. "Do Women Supply More Public Goods than Men?" *Preliminary Experimental Evidence from Matrilineal and Patriarchal Societies*. American Economic Review: Papers & Proceedings 2008, 98:2, 376–381. http://www.aeaweb.org/articles.php?doi=10.1257/aer.98.2.376 (accessed 5 April 2010).

253 Gizelis, Theodora-Ismene. 2009. "Gender empowerment and United Nations peacebuilding." International Peace Research. 46 (4): 505 –523. http://tinyurl.com/6vvqpxv. (accessed 31 May 2012).

254 Hvistendahl, Mara. 2012. "Gender and violence." Science 336: 839-840.

255 Caprioli, Mary. 2003. "Gender equality and state aggression: the impact of domestic gender inequality on state first use of force." International Interactions 29:195–214; 2005. "Primed for violence: the role of gender inequality in predicting internal conflict." International Studies Quarterly 49: 161–178; 2001. Caprioli, Mary and Mark A. Boyer. "Gender, violence, and international crisis." Journal of Conflict Resolution 45:503–518.

256 Melander, Erik. 2005. "Gender equality and intrastate armed conflict." International Studies Quarterly 49:695-714. http://www.iepcd.org/files/Download/genderequality.pdf. (accessed 31 May 2012.)

257   Hudson, Valerie M., Bonnie Ballif-Spanvill, Mary Caprioli, and Chad F. Emmett. 2012. *Sex and world peace*. NY: Columbia University Press.

258   Fisher, Helen. 1999. *The First Sex: The Natural Talents of Women and How They Are Changing the World*. NY: Random House; McDermott, R., and J. Cowden. 2001. "The Effects of Uncertainty and Sex in a Simulated Crisis Game." International Interactions 27: 353-380.

259   Hand, Judith L. 2010. "Sarah Palin and why all women are not progressive." http://tinyurl.com/2c2o2tl. (accessed 5 April 2012).

260   Hand, Judith L. 2009. "To date, nonviolence movements were "before their time." Now they are poised to change history." http://afww.org/NonviolentMovements. html. (accessed 1 April 2012).

261   Fukuyama, Francis. 1992. *The end of history and the last man*. New York: Free Press.

262   Hand, Judith L. 2003 *Women, Power, and the Biology of Peace*. San Diego, CA: Questpath Publishing. p. 127.

263   Hudson, Rex A. 1999. "The sociology and psychology of terrorism: who becomes a terrorist and why?" Prepared by Library of Congress, Federal Research Division. See: www.loc.gov/rr/frd/pdf-files/Soc_Psych_of_Terrorism.pdf. p.50 "Terrorists are generally people who feel alienated from society and have a grievance or regard themselves as victims of an injustice." (accessed 10 April 2012).

264   ibid.

265   Layard, P. Richard G. 2005. *Happiness: Lessons from a New Science*. NY: Penguin Press.

266   *Primate Reconciliation. A review of Peacemaking Among Primates*

267   Silk, Joan B. 2002. "The form and function of reconciliation in primates." Annual Reviews of Anthropology 31: 21-44. doi:10.1146/annurev. anthro.31.032902.101743; Verbeek, P. 2008. "Peace ethology." Behaviour 145: 1497-1524.

268   The Economist. 2012. The Anthropocene. A man-made world. The Economist. http://www.economist.com/node/18741749 (accessed 10 April 2012).

269   Sachs, Jeffrey D. 2005. "Can extreme poverty be eliminated?" Sci. Am. 293:56-65; Lovins, Amory B. 2005. "More profit with less carbon." Sci. Am. 293:74-83: Daly, Herman E. 2005. "Economics in a full world." Sci. Am. 293:100-107.

270   Korten, David. 2009. *Agenda for a new economy. From phantom wealth to real wealth*. San Francisco, CA: Barrett-Koehler Publishers.

271   Eisler, Riane. 2007. *The Real Wealth of Nations. Creating a Caring Economics*. San Francisco, CA: Berrett-Koehler Publishers, Inc.

272   Weiner, Eric J. 2012. "Not their fathers' economics." Los Angeles Times, April 11.

273   Radcliff, Benjamin. 2013. *The political economy of human happiness: How voters' choices determine the quality of life*. Cambridge, MA: Cambridge University Press.

274 Mustafa, Nadia. 2005. "What about gross national happiness?" Time/Health http://tinyurl.com/4krm4 (accessed 12 April 2012); Thottam/Thimphu, Jyoti. 2012. "The pursuit of happiness." Time Magazine-Business Section, October, pp. 1-5.

275 http://www/grossnationalhappiness.com.

276 Gibbs, W. Wayt. 2005. "How should we set priorities?" Sci. Am. 293:108-115.

277 ibid

278 Daly, Herman E. 2005. "Economics in a full world." Sci. Am. 293:100-107.

279 Diamond, Jared. 2005. *Collapse. How societies choose to fail or succeed*. NY: Viking.

280 Daly, Herman E. 2005. "Economics in a full world." Sci. Am. 293:100-107.

281 Hand, Judith L. 2003. *Women, Power, and the Biology of Peace*. San Diego, CA: Questpath Publishing.

282 Daly, Martin & Margo Wilson. 1988. *Homicide*. Hawthorne, NY: Aldine de Gruyter; Tiger, Lionel. 2001. "Osama Bin Ladin's Man Trouble." http://tinyurl.com/7wccyxq (accessed 10 April 2012); Zakaria, Fareed. 2001. "Why do they hate us?" Newsweek: Oct. 15th; Wilson, M. & Daly, M. 1985. "Competitiveness, risk-taking, and violence: The young male syndrome." Ethology and Sociobiology 6:59-73; Schlegel, Alice, and Herbert Barry III. 1991. *Adolescence: An anthropological inquiry*. NY: Free Press..

283 Hiraiwa-Hasegawa, Mariko. 2005. "Homicide by men in Japan, and its relationship to age, resources and risk taking." Evolution and Human Behavior 26: 332-343.

284 Nyborg, H. 1994. *Hormones, sex and society*. Westport, Conn.: Praeger.

285 Zakaria, Fareed. 2001. "Why do they hate us?" Newsweek: Oct. 15th

286 U.S. Navy. 2012. "America's Navy. A Global Force for Good." http://www.youtube.com/watch?v=h3wtUCPWmeI (accessed 10 April 2012).

287 Perry, Tony. 2012. "Marine Corps adjusts its recruiting mission." Los Angeles Times, 11 March.

288 Barry, Kathleen. 2011. *Unmaking war. Remaking men*. Santa Rosa, CA: Phoenix Rising Press.

289 Taken from Cohen, D. (Ed.). 1991. *The circle of life—rituals from the human family*. London: The Aquarian Press.

290 Hand, Judith L. 2001. *Voice of the Goddess*. San Diego, CA: Pacific Rim Press.

291 Evans, Sir Arthur. 1921-35. *The palace of Minos: An account of the early Cretan civilization as illustrated by the discoveries at Knossos*. London: Macmillan.

292 Lancaster, Chet S. 1981. *The Goba of the Zambezi: sex roles, economics and change*. Norman: University of Oklahoma Press; Sanday, Peggy Reeves. 2002. *Women at the center: Life in a modern matriarchy*. Ithaca, NY: Cornell University Press.

293 Hand, Judith L. 2003. *Women, Power, and the Biology of Peace*. SanDiego, CA: Questpath Publishing. pp. 68-70.

294 ibid. pp. 70-73.

295 Cited in McDonnell, Patrick J. 2012. "Pope calls for Christian, Muslim unity against war." Los Angeles Times. 16 September.

296   Hand, Judith L. 2003. *Women, Power, and the Biology of Peace*. San Diego, CA: Questpath Publishing. pp. 59-64.

297   Fry, Douglas P. 2006. *The Human Potential for Peace. An Anthropological Challenge to Assumptions about War and Violence*. NY: Oxford University Press. p. 63.

298   Lakey, George. 2012. "How Swedes and Norwegian broke the power of the '1 %.'" Nation of Change. http://www.nationofchange.org/how-swedes-and-norwegians-broke-power-1-percent-1327762223 (accessed 28 April 2012).

299   Brock. Peter. 1992. *A brief history of pacifism from Jesus to Tolstoy*. Toronto: Syracuse University Press.

300   Goldstein, Joshua. 2011. *Winning the war on war: the decline of armed conflict worldwide*. New York: Dutton; Pinker, Steven. 2011. *The better angels of our nature: why violence has declined*. New York: Viking.

301   I;bid, p. 691.

302   World Bank. http://tinyurl.com/7hqrfhd (accessed 11 April 2012).

303   Potts, Malcolm and Thomas Hayden. 2008. *Sex and war*. Dallas, TX: Benbella Books.

304   http://en.wikipedia.org/wiki/Spittoon.

305   Holman, Jeanine. 2010. "Bound feet." http://www.josephrupp.com/history.html (accessed 17 June 2012).

306   Johnson, M. Alex. 2005. msnbc.com. 18 April. In "The Culture of Einstein" Johnson states that the quote is from a letter to President Harry S. Truman.

307   See Appendix I for brief lists of examples of such organizations.

308   Annan, Kofi. 2000. United Nations address to "Women 2000." 5 June.

309   Kristof, Nicholas D. and Sheryl WeDunn. 2009. *Half the Sky: Turning Oppression Into Opportunity For Women Worldwide*. New York: Alfred A. Knopf.

310   See, Carolyn. 2009. "Carolyn See reviews Kristoff and WuDunn's 'Half the Sky.'" Sept. 11. http://tinyurl.com/6uayu3u. (accessed 17 June 2012).

311   Ellison, Jesse. 2011. "The Global Women's Progress Report." Newsweek, September 26, 2011.

312   Aker, Dee (ed.) and Emiko Noma, Laura Taylor and Susan Van Schoonhoven. 2007. "Is Peace Possible? Women PeaceMakers in Action." San Diego, CA: Joan B. Kroc Institute for Peace and Justice. http://tinyurl.com/7cvmkzj (accessed 12 July 2012).

313   http://www/nobelwomensinitiative.org.

314   Internet Encyclopedia of Philosophy (IEP). http://www.iep.utm.edu./justwar/#H2. (accessed 1 April 2012).

315   Zinn, H. 1990. "A Warrior Turns Pacifist." In: *Strength Through Peace: The Ideas and People of Nonviolence*. McCarthy, C. Ed. Washington, D.C.: Center for Teach Peace.

316   English, J.J. 2007. *Collapse of the War System. Developments in the Philosophy of Peace in the Twentieth Century*. Ireland: Saor-Ollscoil Press in association with Choice Publishing. pp. 65-68, 83-86.

317 Zinn, H. 1990. "A Warrior Turns Pacifist." In: *Strength Through Peace: The Ideas and People of Nonviolence.* McCarthy, C. Ed. Washington, D.C.: Center for Teach Peace.

318 Goldberg, Nicholas. 2009. "Parsing the rules of war." Los Angeles Times. July 26.

319 Grotius, Hugo. 1623. *The rights of war and peace.* Translated by A.G. Campbell. London: Universal Classics Library. 1901.

320 McCarthy, Coleman., Ed. Undated. *Strength through Peace: The ideas and people of Nonviolence.* Washington, D.C.: Center for Teaching Peace.

321 English, J.J. 2007. *Collapse of the War System.* Ireland: Saor-Ollscoil Press in association with Choice Publishing; Fry, Douglas P. 2006. *The Human Potential for Peace: an Anthropological Challenge to Assumptions about War and Violence.* New York: Oxford University Press; Fry, Douglas P. 2007. *Beyond War: The Human Potential for Peace.* New York: Oxford University Press; Goldstein, Joshua. 2011. *Winning the war on war: the decline of armed conflict worldwide.* New York: Dutton; Hinde, Robert & Rotblat, J. 2003. *War No More. Eliminating Conflict in the Nuclear Age.* Stirling, VA: Pluto Books; Horgan, John. 2012. *The end of war.* San Francisco, CA: McSweeney's Books; Swanson, David. 2013. *War no more. The case for abolition.* Charlottesville, VA: David Swanson.

322 Haidt, Johnathan. (accessed 17 June 2012). http://people.virginia.edu/~jdh6n/home.html.

323 Sharp, Gene, Paulson, J., Miller, C.A., & Merriman, H. 2005. *Waging Nonviolent Struggle: 20th Century Practice and 21st Century Potential.* Manchester, NH: Extending Horizons Books.

324 Butler, Smedley. 1935. *War is a Racket.* New York: Round Table Press. See also: http://www.ratical.org/ratville/CAH/warisaracket.html. And YouTube: http://www.youtube.com/watch?v=F3_EXqJ8f-0

325 Ehrenreich, Barbara. 1997. *Blood Rites: origins and history of the passions of war.* New York: Henry Holt. pp. 150-154.

326 Hand, Judith L. 2003. *Women, Power, and the Biology of Peace.* pp. 136-141; Wilson, Marie C. 2004. *Closing the leadership gap: why women can and must help run the world.* New York: Penguin..

327 Walton, Mary. 2010. *A Woman's crusade: Alice Paul and the battle for the ballot.* New York: Palgrave Macmillan.

328 Nagler, Michael N. *Hope or Terror? Gandhi and the Other 9/11.* Minneapolis, MN: Nonviolent Peaceforce and Tomales, CA: Metta Center.

329 Hand, Judith L. 2010. "To Abolish War." Journal of Aggression, Conflict, and Peace Research 2(4): 44-56.

330 Hand, Judith. 2011. "Shaping the Future: A Proposal to Hasten a Global Paradigm Shift for the Security and Well-being of All Children Everywhere." www.afww.org/ShapingTheFuture.html. (accessed 28 March 2012).

331 ibid.

332 Sharp, Gene. 2005. *Waging Nonviolent Struggle. 20th Century Practice and 21st Century Potential.* Boston: Porter Sargent Publishers. pp. 18-19.

333   Nagler, Michael N. *Hope or Terror? Gandhi and the Other 9/11*. Minneapolis, MN: Nonviolent Peaceforce and Tomales, CA: Metta Center; Sharp, Gene. 2005. *Waging Nonviolent Struggle. 20ᵗʰ Century Practice and 21ˢᵗ Century Potential*. Boston: Porter Sargent Publishers; Stephan, Maria J. and Erica Chenoweth. "Why civil resistance works. The strategic logic of nonviolent conflict." International Security 33 (1): 7-44. http://tinyurl.com/5ko7s9. (accessed 17 June 2012).

334   ibid. p. 23.

335   Much of the following section is taken from J. Hand, 2011. www.afww.org/ShapingTheFuture.html. (accessed 28 March 2012).

336   Williams, J., S. Goose, and M. Wareham. 2008. *Banning Landmines: Disarmament, Citizen Diplomacy, and Human Security*. Lanham, Md.: Bowman & Littlefield Publishers, Inc.

337   Kania, John, and Mark Kramer. 2011. "Collective Impact." Stanford Social Innovation Review. Winter. http://www.ssireview.org/articles/entry/collective_impact. (accessed 8 August 2012.)

338   Peggy Lang. (personal communication).

339   Machel, G. 1996. *Impact of armed conflict on children*. NY: United Nations Department of Policy Coordination and Sustainable Development (DPCSD).

340   Sharp, Gene, Paulson, J., Miller, C.A., & Merriman, H. 2005. *Waging Nonviolent Struggle: 20th Century Practice and 21st Century Potential*. Manchester, NH: Extending Horizons Books.

341   Williams, J., S. Goose, and M. Wareham. 2008. *Banning Landmines: Disarmament, Citizen Diplomacy, and Human Security*. Lanham, Md.: Bowman & Littlefield Publishers, Inc.; Williams J, and S. D. Goose. 2008. "Citizen diplomacy and the Ottawa Process: a lasting model?" In *Banning Landmines: Disarmament, Citizen Diplomacy, and Human Security*. Lanham, Md.: Bowman & Littlefield Publishers, Inc. – these describe how this project was assembled, how it worked, problem areas and how it is still working.

342   Hand, Judith. 2011. "Shaping the Future: A Proposal to Hasten a Global Paradigm Shift for the Security and Well-being of All Children Everywhere." www.afww.org/ShapingTheFuture.html. (accessed 28 March 2012).

343   Tipton, Paul. 2012. "Science—it takes a global village." Los Angeles Times. July 9.

344   Hand, Judith. 2011. "Shaping the Future: A Proposal to Hasten a Global Paradigm Shift for the Security and Well-being of All Children Everywhere." www.afww.org/ShapingTheFuture.html. (accessed 28 March 2012).

345   ibid.

346   ibid.

347   Disney, Abigail and Gini Ritiker. 2009. *Pray the devil back to hell*. A film.

348   Goldstein, Joshua. 2011. *Winning the war on war: the decline of armed conflict worldwide*. New York: Dutton. Chapter 12.

349 Hand, Judith. 2009. "Changing the Biological Chemistry of Nonviolence Movements: Women on the Front Lines." http://wp.me/p45hl-8F (accessed 1 April 2012).

350 Hand, Judith. 2009. "Liberian women demand and get peace." http://tinyurl.com/2aq2xe6 (accessed 1 April 2012).

351 Beenish Ahmed. 2011. "Revolutionary Women." The American Prospect. http://tinyurl.com/4fenueg (accessed 1 April 2012); Deutsche Welle. 2011. "The unseen factor: Egypt's women protestors." http://tinyurl.com/4862619 (accessed 1 April 2013); The RFE/RL, Inc. 2011. Spero News – "Egyptian women play vital role in anti-mubarak protests." Reprinted with permission of Radio Free Europe/Radio Liberty. http://t.co/12PnwWa (accessed 1 April 2012).

352 Pinker, Steven. 2011. *The better angels of our nature: why violence has declined.* New York: Viking. p. 671.

353 Coca-cola Television Advertising Web Page. "The 'Hilltop' Ad: The Story of a Commercial." http://memory.loc.gov/ammem/ccmphtml/colaadv.html. (accessed 10 April 2012).

354 Hinde, Robert & Rotblat, J. 2003. *War No More. Eliminating Conflict in the Nuclear Age.* Stirling, VA: Pluto Books. p. 216.

355 Crisp, Richard J. and Rose Meleady. 2012. "Adapting to a multicultural future." Science 336: 853-855.

356 Fry, Douglas P. and Anna Szala. 2013. "The evolution of agonism: the triumph of restraint in nonhuman and human primates." In *War, peace, and human nature: the convergence of evolutionary and cultural views.* Douglas P. Fry (ed.). New York: Oxford University Press.

357 Grossman, Lt. Col. Dave. 2000. "Teaching kids to kill." Phi Kappa Phi National Forum. Fall issue. http://www.killology.org/print/print_teachkid.htm. (accessed 2 May 2012); Grossman, David A. 2009. *On Killing: the psychological cost of learning to kill in war and society.* Boston, MA: Back Bay Books; Lorenz, Konrad. 1974. c1966. *On Aggression.* Translated by Marjorie Kerr Wilson. NY: Harcourt Brace Jovanovich; Verbeek, Peter. 2013. "An ethological perspective on peace." In *War, peace, and human nature: the convergence of evolutionary and cultural views.* Douglas P. Fry (ed.). New York: Oxford University Press.

358 Barry, Kathleen. 2011. *Unmaking war. Remaking men.* Santa Rosa, CA: Phoenix Rising Press.

359 Fry, Douglas P. and Anna Szala. 2013. "The evolution of agonism: the triumph of restraint in nonhuman and human primates." In *War, peace, and human nature: the convergence of evolutionary and cultural views.* Douglas P. Fry (ed.). New York: Oxford University Press; Kelly, Raymond C. 2000. *Warless societies and the origin of war.* Ann Arbor, MI: University of Michigan Press.

360 Lorenz, Konrad. 1974. c1966. *On Aggression.* Translated by Marjorie Kerr Wilson. NY: Harcourt Brace Jovanovich.

361 Hand, Judith L. 2012. "Rick Santorum is a U.S. Presidential Candidate – and a Warmonger." http://wp.me/p45hl-el (accessed 1 April 2012).

362   Horgan, John. 2012. *The end of war*. San Francisco, CA: McSweeney's Books. p. 98

363   Anderson, Mary B. and Marshall Wallace. 2013. *Opting out of war*. Boulder, CO: Lynne Rienner Publishers, Inc.

364   Ehrenreich, Barbara. 1997. *Blood Rites: origins and history of the passions of war*. New York: Henry Holt. p. 118.

Ehrenreich, Barbara. 1997. *Blood Rites: origins and history of the passions of war*. New York: Henry Holt; Goldstein, Joshua. 2001. *War and gender*. Cambridge, UK: Cambridge University Press.

365   Bennett, Brian. 2012. "More pilots wage war from home." Los Angeles Times. July 29.

366   Mead, Margaret. 1940. "War is Only an Invention – Not a Biological Necessity." ASIA, XL (accessed at http://www.andrew.cmu.edu/user/jdegolia/Interpretation%20and%20Argument/Suggested%20Readings/Mead.pdf_- 20 March 2012.

367   Hand, Judith L. 2009. "Locked in the embrace of male biology: a barrier to positive paradigm shift." http://afww.org/EmbraceOfMaleBiology.html. (accessed 1 April 2012); Wilson, Marie C. 2004. *Closing the leadership gap: why women can and must help run the world*. New York: Penguin.

368   Pinker, Steven. 2011. *The better angels of our nature: why violence has declined*. New York: Viking.

369   ibid pp. 680-692.

370   ibid pp. 678-680.

371   ibid p. 681.

372   ibid p. 683.

373   ibid p. 684.

374   ibid p. 683.

375   ibid p. xxvi.

376   ibid p. 685.

377   ibid p. 686.

378   Hand, Judith L. 2009. "Locked in the embrace of male biology: a barrier to positive paradigm shift." http://afww.org/EmbraceOfMaleBiology.html. (accessed 4 April 2012).

379   Hand, Judith L. 2007. "Essential Human Goodness." http://afww.org/EssentialHumanGoodnesshtml. (accessed 4 April 2012.); Waal, Frans de. 2009. *Primates and Philosophers: How Morality Evolved*. Stephen Macedo & Josiah Ober (eds.). New York: Princeton University Press.

380   Pinker, Steven. 2011. *The better angels of our nature: why violence has declined*. New York: Viking. p. 690.

381   ibid p. 691.

382   ibid p. 690.

383   ibid p. 691.

384   Fry, Douglas C. 2012. "Life without war." Science 336: 879-884.

385   Irwin, Robert A. 1988. *Building a peace system: exploratory project on the conditions of peace.* Washington, D.C.: Expo Press.

386   Fry, Douglas C. 2012. "Life without war." Science 336: 879-884.

387   Hvistendahl, Mara. 2012. "Gender and violence." Science 336: 839-840. p.840.

Index

Made in the USA
Lexington, KY
09 September 2014